Domain of the Cavemen

Visitors in the Ghost Room, 1945. Photo by Ralph Gifford, Oregon Caves National Monument (OCNM) Museum and Archives Collections.

Domain of the Cavemen:

A Historic Resource Study of Oregon Caves National Monument

by Stephen R. Mark
Historian

National Park Service   Pacific West Region   2006

A view of Joaquin Miller's Chapel in the Oregon Caves by Ralph Gifford, 1937. (Photo courtesy of Oregon State University Archives.)

Cover Photos:

(top) High jinks at the crossing of the River Styx, 1950s. (Photo courtesy of the Josephine County Historical Society.)

(bottom) Billboard in Cave Junction, 1957. (Photo courtesy of Chas Davis.)

For sale by the Superintendent of Documents, U.S. Government Printing Office
Internet: bookstore.gpo.gov Phone: toll free (866) 512-1800; DC area (202) 512-1800
Fax: (202) 512-2250 Mail: Stop IDCC, Washington, DC 20402-0001

ISBN 978-1-78039-030-7

Great blocks of rock hang as by a thread from the ceiling, while on every side rocks of equal size lie in all conceivable shapes. Standing at the point of entry one looks at the opposite side and sees great cracks, yawning cavities with open mouths of blackness, dismal shadows, to which flickering lights give a ghoulish, dance-like appearance. Yes, the devil seems to be holding high carnival, while his imps would dance the night away.

W. G. Steel, describing the Ghost Room
in "Josephine County Caves" (1888)

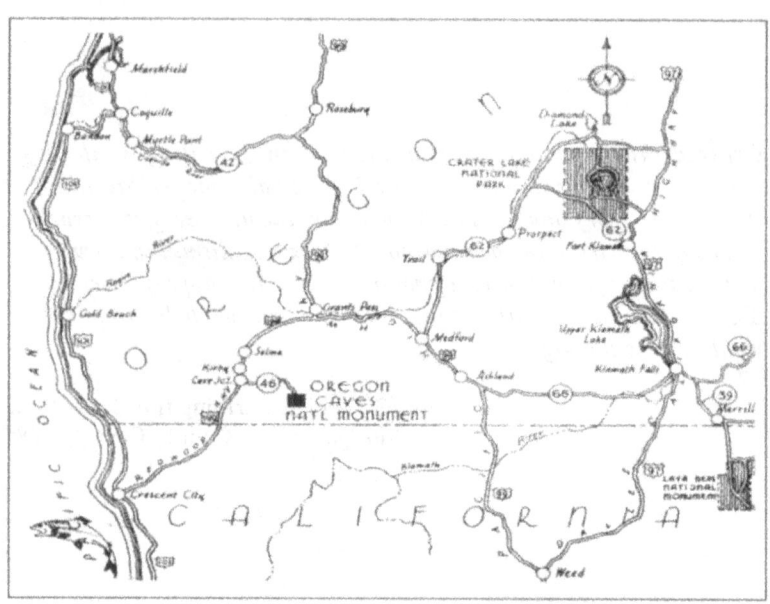

Maps in National Park Service brochure, 1936, by L. Howard Crawford. (OCNM Museum and Archives Collections.)

Contents

Preface ix

Acknowledgments xiii

Introduction: The Marble Halls of Oregon 1

1. Locked in a Colonial Hinterland, 1851-1884 13
  Exploration and westward expansion 14
  Cultural collision and its consequences 16
  Social and economic transition 22
  Discovery of the Oregon Caves 27

2. The Closing of a Frontier, 1885-1915 33
  Developing a "private" show cave 36
  Into a void 41
  The advent of federal land management 45

**3. Boosterism's Public-Private Partnership,
  1916-1933** 62
  Highways to Oregon Caves 63
  Beginnings of a recreational infrastructure 68
  Transfer to the National Park Service 86

4. Improving a Little Landscape Garden, 1934-1943 89
  New lights, but an old script 91
  Camp Oregon Caves, NM-1 95

Development of Grayback Campground 97
CCC projects at Oregon Caves 100
Expanded concession facilities 110
NPS master plans for Oregon Caves 112
Other vehicles for shaping visitor experience 114

5. Decline from a Rustic Ideal, 1944-1995 126
Postwar park development 129
Changes in the forest 134
More visitors and new constituents 138
Attempts to recast the monument 144

6. Recommendations 148
Eligibility for the National Register of Historic Places 149
Interpreting the past at Oregon Caves 158
Additional research 162

Notes 166

Bibliography 216

Appendix 1 – Tour of the Oregon Caves Chateau 220

Appendix 2 - Widening Perceptions and the Viability of
Developing Show Caves, *John E. Roth* 224

Appendix 3 – Road and Trail System 230

Index 232

Preface

Fostering appreciation of historic resources as worthy of preservation is dependent on people seeing them as part of their heritage, and thus worth keeping. This study thus aims to convey the larger story behind material manifestations of the past, especially those still evident in a rugged corner of the Siskiyou Mountains, so as to show their significance or value to the present. A larger goal of this Historic Resource Study is to shed additional light on how cultural perceptions of nature and the resulting trends in tourism have shaped Oregon Caves and the area around it over the span of more than a century. This is a way of attempting to break the habit, which is all too common in agency-funded historical studies, of presenting the park as an island surrounded by a sea where there is little life other than some directive coming from the administering bureau's central offices. A Historic Resource Study should also allow for showing how larger forces (in this case, those beyond the NPS) have affected a place like Oregon Caves and in so doing, allow for building a "land bridge" between the monument and the social, political, and economic patterns governing its historical context.

Despite the name "Oregon Caves," this national monument contains only one cave system. It is located in southwest Oregon, just seven miles north of the state's border with California and some 50 miles inland from the Pacific Ocean. Road access to the coast, however, is limited since the topography is so steep and daunting that the access road (SR 46, the Oregon Caves Highway) is the only unit of state highway system to terminate with a dead end. Trails penetrate further into the mountainous Siskiyou hinterland, most of which is characterized by complex geology and enclaves of mixed-conifer forest. Ranging from 3,680 to 5,280 feet above sea level over just 480 acres, the monument proper (eight acres are located in the town of Cave Junction) is dominated by an overstory of Douglas-fir and other species like Port Orford-cedar, amid small streams or seasonal drainages. A total of some 400 individual plant species in such a small area indicate that conditions are suitable for some endemic flora and fauna. The endemic animals, however, are found within the cave system which consists largely of limestone and marble.

Despite the remote setting of Oregon Caves National Monument, it has occupied a prominent place in the identity of people living in the surrounding area. Promotion of the Oregon Caves included formation of a booster group in Grants Pass, the seat of Josephine County, where members of the "Oregon Cavemen" were linked with the concession company which operated the guide service and other commercial visitor services at the monument from 1923 to 1976. Overseen first by the U.S. Forest Service and later by the National Park Service, the company set important precedents in developing the cave entrance area into a resort containing a hotel, cabins, and other structures within a visually unified designed landscape. One of these structures exemplified the use of "rustic architecture" so well that it achieved the status of national historic landmark in 1987.

National historic landmarks are afforded the highest level of protection in accordance with direction from Congress under the Historic Sites Act of 1935 to "preserve for public use historic sites, buildings, and objects of national significance." Passage of the National Historic Preservation Act (NHPA) in 1966 came with the directive to federal agencies in Section 110 they should nominate all eligible properties (such as sites, structures, districts and objects) under their administrative control to the National Register of Historic Places established by NHPA. This Historic Resource Study is a tool for identifying important properties that qualify for listing on the National Register, as well as relevant themes or "historic contexts," so that managers at the monument can meet their obligations under Section 110 of NHPA; that is, to list eligible properties. Congress did not dedicate funding specifically for this purpose, and given the reality of some bureaus managing millions of acres, the task of inventory and evaluation is still ongoing. Listing of federal properties (which can range from locally to nationally significant) on the National Register has thus tended to be sporadic, especially in the wake of identifying new property types sometimes far removed from the historic buildings that traditionally have dominated the National Register and its more rarified subset of national historic landmarks.

Amendments to NHPA in 1992 removed the need for comprehensive studies and inventory efforts aimed at complying with Section 110 within a set timeframe. Despite that fact, the National Park Service (NPS) continues to undertake assessments of historic resources (generally defined as eligible for the National Register) associated with the park areas it manages. Such undertakings seem to work well in small units like Oregon Caves, especially when they are preceded by context studies written with an eye to the National Register. The most pertinent to Oregon Caves of the latter group is a study by Linda McClelland in 1996 which covered the national park system and facilities in some state parks. This work was subsequently published two years later under the title *Building the National Parks: Historic Landscape Design and Construction* (Baltimore: Johns Hopkins University Press, 1998). McClelland focused on the period between 1916 and 1942, a time when rustic architecture and naturalistic landscapes dominated the design of facilities at Oregon Caves National Monument and other park areas.

McClelland's study supplied context for understanding the breadth of historic resources in national and state parks in the aforementioned period of significance, but it did not offer guidance in formatting subsequent National Register nominations—particularly where resources such as roads and trails are linear in character. This is why nominations of historic properties such as the Oregon Caves Historic District highlighted the buildings and their immediate surroundings as designed landscapes. These have not extended beyond the confines of a polygon drawn to indicate the boundaries of what is "historic" as opposed to what lies beyond it—in many cases the latter is most of a park area which is often classified in this type of zoning as "natural."

As of 2004, concern about historic properties at Oregon Caves has, for the most part, remained within a rather oddly shaped polygon that embraces the seven contributing resources (five buildings and two structures) in the existing historic district.[1] Evaluation of the road and trail system developed between 1916 and 1942 has heretofore not taken place, nor has the identification of contributing resources associated with contexts that are outside of historic landscape design associated with the interwar period. Identifying contributing elements and historic properties in general is generally tied to the four main National Register criteria. These are: (A) those properties associated with events that have made a significant contribution to the broad patterns of American history; or (B) properties associated with the lives of persons significant in our past; or (C) properties that embody the distinctive characteristics of a type, period, or method of construction, or that represent the work of a master, or that possess high artistic value, or that represent a significant and distinguishable entity whose components may lack individual distinction; or (D) properties that have yielded, or may be likely to yield, information important in prehistory or history.[2]

The NPS has developed a thematic framework to address the breadth of most, if not all, historic resources that might need to be assessed against the four main National Register criteria. Locally relevant themes or their facets can be derived from the framework, as might a period of significance. Although the two most recent thematic frameworks have varied drastically with respect to their level of detail, they still form a framework in which to fit a historic property and then evaluate it for possible listing on the National Register.[3] As such, listing is an acknowledgment by the federal agency that a historic property is worthy of preservation. It does not preclude changes or even demolition, but managers must follow prescribed steps in what is called the "Section 106 process" in order to assess an undertaking's effect on a historic property and then mitigate it if the effect is adverse.

Perhaps more important than what this study can provide in identifying and evaluating properties eligible for the National Register is how it serves the purpose of interpreting the past. The study is limited to a relatively short span of time, one reflected in the archival record that emphasizes how Oregon Caves became a functioning part of the local economy and the infrastructure needed to support tourism and park management. Nevertheless, even a small national monument located in the hinterland of southwest Oregon has much to convey about the changing nature of heritage and the efforts to preserve it.

Acknowledgements

Funding for this project materialized in 2004, largely due to the efforts of David Louter, Stephanie Toothman, and Gretchen Luxenberg, historians who work for the National Park Service in Seattle. One of the reasons that funding came about when it did was the fact that most of the source material had been gathered already in order to support a future administrative history of Oregon Caves National Monument. I began assembling material for the administrative history in 1997, something I mostly accomplished as part of intermittent travel to the monument from my duty station at Crater Lake National Park. My supervisors at Crater Lake (Kent Taylor and Marsha McCabe) have supported short-term assistance to Oregon Caves as part of my duties as historian for both parks over the past eighteen years, yet this and other writing projects are of sufficient duration to require financial assistance through the Pacific West Region. One of the efficiencies gained by doing a historic resource study this way is that the source material assembled can serve two documents instead of one. It can also virtually eliminate the overhead associated with a contract.

Another advantage of employing me rather than another historian (either through a term appointment with the NPS or a contract) for the study is that I wanted to produce work that could also be used as the basis for a future publication marking the monument's centennial in 2009. The following chapters are thus an experiment in developing a broader context and more thematic approach than some other studies of this type, and will hopefully reflect some depth in an association with Oregon Caves that goes back to 1977. At that time manager Harry Christianson offered me a job for the summer as a cave guide with two years of college under my belt. I did the standard tour known then as the "spiel" until my great aunt heard that I worked at the monument. She recalled renting horses near what is now Grayback Campground and riding with a friend of hers to the caves in 1917 for a tour led by Forest Service guide Dick Rowley. Her recollection of the trip taken at a time before any roads reached the monument fired my imagination so that I attempted, however crudely, to interpret past interactions between people and the Oregon Caves. It struck Ann Cordero, a NPS seasonal ranger who provided oversight of the concession-run tour, as rather odd but she let me proceed and even provided a copy of Elijah Davidson's article about his discovery of the cave as reference.

Within little more than a year after being hired as a historian by the NPS, I returned to Oregon Caves in 1989 to start my first big project there. I documented three structures as part of a team who produced a package of measured drawings and other documentation for the Historic American Buildings Survey. Drawing from that experience on my next undertaking, I wrote a nomination to the National Register of Historic Places so that the Oregon Caves Historic District could be listed in 1992. In the lull between projects that followed, I found the archivists stationed at branches of the National Archives branches in Seattle and at San Bruno, California, to be very helpful in assisting me with locating reports and other documents pertaining to Crater Lake and Oregon Caves. During this period archaeologist Janet Joyer at the Siskiyou National Forest loaned a large album of photographs that I copied for the NPS museum collection at the monument. Some of them appear in this study, as do those I borrowed from Chas Davis when he managed the Oregon Caves Chateau. Davis later worked for the NPS, and at one point pursued the story of how an invention that made use of stereoscopic reels with photographs originated at the monument and then alerted me to the importance of View Master. Head guides Jay Swofford and Tom Siewert made some initial contacts with former concession employees who loaned photographs for copying or provided information about operations at the monument, especially those during the decades of the 1930s and 40s.

Other people have also helped my work on this study, albeit indirectly, by periodically sending me material relating to Oregon Caves. Foremost among them are Bill Alley, former archivist and historian at the Southern Oregon Historical Society, Larry McLane, past president of the Josephine County Historical Society, and Florenz "Bud" Breitmeyer, whose knowledge of concession operations during the 1930s and 40s is unsurpassed. Other contributors include Roger J. Contor, Doug Deur, Tom DuRant, William R. Halliday, Carol Harbison–Samuelson, Steve Knutson, Francis G. Lange, David Louter, Martha Murphy, Pat Solomon, and Jerry Williams. NPS employees at Oregon Caves have helped me by providing housing and in numerous other ways, not least by their enthusiasm and patience. In the latter regard, I would like to especially thank Superintendent Craig Ackerman, Chief of Resource Management John Roth, Chief of Interpretation Roger Brandt, and Curator Mary Benterou for their support on this and other endeavors. Ackerman, Roth, and Gretchen Luxenberg read the draft manuscript and made suggestions for improving it. John Roth deserves special thanks for contributing an essay which follows the bibliography, as do Elizabeth Hale for copy editing and Mary Williams Hyde for layout.

FIGURE 1. Civilian Conservation Corps enrollees from Camp Oregon Caves rebuilding the Exit Trail, 1935. (Photo by George F. Whitworth, OCNM Museum and Archives Collections.)

Introduction
The Marble Halls of Oregon

Historic resource studies are generally devoted to providing both context and the means to identify material manifestations of the past that are significant to the understanding of how people have interacted with their environment in recorded time. Most opening chapters in such a study move beyond the bounds of a specific site (in this case Oregon Caves National Monument) and follow a chronological sequence of use and occupation by aboriginal peoples, European exploration, activities related to initial settlement by white Americans as well as the effects of contact with aboriginal peoples, discovery of the future park site by settlers, and the promotional efforts made to bring tourists there. Inherent in this progression is a peculiarly North American notion of the frontier, one often defined as the zone or region forming a margin of settled or developed territory, but then applied to land held back from settlement by industrial nation states like the United States and Canada for purposes that included both the economic and aesthetic. These "reservations" were established for a range of purposes such as perpetuating municipal access to watersheds and furnishing timber. They sometimes contained certain tracts considered to be unique geological features and thus warranted special management because of their potential to attract tourists.

An industrial nation state eventually produced tourism on a mass scale, since the more numerous middle classes steadily acquired the means to travel (as only the elite had previously) for

2 INTRODUCTION

FIGURE 2. Statue of a river god in the Grotto, Stourhead Landscape Garden (England). This figure is pointing toward the Pantheon, another stop on a walking circuit designed to present visitors with idealized nature derived from Greek and Roman mythology.

the purpose of experiencing nature as scenery. In most cases elevation to the status of national park or national monument by the federal government did not come without development of transportation networks that increasingly tied peripheral areas such as Josephine County (which surrounds Oregon Caves), to the core of an American industrial nation state. As pack train gave way to wagon road and then to highway, the infrastructure to support tourism in a remote spot like Oregon Caves responded. Promoters, whether they were private concessionaires or government officials, developed Oregon Caves according to a long-established archetype of the landscape garden centered on a grotto or other shallow "cave." Pitched as a resort situated in steep, rugged country clad in towering forest, the national monument and its setting provided at least an illusion of frontier wilderness—one to be explored by foot or horseback once visitors toured the cave as if it were an art gallery. They moved underground from one sculpture to the next, with formal stops dictated by the width of "rooms" and their suggestive decorations.[1]

Steadily rising visitation to the monument was first tied to better and wider highways, though the expanding populations of both Oregon and California (the two states where most visitors originated) must also be considered. Annual visits reached their peak during the late 1970s and then leveled off, possibly in response to escalating fees for cave tours, a slump in per capita income (adjusted for inflation), and an increasing number of competing attractions located in the less remote parts of southwest Oregon. The frontier, or the unbroken expanse of mountain peaks and trees seen as wilderness, maintained its appeal to Americans—with many national forests located closer to centers of population than the monument receiving more recreational visits through the 1980s than ever before. As logging in the adjacent Siskiyou National Forest expanded to areas near the monument during the 1960s, it obliterated parts of the transportation network (mostly by placing roads on top of older trails) that once brought visitors to Oregon Caves. Some areas on the Siskiyou came away largely unaffected and retained their association with the monument, mainly because they had been zoned for recreation or held only marginal value for timber production. These places are included in the following narrative because historic resources of Oregon Caves National Monument cannot be understood without their inclusion.

Historic resources are those material parts of the past which relate to a larger "story" or interpretation that is significant for explaining the present. What distinguishes them from other kinds of cultural resources (such as prehistoric artifacts, plants with ethnobotanical significance, or cultural landscapes with associative values ascribed to them by indigenous peoples) is their linkage with source material in the archival record. These sources are generally in written form, but also include photographs and oral accounts associated with sites, structures, districts, and objects created after 1827, the date of Euro-American contact with the Indians who lived in the area around Oregon Caves. To understand the monument's historic resources and why they might have value or importance, it is necessary to develop a context or background even if the resulting interpretation cannot be separated from a cultural lens that is relative rather than absolute.[2]

Setting

Oregon Caves National Monument consists of 488 acres located in Josephine County, Oregon. All but eight acres form a rectangle that is completely surrounded by the Siskiyou National Forest. The Oregon Department of Transportation nevertheless maintains a right of way through the national forest as part of State Route 46 (also known as the Caves Highway) which terminates at the monument. The remaining eight acres are located in the town of Cave Junction (though four of which are not in federal ownership), where an interagency visitor center stands next to the Caves Highway. A possible addition to the monument, one proposed by the NPS through a general management plan approved in 1998, follows adjacent ridgelines to encompass another 2,377 acres of what is still national forest land at present.

The national monument is situated within a rugged area whose name *Siskiyou* is generally applied to the mountain complex found north of the state line that is six miles from Oregon Caves. This complex extends well into northwest California (where it is known as the Klamath Mountains) and is characterized by old rocks and diverse geology, botanical richness, and steep topography. These qualities have limited human settlement in the mountains around Oregon Caves due to the lack of arable land, though minerals and game prompted periodic forays lasting from a week to several months during the last half of the nineteenth century. Permanent settlement, whether by Indians or newcomers such as the Chinese or white Americans, was usually confined to the Rogue River and its tributaries, though what became the monument is not all that far from the larger basin drained by the Klamath River.

West of Oregon Caves lies the Illinois River, one of the Rogue's main branches, whose valley serves as the primary gateway for most visitors—especially those who reached the monument once road access became available in 1922. The Illinois Valley contains the incorporated towns like Cave Junction and Selma, along with several smaller communities such as Kerby and O'Brien. Far outstripping the valley's population is Grants Pass, seat of Josephine County, located 50 miles north of Oregon Caves along the Rogue River. Grants Pass has maintained a link with the monument in a variety of ways, most famously by being the home of a booster group called the Oregon Cavemen for much of the twentieth century. A less popular access route to the monument originated from the small town of Williams. Located northeast of Oregon Caves, it lies at the upper end of the Rogue's other major tributary, the Applegate River. Another route connects Happy Camp and habitations along the Klamath River with the Illinois Valley. Like the route from Williams, it provides an alternative for the adventurous motorist bound for Oregon Caves.

Purpose and significance

Within that fuzzy and ill-defined idea realm of land management called "heritage," it is not surprising to find that an area's purpose and significance changes, or at least remains vague, through time. The presidential order establishing Oregon Caves National Monument, for example, began by making reference to "certain natural caves...are of unusual scientific interest and importance, and it appears that the public interests will be prompted by reserving these caves with as much land as may be necessary for the proper protection thereof as a National Monument."[3]

This proclamation then expressed the monument's purpose in only two ways. Both of these provisions referenced what constituted protection. The first stated explicitly that the monument is the dominant reservation over adjacent lands in the Siskiyou National Forest if use of the latter interfered with preservation or protection of the Oregon Caves. The other warned all "unauthorized persons" not to "appropriate, injure, remove or destroy any feature," or to settle any of the lands reserved by the proclamation.[4]

Federal officials eventually interpreted the proclamation to allow for the development of a show cave, one with road access for automobiles and supporting infrastructure that included commercial services like hotel accommodation. During the first quarter century of the monument's existence, it functioned as one of the numerous resorts created on national forest lands in Oregon, where the Forest Service granted monopoly privileges to local concessionaires who ran the operation and made specified improvements. The government's role at Oregon Caves largely consisted of supplying infrastructure where its concessionaire could not, with enforcement of the proclamation's provisions for protection almost always limited to when the operator made the Forest Service aware of violations. With Forest Service cooperation, an area of 30,000 acres surrounding the monument functioned at least nominally as a game refuge between 1926 and 1948. Activities such as camping and logging could take place in the refuge, though these uses remained at minimal levels and had negligible impact on the monument due to the lack of road access beyond the Caves Highway during that period.

The monument remained under Forest Service administration during the first 25 years of its existence, yet the agency promoted its recreational appeal resulting from improvements made there rather than any inherent distinctions which bestowed national significance on Oregon Caves. According to one guide aimed at promoting the recreational possibilities in Oregon's national forests, the completion of a road to the monument in 1922 made it a major scenic attraction, instead of "an interesting but inconveniently accessible local attraction" known only to a few people.[5] Even as a major attraction for visitors, however, the monument's appeal centered on the cave tour. This was where the marble formations bore a "more or less striking resemblance to a great variety of objects," according to a promotional folder issued by the Forest Service during the mid 1920s.[6]

By contrast, the NPS saw a need to develop more rational justifications for why Oregon Caves merited the status of national monument once it assumed control of the area in 1934. Much of the agency's reasoning lay rooted in its past, when the NPS had to sift through numerous proposals to establish national parks and decide which ones deserved legislative support shortly after Congress created the bureau in 1916. Oregon Caves received a lukewarm endorsement from Roger Toll, then the main NPS reviewer of candidate areas for the national park system, in 1932. Toll saw the formations as interesting and varied, though the cave's rooms were small and its connecting passages described as narrow. Carlsbad Caverns in New Mexico (which contained the largest room known at the time and some very tall formations) furnished an enviable standard for comparison in what he called the "national interest," but Oregon Caves also possessed a scenic

FIGURE 3. Scenic photography drew its conventions (such as juxtaposing human figures next to much larger sublime elements like enormous trees) from earlier landscape paintings. Frank Patterson took this postcard view next to Big Tree in 1923. (OCNM Museum and Archives Collections.)

setting of forested mountains where varied plant life piqued the curiosity of botanists. Toll also noted that "several types of flora merge here and a number of rare species are found."[7]

The next attempt by the NPS to formally describe the significance of Oregon Caves came during an update of the master plan for the monument in 1945. By that time the plan had evolved from a roll of drawings first produced by NPS landscape architect Francis Lange in 1936 showing how the monument could be further developed. Within a decade the master plan assumed a largely narrative format containing information about resources, interpretive themes, circulation patterns, facilities, and projected needs. The significant "theme" included the monument's mountainous setting as an "outstanding scenic attraction of southern Oregon," the rare plants living in that setting, a large Douglas fir 14 feet in diameter known as "Big Tree," and the geological story covering "a vast period of time." NPS planners placed the cave formations within the envelope of geological processes, describing them as largely products of solution. This characterization (one that could be understood by those having only the slightest acquaintance with science) did not subsume the older view of caves. The resulting calcite deposits were thus said to sometimes assume "fantastic or grotesque shapes" and in others "beautiful or inspirational forms."[8]

By 1952 the NPS began to prioritize the elements of significance in its master plan for the monument, placing geological and biotic distinctions of the Klamath – Siskiyou region at the top. As the "oldest permanent land mass adjacent to the present Pacific shoreline," the extent and magnitude of the story evident in the endemic plants or rock types at Oregon Caves and vicinity had no exact parallels, but were somewhat analogous to the Great Smoky Mountains as a focal point for studying evolution. The cave was still "spectacular," but NPS officials placed greater emphasis in the plan on expanding the monument to include 2,910 acres of adjacent national forest land, where Brewer spruce and Port Orford-cedar were "rapidly being depleted."[9] Just three years later, however, the superintendent of Crater Lake National Park (who had management oversight of the monument at the time) disputed the notion of Oregon Caves possessing national significance. At a time when legislation to expand it appeared to be "imminent," he recommended disposing of the area since Oregon Caves possessed little (in his view) to justify the status of a national monument.[10]

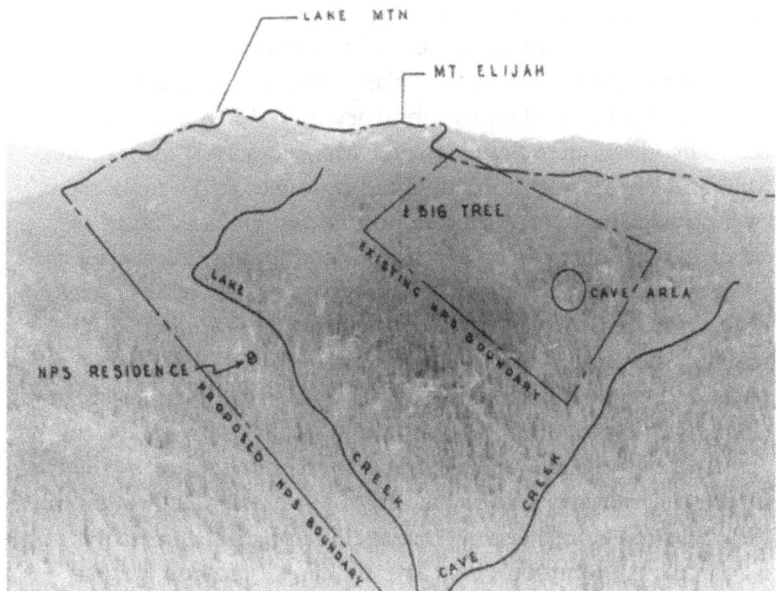

FIGURE 4. Aerial view of Oregon Caves and vicinity, 1949. (OCNM Museum and Archives Collections.)

The first prospectus for Mission 66 (a massive ten year development program aimed at improving park infrastructure in anticipation of the fiftieth anniversary of the NPS in 1966) thus characterized the cave as "mediocre," and disparaged the monument's geological story as "not unusual."[11]

Subsequent master plans tied to the Mission 66 program removed the overtly negative language about Oregon Caves, but statements of significance were short and terse, while any praise for the monument remained faint.[12] By 1975 master plans had become public documents, but the NPS opened the plan's "resource evaluation" section by characterizing the cave as small and incapable of handling large numbers of visitors when compared with other well-known caves in the United States. Against that standard (and probably because of its moderate size), Oregon Caves possessed a "relative lack of significance," though it remained a "major regional resource" providing an educational experience through guided tours. As if to compensate for the cave's "inadequacies," the master plan stated that the monument also preserved an example of primeval forest, one whose value might become increasingly important for sightseeing and scientific studies as the surrounding area was utilized for timber production and other consumptive activities.[13]

The master plan's assessment of the monument in 1975 remained unchanged in agency planning circles throughout the 1980s, at least according to subsidiary NPS documents such as the internally distributed Statement for Management.[14] An updated SFM in 1994, however, highlighted processes at the monument over comparisons with the size, beauty, and endemic fauna of other North American caves. It also attempted to tie surface features such as old growth forest to cave processes, but omitted the built environment even after the Oregon Caves Chateau had attained national historic landmark status in 1987 and then became the centerpiece of a district listed on the National Register of Historic Places in 1992.[15]

Acknowledgement of historic resources being tied to the monument's significance had to wait until December 1997, when the NPS released a draft general management plan document for public comment. Mention of the five buildings (chateau, chalet, ranger residence, guide dormitory, checking station/kiosk) and their designed landscape features as being listed on the National Register came in a separate paragraph which followed wording that closely resembled language about the importance of cave processes and old growth forest found in the earlier SFM.[16] According to the general management plan draft, paleontological discoveries made in 1995 contributed to making the monument a "nationally significant site for well-preserved Pleistocene mammals," though the cave system and tour route were also deemed nationally significant by the time the plan assumed final form in August 1999.[17]

Organization of this study

The following chapters are organized chronologically, as in most historical narrative, but also thematically in order to structure interpretation of the past which provides context and significance for historic resources. In order to tie the study together around a general theme, this work is built around the idea that Oregon Caves is part of larger regional development in the western United States. That development has had to be subsidized, in large part by the federal and state governments, in order for industries like tourism to help a local economy dependent on primary production (mining, logging, agriculture) and services. Tourism, especially

FIGURE 5. Cavemen in front of the Oregon Caves Chateau, 1952. (Photo courtesy of the Josephine County Historical Society.)

the type open to the average person, requires subsidies in form of building transportation infrastructure (usually highways) to be a viable part of an economy. This is a precursor to government projects to develop utility connections or facilities that are aimed at expanding the recreational appeal of an area, as well as the use of private investment capital to develop commercial visitor services such as those found within Oregon Caves National Monument.

Each chapter in this study is tied to what is really an associated subtheme, starting with the Pacific Northwest in general (and Josephine County in particular) being a remote but internal colony in relation to the larger nation state for much of the nineteenth century. Its importance increased with the dawn of transportation links that accelerated the growth of a market economy, a topic highlighted in the second chapter, something which expanded to eventually include tourism. For Oregon Caves to contribute to that economy in any significant way, however, government had to forge a partnership with local boosters to obtain the necessary infrastructure. With chapter three as backdrop, chapter four delves into the specifics of how the monument and its immediate surroundings were developed and marketed as an experience having its origins in the earlier landscape gardens of western Europe. Postwar changes at Oregon Caves are the focus of chapter five, with special emphasis on its place in an expanding local tourist economy, mainly to show how both the built environment and other factors affecting visitor experience have changed over the half century that elapsed since World War II ended. Although a major planning effort served to bring about a dramatic shift in management direction over the intervening decade, the end date of 1995 was chosen because a cave restoration project culminated that year. Recommendations derived from this study furnish something of a conclusion, though they should also be seen as a starting point to examine how past events affecting Oregon Caves might be viewed more critically.

CHAPTER 1

Locked in a Colonial Hinterland, 1851-1884

The title of this chapter is derived from how historian Carlos Schwantes has described the Pacific Northwest, as a region that has supplied raw materials for a national and international market controlled by investment capital located hundreds or thousands of miles away from it. Residents rarely, if ever, derive the full value from foodstuffs, wood products, and minerals produced in the region since there is so little manufacturing in the Pacific Northwest, nor are there retail outlets to match those of the San Francisco Bay Area, Los Angeles Basin, East Asia, Europe, or the eastern seaboard of North America.[1] Josephine County, more especially the area around Oregon Caves, occupies a marginal place within the larger region. The county, with only one urban center in Grants Pass, has usually held one of the bottom few places among the 36 Oregon counties in measures of per capita income. Although primary production in the form of logging, farming, and mining still plays a role in its economy, Josephine County has become largely dependent on the service sector. That sector (which includes tourism, health care, and education) largely relies on government funding. There are some transfer payments in the form of income generated outside of the county through proceeds from investments, but also welfare payments of various kinds.

Initial reliance on primary (generally extractive) means of production for an economic base during the last half of the nineteenth century came about as Josephine County underwent a dramatic and fairly rapid transformation after initial contact between indigenous Indians and white settlers in 1851. White Americans did not know of Oregon Caves and its immediate surroundings until Elijah Davidson's visit there in 1874, but transformation was well underway in the upper Applegate Basin and Illinois Valley (the two areas considered nearest to the future national monument for purposes of this study) by that time. What makes this vicinity and Josephine County unusual within the larger regional context is the absence of the usual precursors to physical transformation—a neat linear progression consisting of exploration, the fur trade, and linkage to the outside by emigrant trails. The process of settlement in southwest Oregon literally began with the first gold discovery in 1851. This chapter will thus emphasize how mining triggered physical changes on the land in what became Josephine County, especially within the Illinois Valley located west of Oregon Caves and along Williams Creek to the northeast.

Miners were soon joined by farmers who grew crops and reared livestock for both a local market (at least initially) and ones reached via pack trains going to Crescent City, California, where animals could be shipped by sea. Reaching distant markets by transporting commodities over difficult terrain slowed the pace of land clearance and other changes associated with farming, as did a precipitous decline in gold production once the richest placer deposits had been extracted. These factors are reflected in the drop of Josephine County's human population from 1,623 in 1860 to only 1,123 fifteen years later.[2] Mining increased the turbidity of streams and thus damaged fish runs even before the advent of hydraulic mining in the 1880s, but they also depleted deer and elk populations by hunting to supplement what they could purchase from nearby farmers. Grazing animals and crops displaced native grasses, but they also reduced the supply of camas and acorns found on bottom land suitable for agriculture. This lead to conflict with local Indians who saw these staples as crucial to their diet, and by 1856, most of the indigenous peoples had been removed from southwest Oregon.[3]

Exploration and westward expansion, 1827-1851

Regional histories of the Pacific Northwest and their more local derivatives typically follow a chronological format that begins with a discussion (however cursory), of Indian peoples prior to contact with white Americans, which is often derived from ethnological and/or archeological evidence. After this "prehistory" is the European and American exploration by sea and land prior to settlement, then some detail about the fur trade, along with Christian missionary activity among the Indians. The narrative usually expands with overland migration by white Americans in the 1840s, then continues its linear march by elaborating on settler encounters with Indians, organization of government as part of incorporation into the larger nation state, so that the frontier period concludes sometime around 1890 with discussion of how primary economic activity forged a distinct society within the often strangely delineated political boundaries. In the colonial hinterland around Oregon Caves and that of Josephine County, however, any such linear progression has been truncated, starting with how Indian removal severely limited the amount of ethnohistorical information that could be collected during the late nineteenth or early twentieth century. Early explorers bypassed the area, as did fur traders, missionaries, and those settlers crossing the continent overland in the 1840s. Miners on Josephine Creek made the first contact with Indians in 1851 and were followed by farmers who began to secure donation land claims less than two years later. Formation of Josephine County as a distinct governmental entity came in 1856, when it split from adjoining (and always more populous) Jackson County.

Exploration of a sort began with a party of Hudson's Bay Company trappers led by Peter Skene Ogden in the late winter of 1827. Ogden departed Fort Vancouver the previous year to implement the company's plan to create a vast fur "desert" devoid of beaver in order to hamper American competition in the fur trade throughout the Pacific Northwest. After going south to the Klamath Basin and toward Mount Shasta, Ogden continued west along the Klamath River and over the crest of the Siskiyou Mountains. He and his group passed along Bear Creek in the Rogue River drainage and traveled to Onion Creek's confluence with the Applegate River (near where the town of Murphy subsequently developed) and then into the middle portion of this watershed. They made camp near the spot where Thompson Creek flows into the river (close to what is now the community of Applegate) but Ogden and his companions furnished almost no description of what they saw, though their leader noted the scarcity of beaver.[4]

Of the early Hudson's Bay Company forays into southern Oregon, Odgen's party came nearest to either the Illinois Valley or the vicinity of Williams. Their characterization of the Applegate Valley as a place ill-suited to trapping beaver left much of what later became Josephine County as a *terra incognita* for the following two decades. This is largely due to its location away from a Hudson Bay Company "trail" that connected the Willamette Valley with the Sacramento River. The "trail" route (which made use of a network of faint traces made by Indians during trade activities) went through the Rogue River Valley in what later became Jackson County, but getting no closer than the area surrounding the future Grants Pass. Travelers like Ewing Young, who in 1834 brought cattle north from the Sacramento Valley to settlers occupying parts of the Willamette Valley, kept fairly close to the Hudson Bay trail. So did a party dispatched from the United States Exploring (Wilkes) Expedition who sought the most practical inland route from Oregon to California in 1841.[5]

In no case could the north-south travel "corridor" be described as a major artery for settlers or commerce, even when a part of the Southern Emigrant Route (Applegate Trail) began running through the same portion in what later became Jackson and Josephine counties in 1846. The California Gold Rush that commenced two years later spurred the building of a rough wagon road to move Willamette Valley grain southward to a suddenly lucrative market. It also helped to move newly arrived Americans who had previously come to Oregon by sea or overland, but then sought their fortunes in California as "Argonauts." Few of these emigrants saw the Rogue Valley and southern Oregon as a place to settle, at least initially, since the goldfields of 1848 and 1849 lay no closer than Sutter's Fort on the American River near Sacramento or in the foothills of the Sierra Nevada. Not until 1850, when prospectors found gold in the Klamath River drainage, and then the following year further north near what became Jacksonville, did the wagon road really begin to bring large-scale changes to the Rogue Valley and outlying areas.

Cultural collision and its consequences, 1852-1856

Within the area of southwest Oregon and northwest California dominated by the Klamath Mountains, the first five years of contact between white miners and the indigenous population quickly

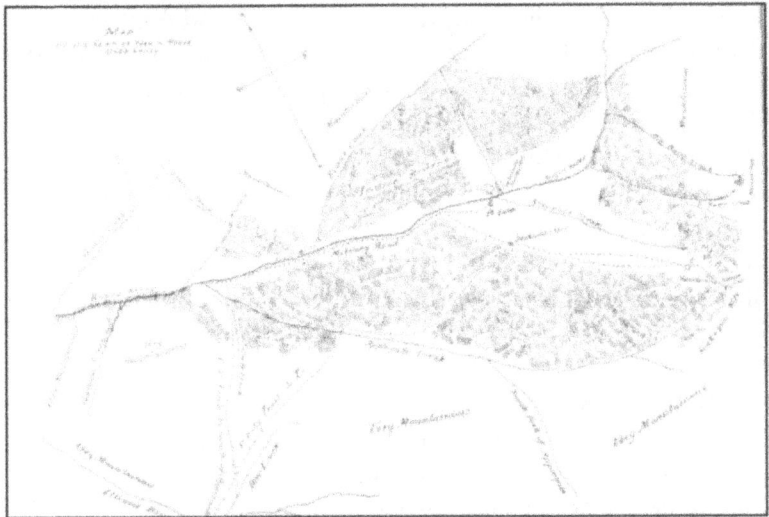

FIGURE 6. Sketch depicting theater of war in the Rogue and Illinois basins, c. 1857. (Courtesy of the Josephine County Historical Society.)

degenerated into chaos. Although sometimes flavored by murder and depredations on both sides, most of the recorded atrocities that took place during this period occurred outside the area of Oregon Caves.[6] One battle, however, was fought on the Applegate River at Murphy Creek in January 1856, and then followed by another at Eight Dollar Mountain in the Illinois Valley two months later. In all probability more devastating, at least from the Indian point of view, and proceeding armed warfare, were the small pox outbreaks. The first swept south from seafarers by way of the Columbia River during the 1780s, with more pestilence of shorter duration coming north from the California coast in 1837-38.[7]

The available evidence indicates that Indians living in what became Josephine County numbered considerably fewer than those of the Rogue Valley in Jackson County at the time of contact with white settlers. What might have been the case before that time is purely conjecture, as the archival records rarely yield even a little information about the linguistic or cultural affiliation of the Indians that American settlers or others of European extraction encountered in the five years following 1851. At minimum, severe disruption to Indian lifeways resulted from five years of conflict in the Illinois Valley, upper Applegate drainage and along the Klamath River. By the end of 1856 many (if not most) of the

Indians from the valleys of the Rogue, Illinois, and Applegate rivers were forcibly removed from their homelands and then relocated on the central Oregon coast. Indians native to the Willamette Valley, previously decimated by diseases and then so overwhelmed by white settlers that they could not offer even token resistance, reluctantly joined their neighbors from southwest Oregon on a reservation that shrank dramatically over the ensuing decades. Some of the Takelma, Dakutebede (Athapaskans), and Shasta of southwest Oregon chose other forms of exile such as intermarriage with white miners or refuge among other Indians in California.

Native peoples situated along the lower reaches of the Klamath River, by contrast, were allowed to remain in scattered villages or "rancherias," even though the effects of war on them during the 1850s proved to be just as devastating. These settlements of Shasta, Karok, and Yurok persisted past the period of initial contact due to their remoteness, as it still required several days travel in 1890 for a person in Happy Camp to reach Yreka or Grants Pass. In addition, Indians living along the Klamath River were supposed to be more numerous than those in the Illinois Valley or upper Applegate even in aboriginal times.[8] Indigenous inhabitants of the lower Klamath could thus inform ethnohistorical work on native lifeways throughout the late nineteenth and early twentieth centuries. Ethnographers and linguists seeking similar insights to aboriginal southwest Oregon labored under more severe, if not crippling, handicaps due to their few consultants suffering extended and usually permanent geographic displacement.[9]

The tragic plight of indigenous peoples who were removed from southwest Oregon in 1856 should be understood at three levels. First is the national context, where efforts to clear lands of Indian title in the southeastern United States and old Northwest culminated in a formal government policy by 1830 of removing tribes. Congress passed legislation that year to establish districts west of the Mississippi River from which Indian title had been removed, and to exchange those tracts for Indian-held lands in the eastern states. Its "success" was reflected in the fact that over the next decade most of the indigenous people within the boundaries of the United States found themselves west of the Mississippi, such that the bulk of relocated Indians settled in what policy makers called a "permanent" frontier along the western border of Missouri and Arkansas. Further westward expansion meant modi-

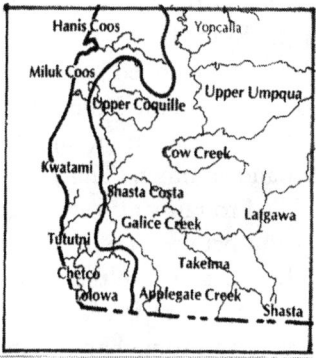

FIGURE 7. Displacement of Southwest Oregon Indians. The diagram at left depicts the location of the Siletz and Grand Ronde reservations in relation to the generalized movement of peoples from their homelands. Names of aboriginal groups and their approximate ancestral territories are highlighted at right for southwestern Oregon. Derived from Jeff Zucker, et al. *Oregon Indians: Culture, History and Current Affairs* (Portland: Oregon Historical Society Press, 1989), 92.

fying the idea of Indian frontier, to where Indians might be concentrated on small reservations of land made for them. This "reservation system" was envisioned to be temporary, with government aid to Indians intended only for a limited period, until those on reservations could support and assimilate themselves into mainstream society.[10]

What took place during the 1850s in southwest Oregon manifested both ideas. An act of Congress dated June 5, 1850, directed an appointed Indian agent to negotiate treaties as part of purchasing Indian lands in western Oregon.[11] The government's intent was to remove indigenous peoples in western Oregon to lands located east of the Cascade Range, but Indians refused to go (they preferred smaller reservations in their own territory instead) so the 19 treaties negotiated by the Indian agent in 1851 remained unratified by the United States Senate. This state of affairs led to appointment of a new Indian "commissioner" for the Oregon Territory in 1853, a person invested with considerable latitude in treaty making. Joel Palmer negotiated treaties in southwest Oregon even before his authorization by Congress to do so. But these treaties were subsequently ratified, thus legitimizing cessions made by groups such as the "Rogue River" (Takelma) and the "Shasta Costas" (Athapaskan).[12] Only the Takelma received a "temporary" reservation of roughly 100 square miles, one that lay between Evans Creek and the Rogue River, though it lasted only until the end of open hostilities between Indians and whites in 1856. By that time Palmer had developed a plan for mass removal to a coastal reservation, one that the military carried out that spring and summer. This occurred despite the fact that Congress had failed to ratify a treaty negotiated by Palmer that covered an area lying between California and the Columbia River, one that included lands where the Siletz Indian Reservation had been created by executive order.[13] A few indigenous people escaped the roundups and some bands remained in their coastal villages, but the Illinois Valley and upper Applegate had effectively been cleared of their native inhabitants.[14]

The dire reality of life in a new place constitutes the second level of consequences stemming from the removal policy, since the Siletz Reservation posed a stark challenge to the survival of both its inhabitants and their cultures. It originally encompassed more than 1.4 million acres, but was poorly suited for agriculture even if the Indians had wanted to become farmers or ranchers as the government intended. Most of the early attempts at agriculture were necessarily experimental, as no one knew which crops might succeed. Most failed, and with rapid depletion of game animals (as well as poor fishing) the human population plummeted. The

Takelma population, for example, declined from 590 in 1857 to 350 just a year later. Some Takelmas received annual annuities in food and clothing since Congress had ratified their treaty. This distinction made them slightly more fortunate than the majority of Indians on the reservation, people who had no ratified treaty and thus did not qualify for assistance. Many Indians tried to return to their home territories, but soldiers stationed at nearby forts were ordered to bring them back.[15]

For those who continued to live on the reservation, it meant a mandatory amalgamation of all western Oregon Indians. Children were forced to attend school, where they could not speak their native languages or engage in traditional practices. Reductions in the size of the Siletz Reservation accompanied these barriers to cultural transmission. Congress chopped it to some 225,000 acres in 1875 once individual Indians received allotments of land.[16] By 1900 just 483 people remained on the Siletz Reservation which lost another 190,000 acres in 1894, so it is not surprising that the total number of Takelma-speaking informants on which anthropologists of the time could base their work consisted of just three or four older women.[17]

The Takelma and their Athapaskan-speaking neighbors were shattered by a sequence of warfare, removal, and life on a distant reservation—all in the space of perhaps two decades. It is worth asking what might have happened had they been allowed to return to their homelands as more than marginalized victims of conquest.[18] The idea of "contested space" provides a third level with which to understand this collision of cultures. The rush by miners during the early 1850s to the Illinois Valley, upper Applegate drainage, and the lower basin of the Klamath River Basin for placer gold came with impacts in the form of increased turbidity, sedimentation, and bed alteration in the streams. Indians certainly would have noticed the devastating effects of mining on the numbers of anadromous fish, particularly the fall runs of chinook and coho salmon.[19] Game such as deer and elk disappeared where gold could be extracted in sufficient quantity to create centers of mining activity like Waldo and Althouse. The advent of farming as early as 1853 in places like the Illinois Valley constituted something of a double whammy to native peoples. Even if agriculture was restricted to a smaller area than mining, it corresponded to land that Indians used to collect seeds, acorns, and camas bulbs. Clearing oaks and plowing grass meadows filled with camas deprived Indians of these food sources, as did the swine that white settlers raised on their land claims.[20] Consequently, the prospects for the peaceful co-existence of two drastically different lifeways (or systems of survival), at least during the 1850s, were virtually nonexistent.

Social and economic transition

Although mining could certainly be disruptive to fish runs and riparian areas in general, environmental impacts dating from the 1850s are difficult to assess a century and a half later. The gold discoveries made in the Illinois Valley during the first half of that decade are probably more significant in contributing to the rapid removal of Indians from the region, as well as the political organization of southern Oregon, than as a lasting economic contribution or type of land tenure. After some prospecting on the Klamath River in 1850 and 1851, white miners headed toward the Illinois Valley from the Happy Camp vicinity. They found gold in Josephine Creek and Canyon Creek, then made additional strikes by the spring of 1852 so that mining activity centered on areas such as lower Sucker Creek, the East Fork of the Illinois River, and Althouse Creek. Over the following year an estimated one thousand miners worked on ten miles along Althouse Creek, so that a town called Waldo formed and became something of a rival to another town in the Rogue Valley known as Jacksonville.

The sudden surge in southern Oregon's white population brought by mining activity led to the creation of Jackson County in 1852.[21] It included all of the Rogue, Applegate, and Illinois valleys, so further partition occurred in early 1856 as more miners came to the vicinity of Waldo. At that point the territorial legislature created a new county comprised of largely mountainous terrain which amounted to roughly two fifths (1,625 square miles) of what had been Jackson County. Josephine County is somewhat unique among Oregon counties in being named for a woman, though Josephine Rollins ultimately made her permanent residence in California. As daughter of the man who found gold on a creek located west of Kerby in 1851, Rollins had little choice but to follow her parents to Yreka when Indians attacked soon after the discovery.[22]

She did not return to the Illinois Valley, like so many miners had who called Josephine County home for short periods during

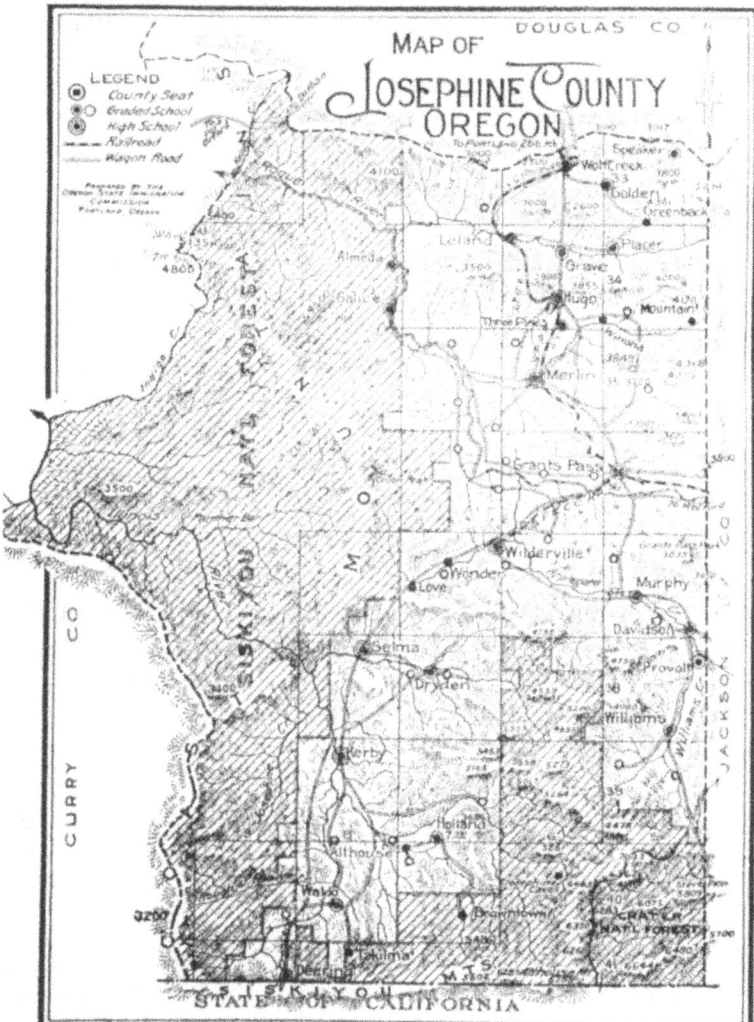

FIGURE 8. Map of Josephine County by the Oregon Immigration Commission, about 1910.

the 1850s. Unlike the Rollins family, however, most gold seekers tended to move toward the most lucrative diggings regardless of Indian troubles. As a group their origins were multi-national, with Chinese miners the largest foreign contingent in 1858, a year when they comprised roughly a quarter of the county's population according to census figures.[23] Over the previous decade the number of miners working at any one time in the county fluctuated greatly, depending upon any number of factors.[24] Some literally "floated" between Oregon and California prior to surveyors locating a boundary line on the ground in 1854, voting in both places and paying taxes in neither.[25]

All of the mining in Josephine County and elsewhere in southern Oregon during the 1850s can be described as *placer*; that is, aimed at deposits held in suspension by sand or gravel laid down by rivers (and sometimes glaciers). This is different from lode mining, where embedded minerals such as gold are extracted from fissures or other gaps within surrounding rocks.[26] Most placer deposits, at least in Josephine County, have been located in riparian areas or along river terraces, usually at the lower elevations. Rich placer deposits within stream channels lasted only a few years, so that gold mining in southwest Oregon hit its peak during the first decade of settlement.[27]

By the end of 1863 one observer described the vicinity of Waldo as "formerly very rich diggings, and some pay yet."[28] To place this statement in context, it is worth considering how the chronological development of mining technology is tied to the need for equipment and capital. The relatively simple placer technologies of panning and wooden boxes graduated in size (going from a rocker or cradle to a much larger Long Tom) allowed individuals and groups with relatively minimal capital to flock to places like Waldo and extract gold until the easily obtainable deposits had been exhausted. Larger cooperative ventures or corporate organization was needed for raising the money required for sluice boxes (essentially a bigger Long Tom that could extend hundreds of feet within a stream) and hydraulic mining. The latter method utilized special equipment and ditches to divert streams, in order for large quantities of water to be directed under high pressure to liquefy soil. Hydraulic mining could thus obliterate hillsides and had an obvious impact on streams and riparian areas. One investment company began building a ditch to divert water from the Illinois River's east fork in 1852 for work around Waldo, and remained in operation for another two years or so.[29]

Accounting for less than a quarter of Josephine County's total gold production over the following century, lode (or "hard rock") mining is even more capital-intensive and specialized since it involves tunnels and other excavation. Prospectors located such a vein in the Althouse vicinity as early as 1861. After digging two tunnels, the company began crushing quartz and then extracted gold with an arrastra, so that the mine produced around $25 per ton through much of the 1860s. Stamp mills being more efficient

FIGURE 9. Early twentieth century hydraulic mining operation at Waldo. (Photo courtesy of the Josephine County Historical Society.)

(yet much more expensive), the new owners worked the vein with this method for a few months in 1875.[30] Fairly rich areas like Althouse allowed for different technologies to be used concurrently so that "a very large number of miners labored there with satisfactory results" for more than 15 years, according to one observer.[31]

Although the era of intensive mining persisted for another couple of decades, its contribution to the population of Josephine County began to wane by 1860. With the easily accessible placer deposits quickly exhausted, some miners headed north to the Fraser River in 1858, and from there to Colorado, Nevada, and eastern Oregon.[32] Put into a national context, Oregon's total production (in which Josephine County played an ever smaller role) never amounted to more than a tiny fraction of the total gold extracted from all western states during the nineteenth and twentieth centuries.[33] Without the boom stemming from low-tech placer mining, Josephine County's population shriveled from 1,623 in 1860 to just 1,204 a decade later. Residents in the Illinois Valley continued to decline during the 1870s, but the county's population surged upward to 2,400 in 1880. The number of people in Oregon, meanwhile, more than tripled during that period (going from 52,465 in 1860 to 174,768 in 1880) while residents of Jackson County also tripled from 3,736 in 1860.[34]

In contrast to the fluctuations associated with mining, farming can be credited with helping to stabilize Josephine County's population, at least to some degree, before the railroad connected it with the Willamette Valley in 1884. Agriculture commenced in 1853, when crops and livestock arrived in the Illinois and Applegate districts, where miners previously had to rely on foodstuffs brought from Crescent City or the Willamette Valley. Most of the early agricultural settlement in Josephine County (this being from 1853 to 1855) resulted from entries made under the Donation Land Claim Act (DLCA) of 1850.[35] Mountain barriers and comparatively poorer soils furnish the main reasons why these claims amounted to considerably fewer in number than those which allocated most of the arable land in western Oregon's interior valleys—the Willamette, Umpqua, and the Bear Creek portion of the Rogue. For example, the Illinois Valley attracted just twenty-two entries for free land, with virtually all of these claims confined to the aforementioned "triangle." Only eight donation land claims could be found in that portion of the Applegate River that included Williams Creek, Missouri Flat, and the mouth of Murphy Creek.[36] Later settlers purchased public land directly in various ways, most commonly under the Homestead Act passed in 1862 or through laws that essentially legalized squatting.[37]

Until 1880 a relatively small amount of viable farm land, as well as the inherent difficulties associated with reaching both of these areas in the absence of a railroad or major wagon road, limited the number of donation land claims and property acquired by any other means. Farmers experienced no difficulties in selling their produce and meat locally when placer mining boomed during the 1850s, but the contraction which followed made them more dependent on access to outside markets. The most lucrative gateway for such intra- or interregional export proved to be Crescent City since it offered access to San Francisco by sea. Crescent City could only be reached by pack trail from southwest Oregon until 1857, when a slightly wider wagon road connected Jacksonville to the coast by way of the Applegate Valley, Kerby, Waldo, and the Smith River.[38] Stages and supply wagons also served farmers and merchants located in the Illinois and Applegate drainages, whether they originated from Crescent City or connected at Jacksonville with the north-south route that linked Portland with Sacramento.[39] The costs associated with this access during the early 1880s were probably the reason why farms in the Illinois Valley (and, by extension, the Applegate drainage) commanded only one half the price of agricultural properties situated in the main Rogue Valley corridor.[40]

FIGURE 10. An early view of Kerby with Eight Dollar Mountain in the background. (Photo courtesy of the Josephine County Historical Society.)

One account published in 1884 described the Illinois Valley as having drifted into decay after the miners began to abandon their placer claims more than two decades earlier.[41] Many of the Chinese miners left to work on building railroads by the early 1880s, taking with them much of the demand for hogs. Farmers who remained grew some crops and ran a few cattle for a basic livelihood that meant bare subsistence in some cases. They hunted, just as the miners had for bears and deer (elk had become scarce by the 1870s), partly to supplement their food supply in addition to reducing threats to livestock.[42] Many farmers became miners in the winter as a way to join the cash economy (gold being convertible to hard currency) and in so doing, brought some measure of stability to a valley containing only a couple of sleepy hamlets.[43]

Discovery of the Oregon Caves, 1874-1884

The same pattern of a boom fueled by placer mines and then slow decline unfolded around Williams, as it had in the Illinois Valley. Gold discoveries in 1859 led to establishment of Williamsburg (the suffix was eventually dropped) which boasted a post office in 1860 and where 6,000 people supposedly resided two years later.[44] Placer deposits played out fairly quickly, but Williams qualified as a mining district, at least according to one source, based on having both hydraulic and quartz mines in 1897.[45] Just as it had elsewhere in Josephine County, mining persisted but lost its central position in the local economy of Williams by the end of the Civil War. A few residents could survive along Williams Creek, making their basic livelihood during the growing season on donation land or a homestead, but they had to spend at least a portion of the wet winter months at their mining claims a short distance away.[46] Most had come to the Williams vicinity by way of the Willamette Valley or California, but they originated from Ohio, Kentucky, Indiana, Illinois, Kentucky, or Missouri—and in most cases being only a generation removed from an earlier trans-Applachian frontier.

Elijah Jones Davidson is representative of both the settlement pattern on Williams Creek and that of other areas in the American West. He was part of a group celebrated by many nineteenth and early twentieth century historians, one who penetrated the unexplored wilds, waging battle with the forces of nature to impose their will on the land. Feted for their self-reliance and emphasis on individual freedom, these "pioneers" embodied the reasons as to why Americans thought they could be considered exceptional, since Davidson and his neighbors were at the forefront of a quickly unfolding settlement wave across the continent.[47] More recently some historians see this group of pioneers as derivative from one of four British folkways that imprinted a specific cultural pattern on the upland (or "mountain") south, as distinct from the tidewater or piedmont regions. Davidson belonged to a group sometimes labeled the "Scotch-Irish," one often characterized by being restless, land-hungry, and having an acceptance of settling sparsely populated areas where their crops and livestock could be located some distance from their neighbors.[48]

Although born in Illinois, Davidson (1849-1927) came to Oregon as an infant in a wagon by way of the overland route. After spending several years trying to farm donation land in what later became southeast Portland (the Laurelhurst Lake vicinity), Davidson's parents settled in Polk County near Monmouth by 1855. They then went south to Williams Creek in 1866 for unknown reasons, though Davidson's father probably went to join a cousin there who filed for a donation land claim in the Applegate Valley as far back as 1854.[49] Elijah married in 1870 and lived around Williams at the time he discovered the Oregon Caves, though he and his wife later moved to Crescent City, and then Bandon, on the Oregon coast. The Davidsons even went to

Nome, Alaska, for several years before returning to buy a farm at Missouri Flat, near Provolt, on the Applegate River.[50]

In the generally accepted version of the cave's discovery, an account written almost fifty years later by Davidson, he described a hunting trip into the Siskiyou Mountains starting from Williams. It began with five other men, yet after one night's camp in the "meadows" on Grayback Mountain, the group split up and each member hunted alone.[51] The only contemporary account, one by Williams resident William W. Fidler, was written in 1877 to document exploration of the cave, but not published until 1887. Fidler simply credited Davidson with accidental discovery while pursuing a wounded deer in company with his dog.[52] Davidson, however, included a bear whose appearance shifted the focus of his hunt and thus became central to the first-person narrative. It concluded with some ingenuity on Davidson's part, in that he placed the dead deer in front of the cave, thereby luring the bear outside with a meal. Davidson could thus return the following day to bag the bruin while it slept after consuming much of the deer carcass.[53] The only divergent account, albeit in a conversation record from the NPS management assistant at Oregon Caves in 1970, summarized the main points given by a Yurok Indian who claimed her grandfather guided the Davidson party. She recalled that William Norris, Sr., one of Davidson's neighbors, helped the party track a bear with dogs. Having chased their quarry inside the cave, three men and a dog entered and eventually killed the bear.[54]

Even if there are some discrepancies concerning the discovery, it is worth noting that the emphasis placed on the priority assigned to Davidson has persisted. Although credited with discovery of the cave in published accounts of the 1880s, Davidson's importance magnified once Oregon Caves could be reached by automobile. A road from the Illinois Valley opened during the summer of 1922, the same year Davidson published his discovery narrative, and brought more visitors to the cave (10,000) than perhaps all previous years combined.[55] At that point Oregon Caves went from a curiosity reached only by mountain trail to a regional draw that attracted private investment capital, though it required a subsidy by way of government-funded additions to infrastructure. Davidson did not stand to benefit from changes brought by the road, though he did supply a promotional vehicle (no matter how the story of discovering the cave was told) that virtually all visitors could understand. Cave tours were already a scripted experience,

FIGURE 11. Elijah Davidson with his gun in Grants Pass, about 1926. (U.S. Forest Service, Siskiyou National Forest.)

in that rooms acquired names for purposes of orientation, while formations elicited comparisons with terrestrial creatures and objects even in 1877.[56] The discovery also provided a starting point for stories, often fanciful, though they served to reduce dissonance among visitors who associated a subterranean environment with gloom and melancholy. As a device for promotion, the Davidson narrative can be taken at face value, as another instance where a western wonder came to light through the lone frontiersman. It can also be appreciated symbolically, where the story's characters of hunter, dog, deer, and bear respectively pertain to male survival, loyalty, paradise, and the wild.[57]

Only a small number of people visited for a decade after Davidson's discovery, with the few surviving accounts each repeating the same elements: disorienting travel through the cave, strangely beautiful formations of varying shapes and sizes, but also the taking of "specimens" as souvenirs.[58] In all probability these parties numbered fewer than ten, given the speed of travel by wagon to Williams and how relatively few people knew about the cave, much less possessed the means or desire to reach it. The absence of a wagon road or passable trail meant that prospective visitors needed to secure Davidson or one of his neighbors as a guide. These limitations effectively restricted touring parties to residents of Jacksonville, still the only town in southern Oregon where residents numbered more than five hundred.

In August 1884, however, a group led by Thomas Condon came from the University of Oregon in Eugene and stopped in Jacksonville on their way to the cave. Condon's lecture at a meeting hall on the geological structure of Oregon, one that outlined changes that took place over millions of years, paid for most of the travel expenses. He and several students continued by wagon to Davidson ranch near Williams, where the road ended, so that Carter Davidson (guide for several previous touring parties and brother of Elijah) could lead them to the cave. They used candles for illumination and noted how white the formations appeared, such that reflected light revealed "millions of sparkling diamonds." One participant mentioned obstacles in the form of slippery rocks, narrow passages, and low ceilings that hampered travel through even a portion of the cave, there being no ladders or other devices to assist visitors.[59]

The prospects for easier access began to change less than a year later, some months after the railroad reached a small hamlet called Grants Pass on Christmas Eve of 1883. One of the Davidsons discussed the cave with Walter Burch, an acquaintance who began to explore the possibilities for a more direct route to it in November 1884. Now that Grants Pass possessed a rail connection from the north, Burch looked at how future visitors might approach what were then called the Josephine County Caves from the Illinois Valley. Instead of going over Grayback Mountain from Williams, he reasoned, a shorter and perhaps easier route might be blazed by way of Sucker Creek or one of its tributaries. Providing improved access with one or more trails was, however, contingent on Burch controlling the cave and land that surrounded it.[60]

FIGURE 12. Cave entrance and creek outflow about 1912. (U.S. Forest Service photo, Siskiyou National Forest.)

CHAPTER 2

The Closing of a Frontier, 1885-1915

The frontier, especially as this concept pertains to the United States, is sometimes defined as a shifting or advancing zone that marks the successive limits of Euro-American settlement. As a cultural construction, this idea resonated with a society that saw its expansion as a political unit in the form of margins in settled or developed territory. Josephine County represented one such margin until 1883 since its access to national and international markets was impeded by the lack of a transportation system capable of profitably carrying heavy loads of agricultural or other commodities over long distances. By better linking western products to a larger market economy, railroads received federal subsidies in the form of land grants to put an end to the farmer's isolation. Their tracks also prompted investors to expand agricultural production in addition to other types of extraction such as minerals, fish, and logs. This fueled population growth, but all of these outcomes were predicated on producers being close enough to the tracks so that additional transport costs (in the form of tolls and freight charges on the relatively few wagon roads suitable for hauling goods in quantity) could be minimized.[1]

Regular stagecoach service that commenced between Sacramento and Portland in July 1860 made a ferry crossing of the Rogue River known as Grants Pass into a station stop. It remained just that until the railroad arrived, whereupon Grants

Pass became a commercial center, but one still in Jackson County. Residents of Josephine County petitioned the state legislature in 1885 to change the boundary in order for Grants Pass and its rail connection to fall within their purview, one that consequently embraced a total of 1.04 million acres (about 1.7 percent of the state; Jackson County was left with 1.78 million acres).[2] Most of Josephine County's population growth during this period occurred in the Grants Pass area, so that few people expressed surprised when it became the county seat in 1886 after a vote where the new city eclipsed its competitors (Kerby and Wilderville) by 116 ballots of the 716 cast.[3] The effect on business generated in the Illinois Valley and from Williams was immediate; instead of their commerce flowing to Jacksonville by stage and wagon as it had since the 1860s, both areas fell further behind communities located in the main Rogue River corridor.[4] Wagon roads connected communities located away from the rail line (one built by the Southern Pacific to connect Oregon with California in 1887, thus finishing a project that had stalled in Roseburg and Redding during the early 1870s), but travel by stage was slow and uncomfortable in comparison to the train, while freight wagons could not approach the capacity of a boxcar. To further illustrate the difficulties associated with being off the main rail corridor, the fastest horse-drawn stages needed 24 hours to go from Grants Pass with Crescent City. Only when automobile stages began their operation in 1914 along this route through the Illinois Valley did the trip take as little as 12 hours.[5]

In the minds of at least two county residents, the portal created by trains stopping at Grants Pass made "the great limestone caves of Josephine County" worthy of developing into a showpiece. As early as 1885, a few people saw the cave's potential to bring tourist dollars from beyond Oregon and thus diversify (if only in a small way) a regional economy still dependent on agriculture and to a lesser extent, mining. These entrepreneurs blazed and opened pack trails to the cave from two directions in the belief that the existing road network could bring visitors in sufficient numbers to recoup a modest investment made in ladders and camping amenities at the cave. They generated some local (and occasionally regional) publicity that made frequent reference to how the Josephine County Caves compared favorably with the Mammoth Cave in Kentucky, but this venture failed, as did the one that followed. Only when public subsidies for automobile

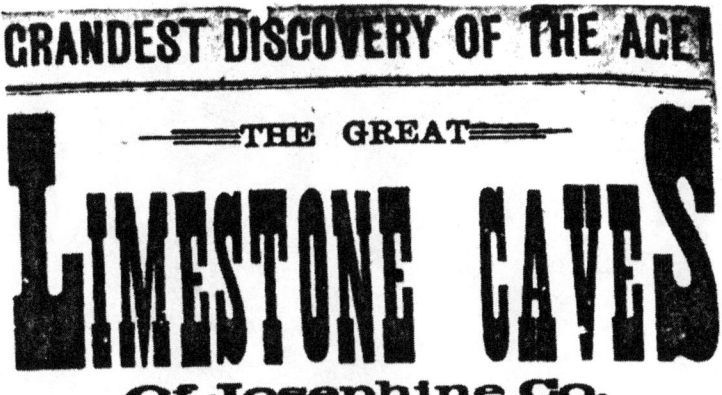

FIGURE 13. Advertisement circulated by Burch and Harkness in 1885. (Courtesy of the Mazamas Library.)

roads and associated infrastructure became available could the Oregon Caves attract sufficient private investment to make tourism at such a remote site represent even a small move away from local dependence on extraction as an economic base.

FIGURE 14. W.G. Steel (center, top) with the Harkness Brothers and S.S. Nicolini (center, front) at the cave entrance, August 1888. (Photo by S.D. Dewert, OCNM Museum and Archives Collections.)

Developing a "private" show cave, 1885-1894

Walter Burch first heard of the cave in 1884 and decided to explore the feasibility of a new transportation route going up Sucker Creek from the Illinois Valley. According to Josephine County historian Larry McLane, Burch found himself in a position to examine the potential of the site as a commercial show cave because he had developed part of the Grants Pass townsite prior to the railroad's arrival.[6] He and his brother-in-law, Homer Harkness, saw the cave's potential as lucrative enough to post a notice of location (the precursor to a mining claim) in the spring of 1885 at the entrance Davidson found, having arrived there by way of Horse Mountain.[7] They attempted to gain title to 160 acres that included the cave under the Timber and Stone Act of 1878, but failed to obtain the required survey, so the claim could not go to patent.[8]

While he and Harkness waited for the survey, Burch hired four men to build a trail up Cave Creek. It took almost six weeks for the crew to construct just over four miles of trail that connected the Sucker Creek "road" with the cave. Once at the entrance, Burch's crew fashioned wooden ladders and then cleared a campground.[9] Work continued the following spring, when Burch and one of the laborers returned to cut a trail from Williams Creek to the cave by way of "Meadows Mountain" and Lake Creek. Burch went back to his base at Grave Creek, near Leland, and brought another man to the cave entrance, this time to build a cabin covered with shakes. Despite these improvements and the advertisements placed in the weekly Grants Pass newspaper, very few visitors came to the cave in 1886 or the following summer.[10] Upon spending an estimated $1,500, the two "proprietors" quit their operation at the cave after 1888.

That year, ironically enough, a feature in a Portland literary magazine provided some favorable publicity about what awaited tourists at the cave. The three Harkness brothers guided a party originating from Portland when they arrived on the train in Grants Pass on August 25.[11] From the account left by one member of the party, William G. Steel, they traveled on a "reasonably good" wagon road to Williams and then labored with two packhorses on Burch's trail to the cave. In many respects no more noteworthy than other journeys to the cave at that time, the party intended to proceed to Crater Lake once they returned to Grants Pass, thus it presaged later regional tours.[12] The party also attempted to take the first photographs in the cave, an endeavor that required the assistance of four men to carry a camera and supplies needed for flash (or "instantaneous") photography. Those images failed to produce prints, but the newspaper accounts generated most likely formed the basis for including the cave in the first tourist guidebook for Oregon and Washington, one published in 1891.[13]

In realizing the need for a larger amount of private investment capital than what Burch and Harkness could provide, the next "owners" decided to promote the cave like a lode mine of the period. W.J. "Uncle Jack" Henderson and Frank M. Nickerson of Kerby, in conjunction with "Captain" Alfonso B. Smith of San Diego, located a mineral claim encompassing the cave sometime between 1889 and 1891. They did so in order to take nominal possession through posting a notice of location, but did not bring the claim to patent.[14] The trio hoped to attract investors through newspaper publicity generated in San Francisco, arguably the West's economic capital for 40 years and the logical center for promoting any middling- or large-scale speculative venture. It was presumably through Smith's efforts that a reporter and photographer from the San Francisco *Examiner* newspaper were dispatched first to Grants Pass and then reached the cave by stage and wagon from the Illinois Valley in June 1891. Two articles on the pair's

FIGURE 15. The cave entrance during the 1890s. (Photo courtesy of the Josephine County Historical Society).

explorations appeared in consecutive daily issues during the following month, an account that quickly offended some readers in Oregon due to an assertion that the cave constituted a recent discovery.[15]

Aside from misrepresenting the cavern's extent, as well as several other distortions concerning previous exploration that were readily rebutted in the Portland papers, the *Examiner* account is notable for effecting a distinct shift toward a new name for the cave. It had previously been known as the "Great Limestone Caves," or more commonly as the Josephine County Caves, usually in the plural because the stream opening and upper entrance were initially thought to lead to discretely different caverns.[16] In his second *Examiner* article, the writer called on a mineralogist to relate what he called the "Oregon caves" to limestone caverns occurring in California. That name gained some currency as Smith pushed formation of the "Oregon Caves Improvement Company" in San Francisco on February 7, 1894.[17]

Publicity generated by the *Examiner* articles served the improvement scheme, given how a "great many people" were reported by one Grants Pass paper to have visited the cave during the summer of 1893. Smith began an outlandish promotion of the cave by December, claiming that 22 miles of it had been explored, in which 600 chambers could be found. In using the

FIGURE 16. "Breaking a passage," drawing in the San Francisco *Examiner*, 1894.

language of those who preferred to mine investors rather than ore, Smith spoke of a "fairy chamber" set in the strata of California diamonds, while a tornado room was visited by a windstorm every twenty-four hours. An ordinary buggy could be driven ten miles into the cave, though he assured one newspaper that the cave entrance could be widened sufficiently to admit a six-horse stage.[18]

Even if some people knew such statements were hogwash, Smith attracted interest from a United States senator from Oregon who supposedly wanted an appropriation from Congress to allow the Smithsonian Institution to explore the cave—as well as renewed attention in San Francisco.[19] Lying squarely at the center of the nineteenth century western economy, San Francisco represented the key to attracting investors who might be gullible enough to underwrite Smith's intention to connect the cave with Grants Pass by building an electric road (one resembling a streetcar line or interurban rail connection) by way of Williams.[20] Smith said he had raised enough money by January 1894 for a road survey and had men working on houses that could serve as temporary lodging near the cave entrance. His immediate aim was to accommodate and publicize another exploring party from the *Examiner*, one set to appear that spring.[21]

Smith's publicity campaign proved convincing enough to attract investors who formed an improvement company in February and reportedly put up $7,000.[22] Whatever amount they actually pledged seemed enough to fuel construction of several supply stations on the "wagon road" from Williams and two buildings at the cave entrance.[23] A party led by four men from the *Examiner* finally arrived by train in Grants Pass one evening in May and were greeted by a large crowd. While the *Examiner* group remained at the cave to explore it further, others in the party returned to Grants Pass and proposed that its residents fund the construction of a road to the cave so that the improvement company could focus its resources on accommodating visitors. City officials appointed a committee to study how feasible a public subsidy like the concessions given to railroad promoters in the 1880s might be. The proposal's credibility hinged on what work Smith's crew had completed thus far, as well as publicity generated by the *Examiner* group exploring the cave with its implied benefits for a growing city.[24]

Previous visitors left their mark on the cave by using torches or taking formations as souvenirs, but the *Examiner* party of 1894 made for an orgy of destruction by comparison. Whereas the envoys from the newspaper in 1891 had merely observed that columns (and presumably other types of formations) had filled some of the potentially passable areas and restricted human movement, virtually every one of their more numerous compatriots in 1894 possessed a "smoky torch" and did not hesitate to satiate their curiosity by breaking soda straws or more rotund formations should these be in the way. To them the scratching of arrows for orientation in the labyrinth they dubbed the "Great Oregon Cave" became a necessity, as was the use of hammers to widen passages or remove obstructions.[25] They justified blasting the "low corridors" between the upper entrance and the cave's largest room, the "Ghost Chamber," by not wanting to waste time with slow travel in areas where previous visitors had gone.[26] Their stay at the cave lasted about ten days, so the group (whose numbers varied from five to eleven) had time to look for new passages. This involved hammering in at least one place to permit entry to the "treasure chamber," but the party found complete skeletons of two large bears, at a place where the men could find no opening from the outside.[27]

The final news article printed in the *Examiner* during June of

FIGURE 17. Man holding a torch in the Oregon Caves during the *Examiner* expedition, 1894.

1894 closed with yet another allusion to Kentucky's Mammoth Cave, but also included speculation about how a little dynamite and a good deal of drilling might yield more in the way of subterranean wonder. Its author connected further exploration with the improvement company's plans to light the cave and build a hotel there, naming Smith as superintendent of the work. Those plans unraveled, however, within days of when this article appeared in the *Examiner*. By August 1894 the company publicly disassociated itself from Smith, who had continued to incur debts on its behalf, such that the directors now levied an assessment of sixty cents a share on the stockholders to remain even marginally solvent.[28] Smith disappeared, and the company quickly collapsed.[29]

Into a void, 1895-1905

Despite leaving some local businessmen in the lurch, as well as those to whom Smith owed wages, ventures like the Oregon Caves Improvement Company were a commonly accepted part of the West's volatile economy during this period. Lode mines, the

FIGURE 18. Grants Pass – Crescent City Stagecoach, about 1900. (Photo courtesy of the Josephine County Historical Society.)

building of railroads, and real estate development were fueled by speculation. Their promoters used newspapers and magazines to lend credence to schemes requiring capital from investors large and small, so it is little wonder that those proclaiming the wonder of potential tourist attractions adopted the same conventions.[30]

Those who wrote about the cave's wonders in the aftermath of the improvement company fiasco of 1894 neglected to mention that debacle, of course, since their purpose was promotion. They carried on with platitudes about how Oregon Caves compared with Mammoth Cave, given the latter's stature as the nation's most famous underground attraction. These accounts also pointed to the need for thorough "scientific" exploration of Oregon Caves in addition to advising would-be adventurers on what to expect during their visit.[31] The writing, as might be expected from Victorian hucksters, sometimes drifted into the florid but consistently attempted to arouse interest in the dark and mysterious features of the cave, though in a way probably best described as Gothic romanticism.[32] None of them triggered any further attempts to develop the cave commercially, though the stage which ran between Grants Pass and Crescent City could arrange a side trip there if a group of paying passengers exceeded eight in number.[33]

Now that the cave lacked an "owner," parties wishing to visit would have to arrange for their own guides—as the articles appearing between 1895 and 1907 took care to emphasize. Most of the ladders placed during the two attempts at commercial operation remained (as did remnants of structures at the cave entrance), but the number of visitors stayed so low without better transportation links that no one bothered to claim the cave. While the prospects for a burgeoning tourist industry with the cave at its forefront seemed dim, if not all together absent, Josephine County did experience some economic diversification during the 1890s. Mining still occupied a place in an economy of a county whose population tripled (to 7,500) between 1880 and 1900, but this activity fell to a distant second behind fruit production of orchards around Grants Pass that exported by rail.[34] Explosive population growth around the San Francisco Bay Area at that time provided an incentive to boost lumber production on the west coast, but the rugged terrain of the Siskiyou Mountains easily defeated attempts to obtain timber inexpensive enough to ship from Josephine County. The county's timber industry remained a local affair, one that could not expand without technological advances that might overcome topographic barriers and distance—especially if the forests of the public domain were to ever play a part in economic diversification.

As part of the public domain, the cave and its surrounding forest land were a "frontier commons" during this period, in the sense they lacked permanent settlement and were thus open to any number of uses. Aside from the relatively few mining claims, an individual could hunt, fish, gather food, use forage, or cut timber without the need to recognize formal ownership boundaries and other types of controls needed to prevent conflicts among users. In short, the "frontier commons" could persist where competition for resources was slight. A shift, however, began during the 1890s in the federal government's role to a more active agent whose willingness to regulate (rather than dispose of) the public domain it still controlled. The most widespread change came in the form of reserving forests, to be accompanied by permits for grazing and prohibitions on activities such as setting fires to improve forage. Impetus for imposing what initially were called "forest reserves" on what the government retained as public domain came from far beyond the Siskiyous, mainly through recognition that eastern forests had been reduced rapidly through land clearance and logging. Ownership of forested land in the United States increased after 1850, for example, to the point where four-fifths of all standing timber had fallen into private hands by 1886—more than doubling the figure alienated from the public domain just 30 years before.[35]

FIGURE 19. This view of visitors in the cave shows the type of ladders and torches in use during the early 1900s. (Photo by Robert Grimmett, courtesy of the Josephine County Historical Society.)

Statutory loopholes and abuses in selling public land led to concentrated private ownership of forests in the east, as well as fraudulent acquisition of timber by syndicates in the western states. Fears of denuded watersheds and a host of uncontrollable impacts following from such an ownership pattern in the 1890s prodded Congress to pass legislation that allowed the President to proclaim forest reserves in unallocated public land containing timber. As a sort of safety valve that might ensure more far-sighted use of natural resources, the forest reserves also sprang from the realization by some that much of the mountainous west remained unsuitable for settlement but might provide an all-important water supply and a resource base that could be managed in perpetuity. Although there were objections to the advent of forest reserves in Oregon, others saw potential investment for community development and praised the idea of allowing permanent public access to the reserves.[36]

Speculators remained a fly in the ointment because they often moved ahead of proclamations and bought up vacant school sections (each township in the public domain contained one where the proceeds from sale went to support local schools) which had to be compensated through exchange of public lands located elsewhere; they were often allowed to choose much more valuable timber according to a "lieu land" provision in the existing law. This loophole allowed those sufficiently capitalized to control vast acreages, especially when the "land rings" hired "settlers" to claim tracts as a homestead under the loosely written Timber and Stone Act of 1878 and then used these for "base" to trade for more valuable sections after the forest reserve was proclaimed. Agents in the General Land Office (who, in conjunction with the U.S. Geological Survey, studied public lands as possible forest reserves during the 1890s) recommended that such abuse could be lessened if the President made temporary withdrawals of forested land. This would effectively suspend mining claims or other types of "entry" by private parties until lands still in the public domain could be studied for their suitability within the authorized boundaries of a permanent forest reserve.

The advent of federal land management, 1906-1915

It took five years for a withdrawal that embraced the public domain around Oregon Caves to take place. As a precursor to a permanent forest reserve, more than a million acres of land situated in Josephine, Curry, Douglas, and Coos counties was studied in 1898. Rancor over the prospect of such a reserve worked to delay even a temporary withdrawal, but it had little to do with effects on the timber industry as it then existed. As mining faded in the Illinois Valley during the 1880s, so did milling activity, subsiding to just one operation on Sucker Creek that produced about a thousand board feet of lumber per day.[37] Small mills existed for local needs elsewhere in Josephine County at that time, but commercial lumber production (that shipped out of southwestern Oregon) existed only in Grants Pass. The city was large enough to provide a ready labor force for several mills, with some specializing in the processing of sugar pine. For the most part, however,

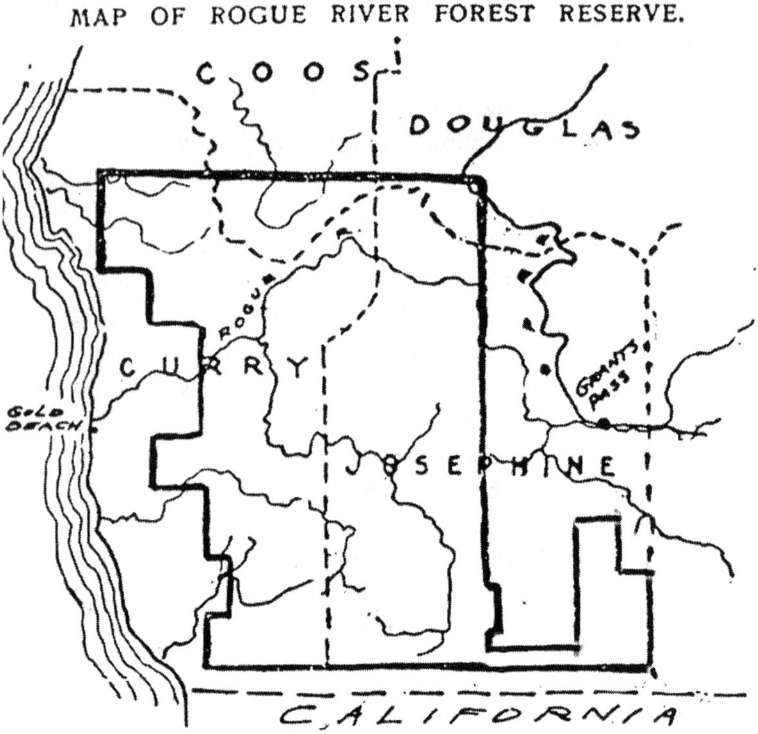

FIGURE 20. The Rogue River withdrawal, as proposed in May 1903.

Josephine County remained unattractive to large-scale milling operations due to the general lack of rail access to timbered stands and a general feeling that it possessed only "light growth" of inferior quality.[38]

What held up the "Rogue River withdrawal" (so named because the prospective forest reserve centered on the river's lower basin) were questions over the disposition of alternate sections in the defaulted Oregon and California Railroad grant. GLO commissioner Binger Hermann also cited some patented homesteads and mining claims being within the proposed reserve as further justification for reporting adversely on a withdrawal in 1902.[39] Hermann's dismissal from his post by President Theodore Roosevelt in 1903 created enough of a void for an opposite view to prevail. H.D. "Doug" Langille, a forest inspector with GLO, made a case for withdrawing some 1.2 million acres in southwest Oregon. His recommendation was endorsed by the Secretary of the Interior and then ordered by Roosevelt on April 29, 1903.[40]

Withdrawal constituted only a first step toward establishing a

FIGURE 21. Many newspapers of the time hailed Theodore Roosevelt as the champion of federal forestry. This cartoon appeared in the Spokane *Review* of 1908.

permanent reserve, though it was intended to be only a temporary measure to permit closer examination of the affected lands. The order halted the land rings for the time being, in that they excluded all forms of entry, but its opponents frequently made the charge that valuable agricultural land had been withdrawn. Others thought that prospecting for minerals should continue on the withdrawn lands, but that the largely mountainous topography precluded any hope of commercial agriculture. One forestry official in 1903 responded by characterizing the opposition as dominated by those who objected to losing their illegal access to free forage and timber.[41]

Proclamation of the Siskiyou Forest Reserve from the Rogue River Withdrawal stalled in the face of complications posed by the inclusion of O&C lands (a minor problem solved by eliminating those sections already granted to a railroad syndicate) and opposition to the reserve in Curry County, where the reserve would have amounted to three-fifths of the land area. This resulted in elimination of roughly 500,000 acres from the proposed reserve in 1906, though 446,000 acres were added to it from other townships by the date of official proclamation on March 2, 1907.[42] Roosevelt acted just two days before he lost the authority to make such proclamations in Oregon and five other western states. The restriction came from legislation backed by opponents of the forest reserves in Congress (one being Senator Charles Fulton of Oregon), though the President's action in creating a number of "midnight reserves" largely rendered such resistance futile.[43]

Even if Roosevelt lost his authority to proclaim forest reserves in some of the west, he retained the power to designate "national monuments" on public land located anywhere in the nation. The so-called "Antiquities Act" passed by Congress on June 8, 1906, stipulated that the boundaries of such monuments should be confined to the smallest area compatible with the proper care and management of the objects to be protected. This provision of the act may have been based on the specific aim of preserving prehistoric Indian ruins in the southwestern states, though the law was applied to encompass a broader range of antiquities from the time of its enactment.[44] In the case of Oregon Caves, its proclamation followed a somewhat similar sequence to that of the surrounding forest reserve, or "Siskiyou National Forest" as it was known from March 4, 1907.

What seems to have triggered the initial withdrawal of the area surrounding Oregon Caves as a future national monument can be tied to the arrival of poet and writer Joaquin Miller in Grants Pass on August 3, 1907. One paper gave readers two days notice before his arrival, stating that the flamboyant Miller intended to meet Ashland attorney Chandler B. Watson (who had once dabbled in railroads, real estate, and timber lands) at the station and then go to the cave.[45] The pair hoped to duplicate for Oregon Caves what Miller and others did for Crater Lake several years earlier. In 1903 the poet helped arouse interest in Crater Lake by joining a heavily publicized "camping trip" organized by Will G. Steel (Watson's one-time business associate) that departed from Medford and included Senator Fulton among its members. Miller's article in *Sunset* magazine (an organ of the Southern Pacific Railroad published in California and aimed at promoting tourism in the west) titled "The Sea of Silence" helped to increase the popularity of newly established Crater Lake National Park.[46]

Miller's arrival in Grants Pass coincided with a telegram to the chief of the United States Forest Service (a bureau in the Department of Agriculture created by Congress in 1905 for managing the forest reserves) requesting an immediate withdrawal of four sections (2,560 acres) around the cave. Forest Supervisor M.J. Anderson wanted to prevent one R.W. Veach from filing a

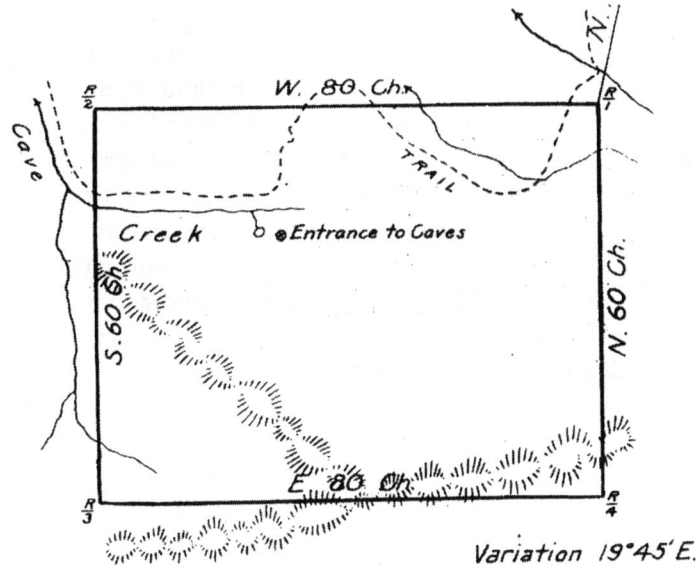

FIGURE 22. Robert Dean's survey sketch for the proposed Oregon Caves National Monument, early 1909.

mining claim in that area as a pretext for controlling the cave.[47] Officials in Washington, D.C. expedited the withdrawal, effective as of August 12.[48] Apparently outmaneuvered, or at least prevented from pursuing a mineral entry, Veach and his associate G.O. Oium applied for a permit to furnish guides, light the cave, and build a hotel at the cave in exchange for full control of some 62 acres inside the withdrawn parcel. The Forest Service took no action on this request, presumably because Anderson had yet to report on the withdrawal or follow through with a survey aimed at determining exact boundaries for a national monument to be created around the cave.[49]

Such tasks were not a top priority for Anderson and his tiny staff of forest guards. They spent most of their time that season trying to ascertain forest boundaries and determining whether claims made under the land laws were fraudulent or not.[50] By November a survey crew had come near enough to the cave in locating a trail, but other work and winter storms delayed any survey for a future national monument until the following year, but even this fairly routine endeavor had to be spurred by Oium making another request for a ten year lease at the cave.[51] Anderson then sent a forest guard, Robert Dean, to survey and report on a proposed national monument. Dean did little more than run corners for an administrative site (the printed form he used for the report had "administrative site" struck in favor of "national monument") thus creating a neat rectangle of about 480 acres, more or less.[52] He contended in the report that "within this tract is situated the Oregon Caves," but Dean offered no evidence that the cave fell within the corners he established. In making only a rough sketch that accompanied the notes pertaining to the running of these lines, Dean located the cave entrance below adjacent ridgelines indicated by some hachures.[53]

Anderson meanwhile tried to make a case for granting Veach and Oium the permit they sought. He wrote to the chief forester that visitors had destroyed formations, even after the Forest Service had posted notices threatening closure of the cave until the necessary means for its protection could be provided.[54] Oddly enough, reference to vandalism had almost vanished from news articles or other published accounts about Oregon Caves during the decade preceding 1906. Miller and his companions nevertheless identified the need to protect the cave from vandals during their visit in August 1907.[55] The argument for national monument status only seemed to gain momentum when Anderson submitted papers containing his report (and presumably Dean's survey) to the district forester's office in February 1909. He explained that visitors had "blown off and carried away" many of the most valuable formations, thus prompting him to recommend that a national monument be proclaimed by the President. Anderson also wrote that the Forest Service rebuilt and improved trails leading to Oregon Caves, not only for better access, but also to more easily protect the valuable forest surrounding them.[56]

In addition to the expediency of withdrawing four sections around the cave in 1907 and then reducing the area encompassed by the proposed monument with a crude survey, potential timber values can help explain why the future Oregon Caves National Monument was destined to remain small.[57] As Anderson explained to the district (later regional) forester in Portland, the withdrawal constituted a temporary measure until a survey of the cave's "exact" location could be made.[58] He and other agency officials knew that at least one previous inventory showed that timber volumes in the vicinity to be among the highest in southwestern Oregon.[59] It made sense (at least to the foresters who saw better

THE CLOSING OF A FRONTIER   51

access to timber in the Siskiyou Mountains on the far horizon) to strictly comply with provisions of the Antiquities Act restricting any national monument encompassing Oregon Caves to the smallest area compatible with proper care and management of the protected objects.[60]

The need for protected status gave the matter of Oregon Caves some urgency, so a proclamation was drafted at the district forester's office in February 1909 and then sent to Washington, D.C. on March 1.[61] It should be stressed that only the President possessed the power to make such a proclamation, but Gifford Pinchot as chief forester seemed eager to allay any charges that a future Oregon Caves National Monument represented a case of administrative fiat—even if it was. As a master politician, Pinchot engineered creation of the Forest Service by working through his friend Theodore Roosevelt and other influential men both in and out of government. Pinchot knew that public acceptance of any regulatory measure often hinged on the Forest Service being seen as reactive to a crisis, even one like Oregon Caves, where prominent citizens or an organization raised an alarm through the media.

As creatures of the Progressive Movement which dominated American politics through the 1920s, he and the Forest Service conducted a clever public relations campaign that preached a "gospel" of efficiency where public lands such as forests held a multitude of "resources" like timber and forage. These were not to be wasted, especially for speculative ventures, but used under the purview of scientifically trained foresters who could arbitrate when conflicting interests had to be reconciled for "the greatest good for the greatest number [of American citizens] in the long run."[62] This kind of forestry, even if only custodial at the time, could promise everything to virtually everyone, despite rarely generating enough revenue to meet its administrative expenses through receipts from mining leases, timber sales, or grazing allotments. Despite its failure to achieve self-sufficiency, Forest Service control brought an end of frontier conditions, at least in part of the public domain. Pinchot and the Forest Service, however, co-opted the language of the frontier to obtain appropriations from Congress aimed at preventing wildfires that, along with unscrupulous forest users, could denude watersheds and needlessly destroy resources that could meet current and future needs.[63]

Buoyed by the success that Roosevelt had in destroying the

opposition to his forest policy at the conference on public lands in Denver in June 1907, Pinchot encouraged the western states to establish what came to be called "conservation commissions." Governor George Chamberlain appointed members for the quasi-public Oregon Conservation Commission in 1908, a body with a nonexistent budget that lobbied for orderly and efficient development of the state. It crafted natural resource policy through formal recommendations, focusing on the potential of water for power, irrigation, and forestry in Oregon.[64] Watson happened to be a member of the commission and seems to have induced the chairman, J.N. Teal of Portland, to write Pinchot in June of 1909 about the destruction caused by vandals and how torches used by visitors defaced the cave.[65] One of Pinchot's assistants replied to Teal on July 6, writing that a proclamation had already been sent to the President (Roosevelt's successor, William H. Taft), who was expected to sign it.[66]

Anderson had already assured the district forester and Pinchot of local support for the proclamation in June by sending a booklet from the Grants Pass Commercial Club, predecessor to the town's chamber of commerce, promoted public ownership of the cave and contained numerous photographs.[67] He and the district forester (as well as Pinchot, presumably) already knew of Miller's article on the cave to be published by *Sunset* in September.[68] The piece reached a wide regional audience, just as his earlier article on Crater Lake had, so no one could accuse the Forest Service of being disingenuous or duplicitous in acting to protect the Oregon Caves.[69]

What made the proclamation as signed by Taft rather curious was its creation of overlapping reservations. The national monument established on 480 acres of the 1907 withdrawal was to be dominant over the surrounding national forest, another reservation created by presidential proclamation.[70] This seems to have been an attempt to make preservation of the cave compatible with expected future use of the Siskiyou National Forest, hence the language in the national monument proclamation forbidding use of the land that interfered with its status as a protected area. The proclamation also included a boilerplate warning about destroying or removing the monument's natural features, as well as a prohibition on settlement. These provisions bore enough resemblance to those in other monument proclamations issued between 1906 and 1911 that one historian has concluded that all such documents, at least in their original form, came from the hand of one employee in the Department of the Interior.[71] In any event, the proclamation establishing Oregon Caves National Monument on July 12, 1909, generated little publicity in the state's newspapers, though the accidental shooting death in the cave of Frank Ellis, a Grants Pass resident, several weeks later certainly did.[72]

Ellis and his companions, like some others among the estimated 360 visitors that summer, had come to the cave without hiring a guide.[73] The Forest Service did not yet provide such service, or for that matter, have a presence at the monument—even if the district forester's office in Portland, upon advising Anderson of the signed proclamation, had asked him to "assume charge at once."[74] That year the Siskiyou National Forest had been divided into districts, though the nearest ranger (who spent much of his time on fire patrol) established his headquarters more than 20 miles away by trail and wagon road, on Page Creek, located near the settlement of Takilma.[75]

Although Forest Service officials expressed token concern about public safety at Oregon Caves in the wake of the Ellis shooting, what finally put a man on site (at least in the summer months) was vandalism. Earlier deliberations about granting a lease in exchange for private parties making improvements became moot, mainly because outlay needed to build a lighting plant or hotel accommodations in such a remote area seemed simply too great. Approximately 300 visitors came to the new national monument in 1910, an insufficient number for recouping an investment in facilities even if a fee was charged for entering the cave, with the levy being on top of what most had already paid their guide for packhorses and camping gear. Anderson and others in the Forest Service meanwhile voiced their concern about damage to formations, especially the discoloration resulting from the use of pitch torches by visitors and their guides. Although granting a lease to private parties who might provide facilities and protect the cave remained a financial impossibility, the idea of employing a guard there to deter those who might violate posted rules began to gain momentum. The Forest Service had to be prodded, however, by a letter from the Oregon Conservation Commission in order to hire its first guard at Oregon Caves, one to be employed for the summer season of 1911.[76]

At a time when the agency began to impose grazing fees and sell timber for building mining shafts, Forest Service officials made

FIGURE 23. Pack train on the trail from Williams to Oregon Caves, about 1915. (U.S. Forest Service photo, Siskiyou National Forest.)

a point to downplay the free guide service provided by the guard.[77] They hired Vickers G. Smith for 60 dollars a month that season and instructed him that tours could be given only once a day, since protection work (which in their view justified the position) came first. His duties thus included installing new ladders inside the cave, realigning the trail to Williams near the monument, and posting numerous warnings as a way to better ensure compliance with provisions in the Antiquities Act. Given how staffing on the Siskiyou was limited to a few guards and even fewer rangers, the new forest supervisor R.L. Fromme nevertheless complained to the district office that Smith could not be made available for fire patrol duty over a wider area.[78]

Small as the appropriations were at the time, federal funding for improving facilities at Oregon Caves and Smith's salary represented a shift from the nineteenth century conception of the frontier commons as *laissez-faire*. So did fire patrol and other management activities on the forest, since they were manifested as tax-supported regulation in the name of expected future returns from conserving natural resources. Federal foresters of the time consistently made a case for maintaining a "bank" of standing timber free from the threat of fire in the expectation that it would eventually become an accessible commodity. Managed properly, national forests might thus help the nation avert a disastrous "wood famine" stemming from wasteful logging and a lack of foresight by those who owned private land.[79]

In the early part of the twentieth century, putting up public funds in the hope of beneficial future returns (albeit in the shorter term) resonated to many people at the local level. Businessmen and other boosters in Grants Pass, for example, understood the value of its rail connection to Portland and Sacramento, but knew that more lines into southwest Oregon's hinterland could open the way for additional prosperity and attract more people to Josephine County. In 1911 Grants Pass boasted slightly over 6,000 inhabitants (in a county whose number of residents totaled about 9,500), and responded enthusiastically to plans announced by a syndicate of "capitalists" from San Francisco and Portland who wanted to build a new railroad line. This one was to run from Grants Pass to the cave by way of the Applegate drainage so that the Williams area might be better developed.[80] City residents raised $60,000 from subscriptions in order for construction to begin in March 1911, but the holding company went bankrupt after building a line for several months along a surveyed route from Grants Pass through the Illinois Valley and toward Crescent City.[81] Construction of the "California and Oregon Coast Railroad" commenced again in 1913 with a $200,000 municipal bond from Grants Pass, though this infusion of public money provided only enough capital for the line to terminate only fifteen miles southwest of town.[82]

Plans for a road from the Illinois Valley to the monument during that period followed a similar trajectory. In early 1912, Grants Pass promoters supposedly induced Portland "parties" to put up $25,000 for a road starting from the hamlet of Holland, with its start contingent upon securing a permit from the Forest Service that allowed them to build a hotel and light the cave. Although he had since resigned from the Forest Service, Anderson's involvement with the scheme provided it with some credibility. Anderson applied to Fromme for the permit, writing that funds secured for a wagon road from Holland to the cave would allow for construction to continue all the way to Williams, so that visitors might pass the cave on their way to or from Crescent City. The Forest Service stalled on granting the permit, citing a competing application for similar privileges and the question of whether exclusive control (which would follow from lighting the cave, since it tied directly to a guide service) could be given to private parties on a national monument.[83] Representatives from all three departments administering national monuments (Agriculture, Interior, and War) met to discuss this question in June 1911 and subsequently reached the conclusion that the government should not allow private parties to develop or manage the monuments, even under departmental restrictions. This decision allowed Fromme to deny Anderson's request for a permit, at least in its existing form.[84]

Undeterred, Anderson circulated a petition asking Congress to establish a national park on the land surrounding Oregon Caves so that private capital could develop a lighting system and build a hotel as part of a lease arrangement.[85] He and supporters in the Grants Pass Commercial Club attempted to gain the backing of Oregon's congressional delegation during a period when two other national park proposals in the state seemed to be gathering momentum.[86] Members of the delegation then introduced bills to establish an Oregon Caves National Park both in the House and Senate during the first week of January 1913.[87] The legislative process directed that these bills were to be reported by the bureau administering the land if already federal, so this task fell to the Forest Service. The new forest supervisor on the Siskiyou, Nelson MacDuff, objected to the Senate version of the bill, which called for transferring an entire township (some 23,000 acres) surrounding Oregon Caves to the Department of the Interior, where its head (the Secretary) had charge of all national parks. His reasons centered on removing merchantable timber from the possibility of future sale, the prohibition on grazing, as well as some doubts about the cave as a scenic attraction.[88] The House bill called for reserving only two and a half sections (1,600 acres) around the cave, so MacDuff did not voice objections based on losing future revenue from timber or grazing. He instead saw advantages to a prospective national park, since a road built to it might permit the transport of logs from the national forest sometime in the future.[89]

Both bills remained mired in committee, buried amid the spate of national park proposals made by western congressmen and senators of the period. Boosters in Grants Pass tried to fuel interest in establishing the park by distributing a booklet of photographs of Oregon Caves, but only succeeded in providing logistical support for the largest gathering at the cave that had been held up to that time.[90] About ninety members of the Mazamas visited from Portland in June 1913 and generated enough publicity for

FIGURE 24. Wagon road between Kerby and Selma, about 1910. (Photo courtesy of the Josephine County Historical Society.)

residents of Josephine County to stage a "Cave Day," an event which attracted two hundred people in June of the following year.[91] As the months passed, however, it became increasingly evident that the proposed national park was dead. Pinchot's successor as chief of the Forest Service, Henry S. Graves, hoped to obtain authority from Congress that might allow the agency to grant permits for hotels and summer homes in the national forests—something that amounted to leasing. Such authority might make it expeditious to rescind the proclamation for Oregon Caves (since the Forest Service continued to assume that it lacked the means to entice private parties to develop facilities for the national monuments), a prospect that quickly garnered support from the Grants Pass Commercial Club.[92]

Left with few other options in the mean time, boosters continued to promote the need for a road to Oregon Caves.[93] Not only did they see the cave as an enticing focal point bound to attract thousands of visitors, but a road to it might augment resource extraction over a wider area. In early 1914, for example, one journalist extolled the superb hunting and fishing opportunities near the monument and then speculated how "investigation" of the "gigantic copper belt" lying between Oregon Caves and the coast would come once the means for tourist travel had been developed.[94]

Although the means seemed to lie in building roads, how to finance such construction in sparsely populated areas remained problematic. In 1910 the Oregon Conservation Commission pointed to how inadequate the prevailing method of using county property taxes for constructing and maintaining roads of any standard. The system was especially unfair where considerable road mileage was needed to serve relatively few residents whose property had low assessed value. Commission members concluded that only the state could finance the amount needed for an adequate road system in Oregon, something that might hopefully be achieved with federal aid.[95]

Despite being a tenet of the "Good Roads Movement" that attracted a broad base of support throughout the United States, state financing of roads in Oregon had so far proven to be elusive. Some local groups who saw economic development as following from the stimulation of tourist travel to scenic attractions located on federal land tried to obtain appropriations for individual road projects from Congress, but met with only limited success.[96] Will Steel was named superintendent at Crater Lake National Park in 1913 largely because he had previously led the effort that resulted in garnering federal money for a system of roads and trails in the park.[97] His efforts culminated in one of the few success stories that resulted from approaching Congress this way, though Steel and other Crater Lake supporters were openly critical of the state's reticence to undertake construction of an approach road from Medford several years earlier. The question of how to finance roads had become hot as early as 1910, when the Oregon Supreme Court ruled the prospective Medford route to Crater Lake constituted "a local affair" (and thus not eligible for funding from Salem), so that the decision raised a furor in the state's newspapers.[98]

Road conditions in Oregon at the time have been described as "primitive" in that only ten percent of the 37,000 miles of road in the state possessed any form of hard surfacing or "base." Oregon contained some 12,000 private automobiles, but the predominance of bad roads confined such travel, especially if it took place outside of cities or beyond the summer months.[99] Promoters of the Columbia River Highway who resided in Portland convinced the Oregon Legislature to take a cautious first step in 1913 toward rectifying the situation by creating a state highway commission. Oregon lagged behind California and Washington in getting even that far, and the body (which in its infancy was largely advisory) did little more than try to drum up local support for counties to issue bonds that could be used to implement plans for a system of trunk roads.[100] None of the cross-state routes ran near Oregon Caves, but Grants Pass paved its Sixth Street in 1910 and this part of the town subsequently became part of the main north-south road in Oregon, the Pacific Highway. In the first years of building this road (which eventually achieved the distinction of being the first to run the entire length of any state west of the Mississippi River), the Pacific Highway nevertheless remained a quagmire between towns, full of torturous curves and other challenges for under-powered automobiles.[101]

Even if horse-drawn grading equipment and gangs of men could slowly improve the Pacific Highway and other trunk routes in Oregon, promoters of a road to the cave faced the stark reality of sparsely populated Josephine County, where elected officials could not fathom issuing bonds for such a project. Illinois Valley residents petitioned to the county in 1914 for $1,000 to push a road further up Sucker Creek, a project touted to shrink the distance to Oregon Caves from 9.5 miles to 4.6 miles.[102] According to the petitioners, farmers and miners intended to spend a like amount, but the proposal went nowhere for two reasons. With revenues derived from a relatively low tax rate and demands for better roads in more populated parts of the county, officials in Grants Pass balked, especially since the projected route would not reach the cave. For that to happen, there had to be some way to finance roads in the national forests. Chief Forester Graves visited Portland in the fall of 1914 to promote his plan to finance such roads with future revenues from resource development instead of using a portion of current receipts. The allure of Oregon's scenery could be used as justification for the proposal (given how

FIGURE 25. Commercial camp at the confluence of Grayback and Sucker creeks, about 1915. (U.S. Forest Service photo, Siskiyou National Forest.)

the state was thought to be so attractive to prospective tourists that such roads could pay immediate dividends), since it aided the development of local communities who were also supposed to benefit from timber revenue once these stands of merchantable trees could be accessed.[103]

At the time, however, fewer than 3,000 miles of road existed in all of the national forests combined. Without federal legislation authorizing the type of finance Graves and others in the Forest Service had in mind, little could be done for better access to Oregon Caves—aside from some improvements to the trails which started where the wagon roads ended. Visitation to the monument in 1915 stood somewhere around 1,000, enough traffic so that a commercial tent camp began a second season of operations where Grayback and Sucker creeks met to become one stream above the Illinois Valley.[104] This type of enterprise should not, as congressman W.C. Hawley assured his constituents in Grants Pass, constitute an impediment on road construction to Oregon Caves. He had since adopted the hopeful tone of boosters throughout the state, stating that a special appropriation from Congress for a road to the monument could be secured, though his proposal to secure the funds had not yet assumed a tangible form.[105]

FIGURE 26. Family group at the cave entrance, 1914. (Photo by George Barton, OCNM Museum and Archives Collections.)

FIGURE 27. At Government Camp near the cave entrance about 1915. (Photo courtesy of the Josephine County Historical Society.)

CHAPTER 3

Boosterism's Public – Private Partnership, 1916-1933

Some Americans have believed that the frontier produced a distinct national character—one based on self-reliance, love of liberty, aptitude for innovation, and belief in progress.[1] Whether this is true or not, such thinking prevailed at the beginning of the twentieth century, at a time when the Forest Service sought to regulate use on what had formerly been (at least since 1850 or so) a frontier commons. Popular fiction during the first couple of decades after 1900 generally portrayed forest rangers as pioneers, who in facing an untamed land alone, constantly faced the threat posed by wildfires and unscrupulous forest users who stole timber, set fires, or otherwise harmed the public interest through self-serving and expedient actions that worked against the long-term vision of conserving natural resources.[2]

In 1910 rangers and forest guards patrolled between 450 and 670 square miles each, but did so with horses and hand tools. For fire protection on the national forests to work, it had to be seen as both an investment and precondition to more intensive management. Long-term success, according to Graves and others in the leadership of the Forest Service, depended upon strategic placement of roads, trails, lookouts, and guard stations—as well as telephone lines, tool caches, and fuel breaks. Even with the constant reminder of the menace that wildfire posed to western communities (1910 was a particularly bad year), federal subsidy in the form

FIGURE 28. Parking area at Oregon Caves in 1922. (U.S. Forest Service photo, Siskiyou National Forest.)

of appropriations for developing infrastructure on the national forests was slow in coming. Private land produced far more timber, and most investments made in the national forests served a relatively small number of constituents, so Congress understandably proved reluctant to provide as much funding as the Forest Service requested. More lavish subsidies for developing the west (which began with grants Congress gave to railroads during the Civil War) were tied to faster returns.[3]

Highways to Oregon Caves

Although the agency saw its primary duty as managing timber, more roads opened the possibility of new uses like recreation tied to the expanding ownership of automobiles, and thus more constituent support. The Good Roads Movement also adopted language of the frontier as it pressed for "new roads over old trails."[4] Even if far from unified, this coalition consisted of farmers, country doctors, traveling salesmen, manufacturers, and urban professionals. Beyond creating new possibilities for touring, the movement also sought to broadcast its message that more and better roads could aid progress by eradicating rural isolation. Consequently, road advocates adapted promotional strategies first developed by the railroads to emphasize how a system of both long-distance and local roads served to unite the nation.[5]

As automobile ownership in America began to surge, the Good Roads Movement and the Forest Service applauded Congress when it passed the first federal highway act in 1916. Some funding became available for the next fiscal year, with a portion of the appropriation made under the act directed to roads and trails in the national forests, such that the Forest Service received ten million dollars for construction over the next decade. The legislation also carried three key stipulations. First, no state could receive federal funds without setting up a highway department. This acted as the impetus in Oregon to begin implementing the plans laid by its highway commission several years earlier for a system of trunk roads. The second stipulation also served to strengthen the idea of state control over highways by requiring that it assume responsibility for maintaining roads financed under the act's provisions. Third, states could not act unilaterally with federal funding for roads, since the Secretary of Agriculture (who oversaw the Bureau of Public Roads (BPR), the agency charged with supervising highway projects crossing federal lands) had to approve project statements submitted by the highway departments.[6]

The small amount of money appropriated by Congress in 1916 boosted prospects for a road to Oregon Caves only a little. It did, however, lead to a reconnaissance survey that examined possible routes up Sucker and Cave creeks to the monument. This undertaking by the Bureau of Public Roads followed their survey of the Hayes Hill section of the Grants Pass – Crescent City wagon road during the fall of 1917.[7] The next step, location work for both routes, was spurred by passage of another act less than two years later. Aimed at funding rural post offices, it also granted another nine million dollars toward development and administration of roads in the national forests. BPR engineers could thus determine and stake the best route from Holland to the monument, one that some observers first thought might ultimately reach Williams.[8]

Actual construction of the road began in August 1921 with clearing over the twelve miles between "Robinson's Corner" and a parking place for 50 cars at the monument, with the latter located about 900 feet from the cave entrance. Grading a roadway eight feet wide with turnouts then ensued from Grayback Creek, with most of the work accomplished by crews of men with hand tools and teams of horses.[9] A "trail" for pedestrians connected the

FIGURE 29. The Oregon Caves Highway prior to widening was little more than a one lane road through the Siskiyou National Forest. Frank Patterson took this view of the Lake Creek Bridge in 1924. (OCNM Museum and Archives Collections.)

FIGURE 30. Paving the Oregon Caves Highway about two miles from the monument in 1931. (Photo courtesy of the Oregon Department of Transportation.)

monument's main parking area to the cave entrance, though it also was built eight feet wide to allow the occasional transport of supplies and equipment. Crews completed virtually the entire job by the following June, thereby allowing motorists access to the monument for most of the 1922 season so that visitation increased by almost ten times (to 10,000) over what it had been in 1921.[10]

Auto travel to the cave that year had still been hampered by the incomplete part of the Oregon Caves Highway, where three miles of road to run north of Sucker Creek (and thus away from Waldo and Holland) had been designed, but not built.[11] Boosters in Grants Pass also wanted a better connection with Crescent City than the wagon road which wound its way over the torturous Oregon Mountain grade and down Patrick Creek in California. Elected officials in Josephine County lobbied the state highway commission to change the road's name in Oregon to the "Redwood Highway" in May 1924 to provide the traveling public with the impression that the route between Grants Pass and San Francisco constituted a major scenic thoroughfare.[12] The highway commission thus voted to improve a section of road between O'Brien and the state line, a project that was financed in part through a bill enacted by the state legislature authorizing the nation's first gasoline tax. In the mean time, several houses appeared at the "Redwood Junction" where the highway met the road to the monument, a place whose promoters dubbed "Caves City."[13]

By the end of 1926, annual visitation at the monument had more than doubled (to almost 21,000) from what it was just four years earlier—even with an impediment in the form of what amounted to a one-lane access road. Boosters in Grants Pass called for widening the Caves Highway and were soon joined by businessmen from the Redwood Empire Hotel Resort Association whose annual convention featured a caravan to the monument that fall.[14] This advocacy quickly paid dividends, though not in the form of a road contract, but BPR engineers supervised widening the road to a 14-foot standard within the national forest over the next three years, beginning in the spring of 1927.[15]

Widening the Caves Highway came as improvements to the Redwood Highway begun in 1924 culminated with a vastly improved road link between Grants Pass and Crescent City.[16] Visitation to the monument thus continued to increase (to more than 24,000 in 1928), coincident with more funding for roads. State highway department crews and county personnel worked together in order to widen the road between the forest boundary and Caves City in 1929. That year BPR made use of a smaller

FIGURE 31. Widening the Oregon Caves Highway did not remove this hairpin curve. (Photo by Frank Patterson, OCNM Museum and Archives Collections.)

federal allotment to enlarge the monument's main parking lot and complete the road widening within the Siskiyou National Forest to 16 feet.[17] Subsequent resurfacing and then paving in 1931 created a dustless road touted to be one of the best in southern Oregon.[18]

Such an investment for highway infrastructure followed a national trend in responding to the spectacular increase in automobile ownership over three decades (going from only 8,000 in 1900 to some 40 million in America thirty years later), but becoming especially acute during the 1920s. What made the Oregon Caves Highway unusual in relation to the state highway system was that it terminated at the monument with no through connection while several trunk roads in Oregon still were either partially or fully surfaced with gravel.[19] Not only could Grants Pass interests argue for improving the monument's approach road based on the economic importance of being a gateway to Oregon Caves, they could also point to the existence of a public and private infrastructure supporting an expanding tourist industry. The appearance of overnight accommodation formed a cornerstone of that infrastructure, as the Grants Pass newspaper reminded readers with its travelogue section in June 1931. Although the cave tour retained top billing in the lead article, the paper ran headers announcing "Oregon Caves Highway Lined With Visiting Sightseers," and "Auto Camps Along Highway Near Caves Junction Delight Tourist."[20]

Beginnings of a recreational infrastructure

Auto camping started as a response from leisure travelers to the freedom presented by owning an automobile, in that they could avoid the cost and restriction of hotels by camping outside towns or anywhere along a road. The auto "gypsy" thus dodged the necessity of making hotel reservations, eating at set times in dining rooms, having to interact with desk clerks (who sometimes looked askance at dusty motorists, as opposed to their clientele who traveled by rail), or paying to park their car in a garage.[21] By 1915 civic boosters in many western municipalities looked to situate an auto camp in a centrally located city park, reasoning that such facilities could attract tourists to local businesses and allow the town to advertise itself as one embracing progress.[22] Like Ashland, Grants Pass opened a free municipal auto camp by the summer of 1915, one that included a community house so campers could cook their meals and socialize with others in Riverside Park. Hotel owners and entrepreneurs who wanted to open private camps viewed a free city-run camp as unfair competition, though it was the sheer popularity of Riverside Park among campers that led to a charge of 50 cents per night in 1923, mainly to offset expense of providing utilities.[23] Cabins appeared in Riverside Park as well as Ashland's Lithia Park by 1925, reflecting a trend of motorists carrying less camping gear.[24] Municipal camps became crowded in the summer and imposed limits on how long people could stay in them by this time, so many travelers found private camps attractive—especially if cabins could be rented.

The first commercial camps in Oregon and Washington appeared during the summer of 1922. Only seven years later, Grants Pass possessed the largest number of such camps (24) among all cities in the Pacific Northwest. Approximately 190 cabins dotted the vicinity of Grants Pass in 1929, but motorists could also find them scattered along the Redwood Highway as well as other major travel routes in western Oregon.[25] These cabins could be built for $200 or less, thus allowing owners to recoup their investment in only a season or two of rentals. Whether situated in town, or on a main road many miles from a central business district, commercial cabins tended to be arranged in a row either parallel or perpendicular to the highway. Rural cabin camps often included a gas station and possibly a store as part of their operation. These differed from resort cabins, which were more substan-

FIGURE 32. Camp near Grayback Creek as it appeared in 1916. (U.S. Forest Service photo by U.L. Upson.)

FIGURE 33. "Grayback Park" in 1924. This photo was used by the Forest Service in the late 1920s to illustrate a typical campground scene in the national forests of Oregon. (U.S. Forest Service photo, Siskiyou National Forest.)

tial since their clientele usually stayed more than one night. Resort camps also placed more emphasis on harmonizing their cabins with the surroundings, often utilizing either foundation plantings or trees for screening and building the structures in irregular clusters. Some proprietors erected resort cabins with exterior details to distinguish one cabin from another and used logs, shingles, or tree bark to imitate the nearby forest.[26]

With hotels and cabins readily available, camping began to be less prevalent in Oregon towns by 1930, with free facilities being a thing of the past. Free campgrounds could be found in the national forests, however, ever since the Forest Service started including automobile-associated recreation as a recognized "use" (supposedly on a par with timber and grazing) in 1916. That year the Forest Service built its first developed campground at Eagle Creek in the Columbia Gorge, a facility that included camp tables, toilets, and a station where campers could register. Situated at the head of a trail built especially for hiking, the campground served as a showpiece in a "Columbia Gorge Park" declared by the Secretary of Agriculture in late 1915.[27] Congress provided funding for more campgrounds in the national forests only hesitantly at first, but by 1925 the Forest Service counted 1,500 of them. Only a third of that number, however, even possessed the most basic facilities. Over the next five years, an annual appropriation that averaged $45,000 for campground development had to be divided among 150 national forests, so improvements made at any single site were generally modest. Some tables, fireplaces, pit toilets, and minimal leveling for tents and parking generally cost in the neighborhood of $200.[28]

Since Oregon Caves National Monument possessed no land level enough to permit camping by motorists (aside from the parking lot which some visitors used for that purpose during the 1922 and 1923 seasons), Forest Service officials decided to layout a public campground below the monument but near the highway. They chose a site on Sucker Creek near its confluence with Grayback Creek in 1922, though Congress still had to pass a bill transferring some revested railroad grant land to the Siskiyou National Forest before clearing for the campground could proceed.[29] Although the Forest Service allocated only $10,000 for recreational improvements in all of the national forests that year, it made this campground enough of a priority during the 1923 season (given how the agency administered only one national monument in Oregon) to fund some tables and fireplaces, as well as a water system and two large restrooms. By September the forest supervisor pointed to the popularity of "Grayback Park" (also called "Sucker Creek" or the "Oregon Caves" forest camp) as justification of the need for an additional twenty tables and fireplaces.[30]

Although funding the campground facilities loomed fairly large within a small budget devoted to recreation, it comprised only one piece of a larger "Oregon Caves Resort" that the Forest Service saw as funded largely from private investors but split between the Grayback site and the monument. Resort development at Oregon Caves and elsewhere in the national forests of the period fit a template that the agency called "recreation centers." These were established as a kind of zoning measure on the national forests, but with several justifications. One asserted that the Forest Service could be the dominant purveyor of recreation on federal land in Oregon and Washington, where there was a considerable amount of old growth timber that the agency did not want transferred to the National Park Service (NPS) or another bureau. Such centers also appeared to be a way of accommodating concentrations of people who wanted to pursue outdoor activities like camping, fishing, hunting, and horseback riding, while also keeping them from dispersing to areas within the national forests where they might inadvertently set fires or otherwise interfere with the management of timber or grazing. In such recreation centers, national forest land could be developed by investors who leased tracts to build resorts near lakes, along rivers, or by tourist attractions like the Oregon Caves.[31]

Privately run resorts were intended to complement government-funded amenities like campgrounds, roads, utility systems, and trails. The Forest Service thus created a private-public partnership on the national forests that also included the state highway department when needed. Agency leadership in Portland moved to publicize this partnership to motorists in 1923 through issuing a free map of the national forests in Oregon, one including descriptions of each recreation center and a list of municipal and roadside campgrounds.[32] The Forest Service supplied more detail about each recreation center by dispensing free leaflets about some of them (one covering Oregon Caves appeared in 1922), though hikers, campers, horse users, and hunters could also buy a handbook covering all of the designated areas in Oregon for a small fee from the Government Printing Office.[33]

Much of the need to stimulate recreational developments in Oregon's national forests of the time did not come so much from the growing city of Portland or the towns in the Willamette Valley, but from a geopolitical battle waged in Washington, D.C., where the Forest Service faced competition from the National Park

Service. Although the Forest Service administered a far greater land base than its younger rival (Congress created the NPS in 1916 and placed it within the Department of the Interior), Park Service leadership pursued expansion aggressively, often at the expense of the USFS. Even if national monuments once under Forest Service administration like the Grand Canyon (transferred to the Park Service in 1919 when it was reclassified as a national park) deserved its new designation, the NPS posed a constant annoyance, if not an outright threat, to the USFS during the 1920s and 30s. The Park Service took the offensive with its unilateral legislative proposals for expanding existing national parks like Crater Lake through transfer of national forest land, but also pestered key congressmen with an insistence that only one bureau (the NPS) should manage all of the national monuments. In seeing itself as the main provider of recreation on federal lands and at one point (in 1922) temporarily succeeded in blocking an appropriation for campground development in the national forests, the NPS viewed such Forest Service expenditures as future competition for the funding of these facilities in the national parks.

Rancor between the two bureaus over park expansion and money for recreational developments had reached such proportions by 1924 that the Coolidge Administration had to set up a "coordinating commission" for the purpose of informing Congress how best to allocate contested areas. When the NPS and its allies succeeded in more than doubling the size of Sequoia National Park two years later by not engaging the commission, however, the Forest Service created a new administrative classification on the national forests called wilderness (or "primitive") areas. Capitalizing on what some people saw as too much road building in the national parks, chief forester William B. Greeley initiated an inventory of the still roadless land the Forest Service administered as a precursor to classification as wilderness by the agency. Although administratively designated wilderness could be revoked (and in some cases, did not prove to be all that restrictive), it worked to stem the tide of successful land transfers, reinforcing what the Forest Service wanted its constituents to believe about the agency's ability to manage both recreation and timber destined to be utilized in the future.[34]

Wilderness areas in the national forests of the time tended to be situated at high elevations, where timber values were negligible in comparison to the costs of providing roads or other access.

FIGURE 34. Hikers on the "Oregon Caves" (Big Tree) Trail in the 1920s. (U.S. Forest Service photo, Siskiyou National Forest.)

Recreation centers identified by the Forest Service, however, could often be situated on the periphery of wilderness areas, as staging areas serving users who preferred a backcountry recreational experience. The privately run resorts could provide beds and supplies to those who wanted such amenities, but the Forest Service could promote the wilderness it controlled as something more "pure" than sometimes crowded national parks, where those who came for solitude might be alienated by an expanding road network and the villages designed to centralize visitor services. Although disaffected park users constituted only a tiny minority of visitors at that time, they could be vocal and through the press helped to fuel the perception of wilderness in the national forests as a legitimate alternative to national parks for backcountry recreation.[35]

One advantage to the Forest Service in its war of public relations with the NPS lay in the fact that the wilderness areas in national forests were situated closer than the national parks to most Oregonians, as was the case for many residents of other western states. As less crowded and thus free of the restrictions that the NPS sometimes had to impose on park users (many of whom represented a non-resident or national constituency in contrast to the local or in-state one the Forest Service courted), wilderness areas also allowed the Forest Service to enhance its image as a federal agency that worked with its constituents to bring federally funded amenities to the designated recreational centers. Even before the Forest Service launched its wilderness inventory in late 1926, the district forester based in Portland wrote that recreational centers in the national forests of Oregon amply met the local and regional demand for a type of "wilderness park" because these areas contained sufficient acreage to offer variety and adventure.[36]

Other types of administrative designations could be used in lieu of the more restrictive "wilderness area" in places with recreational appeal and where sufficient quantities of merchantable timber might make road building viable for commodity production sometime in the future. State game refuges represented one such designation compatible with a "recreation center" like Oregon Caves. Established in cooperation with the state game commission (like most states, Oregon retained the management authority over wildlife within its borders), the refuges theoretically functioned as a safeguard against extreme depletion of breeding stock, whether for big game or migratory waterfowl. These remained closed to hunting all year and could function as a kind of park, especially where the Forest Service had begun developing a trail system for the purposes of fire control and recreation.[37] The agency's leadership thus endorsed setting aside the "Oregon Caves Game Refuge" on 20,000 acres surrounding the monument in April 1926, supposedly as part of a plan described by one newspaper account to have game animals (in this case, deer) as "tame as in Yellowstone."[38]

In their self-appointed role to promote recreation in Oregon, Forest Service officials also had a hand in promoting the spread of state parks. District forester C.J. Buck sat on an advisory commit-

FIGURE 35. By 1919 what became known as "Government Camp" near the cave entrance featured a rudimentary water system and places for tents to accommodate visitors who stayed overnight. (U.S. Forest Service photo, Siskiyou National Forest.)

tee for the state parks, which in 1925 numbered only 28 areas that totaled 1,400 acres. Buck and others in the Forest Service saw their potential, however, to complement recreational developments located in the national forests by serving as rest stops for motorists who used the state's highway system.[39] State park acquisitions (most sites had to be purchased from private owners) in Oregon accelerated by the end of the decade, though their number and size lagged behind California—where the nonprofit Save-the-Redwoods League had spearheaded efforts to establish a chain of parks between Crescent City and San Francisco through buying private timberland. Park sites along that portion of the Redwood Highway were large enough to provide focal points (since most preserved old-growth redwood forest) for northbound tourists who then might continue their journey toward Grants Pass. Members of the Redwood Empire Association and Grants Pass Commercial Club were quick to realize that an existing resort on national forest land at Patrick Creek represented one potential stop near the state line—as did Oregon Caves—since both recreation centers lay either on, or near, the travel corridor between Grants Pass and Crescent City.

Having a road to Oregon Caves from its junction with the Redwood Highway as of 1922 represented a new prospect for investors willing to join the Forest Service in developing a resort for the monument. Until 1915 the agency had interpreted existing law and regulations as prohibiting private development in the national monuments, but this stance changed in the wake of Congress passing the Term Occupancy Act on March 4 of that year. The legislation authorized the Forest Service to lease national forest lands for hotels, camps, or other types of resorts like summer homes. A subsequent solicitor's opinion that the act also allowed the leasing of land within national monuments had Forest Service officials pondering whether to grant requests for permits at Oregon Caves and other higher-profile areas it administered. These could be issued at the agency's discretion, but District Forester George H. Cecil first sought advice about the Oregon Caves situation from a member of his research staff, Thornton Munger. After inspecting the monument in the spring of 1917, Munger recommended that no permit be granted without provisions requiring the prospective concessionaire to spend several thousand dollars on improvements. Munger also convinced Cecil that this simply could not be done until a highway to Oregon Caves was built.[40]

In the meantime, the seven- or eight hundred visitors who reached the monument on foot or horseback each summer needed to bring their own outfit or hire it near the two trailheads. In 1917 it took two hours by car or auto stage to go from Grants Pass to Williams, where the Grants Pass Commercial Club arranged for a private party to maintain a "resort" (meaning that tents could be rented for an overnight stay) at Caves Camp. Visitors needing saddle or packhorses needed to make arrangements with a proprietor at Provolt. Motorists could also go through the Illinois Valley and then to Holland, but the road ended at the confluence of Sucker and Grayback creeks. They could camp near the trailhead, hiring horses and/or guides from either of the two closest ranches.[41] With the number of visitors each year still only a thousand or fewer, the Forest Service facility infrastructure at the monument could best be described as scanty. By 1919 the only improvements outside the cave consisted of toilets near the entrance and some pipes that provided campers with water.[42]

With the located line of the future Oregon Caves Highway now set, the Forest Service had to consider how to make a resort operation work at the monument. The monument's steep topography made for plenty of uncertainty about the feasibility of development, especially when agency officials could not know what patterns might emerge from road access. For the moment, they deferred granting anything more than a temporary permit authorizing a tent camp where the concessionaire provided meals and lodging.[43] By the fall of 1921, however, the Forest Service decided to move cautiously with its long-range planning for Oregon Caves, in the direction of establishing a future government headquarters, an improved campground, and overnight accommodations at Grayback, thus limiting facility development at the monument to that of a parking area, lunch room, and guide quarters. Separating the resort into two units did little to clarify how much private investment might be needed even in the short term, since an as-yet unknown tourist trade would determine the amount of capital that the Forest Service could demand up front from a prospective concessionaire.[44]

When the road finally reached Oregon Caves in June 1922, the Forest Service responded by granting a temporary permit for its concessionaire (a man named McIlveen who had previously managed the Patrick Creek resort) to operate a tent camp and guide service. It worked as an interim measure, though the Forest Service knew that McIlveen lacked the investment capital needed to meet the terms of a concession contract that officials envisioned as lasting ten or more years. Consequently, the Forest Service turned to the commercial club—now renamed as the Grants Pass Chamber of Commerce—to find parties willing to incorporate and put $20,000 toward permanent improvements over three years starting in 1923.[45]

The Forest Service previously tried to entice local contacts like

FIGURE 36. Frank Patterson took this photo of the Chalet in 1927. (OCNM Museum and Archives Collections.)

FIGURE 37. A meeting of the Grants Pass Commercial Club in the Chalet. Manager George Sabin and builder Gust Lium are at bottom left. (Oregon Caves Company album, OCNM Museum and Archives Collections.)

pharmacist George Sabin with placing ten or fifteen thousand dollars toward a hotel, but Sabin and a group of his fellow businessmen wanted to see how things might go in 1922 before they committed to anything.[46] Seven of them incorporated contingent on Forest Service approval of their application for an exclusive privilege to provide guide service and permanent facilities, something granted in March 1923. The Forest Service retained the power to revoke it for unsatisfactory service, but among other things specified that a guide headquarters building be erected at the monument as soon as possible.[47]

Plans for the new structure had to first be approved by the forest supervisor, so the Oregon Caves Company requested the consulting services of Arthur L. Peck, a landscape architect who periodically worked on Forest Service projects and taught at the Oregon Agricultural College in Corvallis. As a preliminary step to drawings, Peck recommended an architectural theme that might unify resort developments at the monument with those planned for the tract on Grayback Creek. He followed in the footsteps of his mentor Frank Waugh, who visited Oregon Caves with C.J. Buck in 1917 as part of a trip to assess the recreational possibilities on the national forests.[48] Little in the way of concrete results came from Waugh's visit six years earlier, but in April 1923 Peck suggested that an architectural theme for the resort should be "Swiss" or "Alpine."[49] Its distinctive feature quickly became the use of the bark of Port Orford-cedar as sheathing, complemented by sugar pine shakes for roofing material. Peck originally put forth the idea of using cedar shakes as siding, but the company experienced difficulty in obtaining sufficient quantities. When one of their "pick and shovel" men who were excavating the building suggested cedar bark as an alternative, Sabin (who had been hired to manage the concession) agreed.[50]

Peck's significance to future development of the cave entrance area was largely confined to locating some building sites, though he conceptualized the first two pieces of a larger development scheme. The first involved a "chalet" to be placed on the terrace named "Government Camp," where Peck thought a "porch" might allow visitors to look down the "valley" of Cave Creek, one that doubled as a gathering area where those taking the tour might meet their guide. As the center of pedestrian circulation, the porch served as a trailhead for an existing footpath to the cave's upper entrance, a route along which one or more small buildings (such as cabins or cottages) could replace the tents and be "arranged as on an irregular street."[51]

Constructed to be a multi-purpose building, the Chalet was intended to house an office, dining area, a changing room for wearing coveralls as part of taking the cave tour, and quarters for

FIGURE 38. Resort cabins or "cottages" at Oregon Caves. (Photo by Frank Patterson, OCNM Museum and Archives Collections.)

guides. The popularity of dining in the Chalet had become so apparent during its first season of operation that Sabin urged that an addition be built. He also wanted to improve the tent houses, erect a stone fireplace for nightly gatherings below the Chalet, and transplant native flora (ferns in particular) to enhance the resort setting. Such enthusiasm made forest supervisor E.H. MacDaniels write to the district forester, in regard to any lingering doubts that the Forest Service might have about renewing the permit, about how unlikely it was that anyone else could match the level of investment and service provided by the company.[52]

Such a statement should be seen in the context of the company having spent more than double what it agreed to invest in the Chalet according to terms of the permit, as a means to begin backing away from putting large sums into the Grayback development. Sabin and the stockholders expressed their reluctance to build a resort hotel at Grayback in the fall of 1923, mainly because they saw the monument as their profit center instead of a site located eight miles away.[53] The company nevertheless erected a store near the campground built by the Forest Service in the first months of 1924. Not only was this building required as part of the permit, but Sabin thought it useful as an "information bureau," where visitors could make telephone reservations for overnight accommodations and meals at the monument.[54] The trend toward building structures at the monument continued that year, with two privately funded buildings added. One was "Kiddie Kave," a nursery for children too young for the cave tour, while a small lamp house (for carbide lanterns in the absence of electric lights) located adjacent to the cave entrance constituted the other addition. The latter also doubled as a "studio" to sell images produced by scenic photographer Fred Kiser.[55]

Increasing dissatisfaction with the appearance of tent houses and their platforms above the Chalet served as the main reason for why Forest Service officials encouraged the company to spend several thousand dollars on constructing new cabins in their place once the summer season ended in 1925.[56] Sited along the "irregular street," the seven units were sheathed in cedar bark and came with separate bedrooms, a toilet, and bath. The cabins were designed and built by Gust Lium (the son-in-law of stockholder Sam Baker) who also undertook a small dormitory for housing male guides by the summer of 1927. Construction of these facilities signaled the end of Forest Service insistence on resort buildings at Grayback.[57] With eleven structures added at the monument since 1923, the company also had to expand its septic system in the fall of 1927. By the beginning of the following year, their investment also included installation of some electric lights to illuminate the area around the Chalet, as well as a service road that went to an incinerator located near No Name Creek.[58]

The Forest Service estimated that the company had expended roughly $35,000 by early 1928, with this figure resulting from what Buck and others described almost six years earlier as the necessity to "successfully exploit Oregon Caves" for tourists.[59] This infusion of private money for developing the monument should be seen against the backdrop of the $130,000 in state and federal funds that financed a road between Grayback and the cave entrance, as well as direct expenditures from the Forest Service budget over a fifteen-year period—which by 1925 had grown to $12,000.[60] About a third of the latter figure consisted of salaries for the forest guards stationed at Oregon Caves between 1910 and 1922, so that actual improvements mostly consisted of the replacing of wooden ladders with iron ones, widening of passageways, and building better trails both in the cave and above ground.[61]

Not that the Forest Service lacked plans that could be implemented with funding from a special appropriation. Electric lighting could eliminate the need for candles and carbide lamps, devices blamed for having detrimental effects on cave formations.[62]

FIGURE 39. Newly completed exit tunnel, 1931. (Photo by Frank Patterson, OCNM Museum and Archives Collections.)

Planning for lights started in the fall of 1920, so that an estimate for a power plant and wiring were incorporated into bills introduced during the 1922 and 1924 sessions of Congress.[63] Both bills failed because officials in the Harding and Coolidge administrations objected to a funding request where lighting accounted for only half of the proposed appropriation ($30,000), with the remainder consisting of unspecified improvements.[64]

FIGURE 40. Crew working on the Chateau's foundation, 1931. (Oregon Caves Company photo, OCNM Museum and Archives Collections.)

A new bill written by the Forest Service and introduced by Senator Charles McNary of Oregon in February 1928 contained more specific language. It earmarked funding for electric lights, a system to wash formations while removing mud from the cave, and for building an exit tunnel. The bill passed in early 1929, mainly because the Forest Service convinced McNary and others in Congress that with rising visitation to Oregon Caves (it almost reached 25,000 in 1928), the contemplated improvements could work to make the monument virtually self-supporting. This could be done, they argued, by having the appropriated amount ($35,000) eventually returned to the Treasury through the government collecting a percentage of the fees paid by visitors to the company for taking the cave tour.[65]

Work financed by the appropriation began in the summer of 1930 with installation of pipe and hose for a washing system in the cave.[66] Excavation for a power generating plant for the lights followed, at a site below the cave entrance in the canyon formed by Cave Creek.[67] This diesel-powered plant was necessary while the Forest Service waited for a private utility to build a transmission line from the Illinois Valley. The exit tunnel affected circulation and visitor experience in the cave even more than electric lights, since prior to its construction visitors had to retrace their steps from the Ghost Room to the upper entrance. This routing made tours more than two hours in duration and required parties going in opposite directions to pass each other. Such a circulation pat-

FIGURE 41. Service station in the main parking area, about 1937. (Photo courtesy of Bud Breitmayer.)

tern proved to be especially difficult on days when more than four hundred people entered the cave, but the Forest Service made no firm decisions about the route of an exit tunnel until the spring of 1930.[68] At that point the agency's surveyors compiled the first profile map of Oregon Caves, but also shot a transit line which indicated the most feasible route required 500 feet of excavation above the Ghost Room.[69] This project then went to contract, but construction proved so expensive and difficult for the winning bidder that he defaulted. The Forest Service now had to hire day labor to finish a job that consumed nine months instead of the expected five.[70]

Completion of the tunnel came in February 1931, just as the company (which was now calling itself the "Oregon Caves Resort") pressed the Forest Service to renegotiate. Instead of an annual permit, they wanted to obtain a term agreement, or what amounted to a twenty-year contract, something contingent on completion of a specified program of improvements within three years. For several years Sabin and the stockholders had openly expressed their desire to build a hotel in the ravine below the cave entrance, a location that might permit water from Cave Creek to run through the dining room.[71] By December of 1928 they had publicly promoted the allure of an ample lobby, heated rooms, and larger dining facilities than those in the Chalet.[72] When they began to ask the Forest Service for at least 20 years of operation at the monument to be more or less guaranteed by a term permit, Forest Supervisor J.H. Billingslea took the hotel idea seriously enough to begin discussions about design with Sabin, Lium, and Peck in September 1929. Peck pointed to how such a building might enhance a view of the distant ridgeline, while possibly relieving pedestrian and vehicular congestion below the Chalet if a "forecourt" filled the head of the ravine. A rustic bridge could be built to allow visitors access to the hotel site, making it in Peck's words, "the hub of all further improvements."[73]

What delayed the start of hotel construction for another two years was linked to the insistence of company stockholders on what the Forest Service saw as financing a $50,000 building project with future profits derived from visitors paying fifty cents each to go through the cave with a guide. The Forest Service nevertheless granted the company exclusive rights to the guiding concession, as well as those for food service and accommodation at the monument for a period of twenty years in October 1931.[74] Crews had already begun pouring concrete for walls and the bottom floors of the hotel by that time, work that represented an act of faith on the company's part since it came during the worst period of the Great Depression.

Despite some uncertainty over how the project might be financed, Sabin and the stockholders remained confident. A record number of people (28,000) visited Oregon Caves in 1931, partly because they could reach the monument on a recently widened and paved highway. The company anticipated increased business in coming years by erecting a service station at the monument's main parking area according to plans prepared by Lium and approved by the Forest Service. Sheathed in cedar bark like the other structures, it included a garage and enough space to bunk four employees in an upstairs room. The station also provided a way for the diesel house built for lighting the cave to generate revenue for the company, in that the mechanic hired to maintain it could also run the service station. Having gasoline available at the monument proved acceptable to the Forest Service, since officials knew that the Oregon Caves Highway lacked any such facilities for motorists.[75] The company encountered no difficulties when they built the service station in June, but financing the hotel required that they sell $25,000 of stock in order to raise half of the construction cost. Enticing new investors at that time proved to be more difficult than anticipated, so the work supervised by Lium slowed with no more than twenty men on hand at any one time.[76]

While crews poured concrete for the hotel, the company also

augmented their need for additional water by building a cylindrical reservoir holding some 17,000 gallons in the "gulch" above the Chalet.[77] This privately funded addition to the monument's utility infrastructure went unseen by most visitors, though Sabin and the stockholders made sure that newspapers publicized the distinctive features of the "Chateau," then under construction. In addition to a portion of Cave Creek flowing through the dining room, prospective guests could anticipate enjoying a sunken garden that featured a pool bordered by native plants. Sabin promised steam heat and baths in all of the hotel rooms, with guests to be greeted by an imposing marble fireplace in the lobby of the six-story structure.[78]

Transfer to the National Park Service

With financing difficult enough that the Chateau's completion had to be delayed until the spring of 1934, the company wanted to renegotiate, or at least defer, that provision in their term permit which required half of net proceeds from cave tours be paid to the government each year.[80] The Forest Service agreed to a deferment but would not renegotiate, so Sabin attempted (in a somewhat indirect way) to court the NPS who he thought might further develop the monument's infrastructure without these kinds of strings should the administration of Oregon Caves ever be transferred. Park Service director Horace Albright ordered Roger Toll (the superintendent of Rocky Mountain National Park, but who also reported on the worthiness of new areas for possible transfer to the NPS) to make a "general study of caves" in September 1931, an assignment that included a visit to the monument.[81] Toll's report was lukewarm in that it made no recommendation for or against transferring administration of Oregon Caves, but Sabin felt he had nothing to lose by baiting the Forest Service with an observation that NPS officials sometimes failed to cooperate in promoting scenic attractions outside of their jurisdiction.[81] Taking care to cite no one by name, he asked the Forest Service to secure Albright's opinion about a policy of "mutual co-agency" and its benefits for Oregon Caves and other areas on the Pacific coast. Albright's eventual reply was cordial, pledging that more effort would be made to promote Oregon Caves, but this gave Sabin an opportunity to write a gracious letter in return.[82]

On the surface, this exchange between Sabin and Albright

FIGURE 42. The Chateau under construction in 1933. (OCNM Museum and Archives Collections.)

amounted to nothing more than pleasantries and an opportunity to explain Sabin's apparent misperception. Yet it also served to keep Oregon Caves on the NPS radar screen while an executive order from President Franklin D. Roosevelt was being drafted in response to legislation passed by Congress on March 3, 1933, requiring him to investigate how reorganizing federal agencies might best serve the functions assigned to the Executive Branch. In reference to what the NPS might gain, much of the order issued on June 10 was explicitly worded to authorize the transfer of battlefields and other historic sites (which were a keen interest of Albright's) from the War Department to Interior. The order also provided for all national monuments (including the 16 administered by the Forest Service under the Secretary of Agriculture) to go to the NPS if Roosevelt heard no objections within 60 days.[83] A conference between Forest Service and Park Service officials in Washington resulted in a misunderstanding of what each agency thought about how many were to be transferred.[84] The President then transferred all of the ones administered by the Forest Service in August, though the NPS did not assume control of them until the following April.[85]

Unlike most of the 16 monuments (where Forest Service expenditures remained minimal at best), the transfer of Oregon Caves represented a blow to agency prestige. The Forest Service wanted to show that a wise investment of federal funds had gone toward developing a national monument under its care, money that in concert with private capital might even put such recreational improvement on a self-supporting basis. While Forest Supervisor G.E. Mitchell acknowledged that the company could fare better under NPS administration, since that agency seemed to have more success in landing appropriations for development where no return to the government was expected. He nevertheless contended that the public interest was better served by the Forest Service, citing the small amount expended on administering Oregon Caves could be directly tied to the efficiency gained by the monument being part of Siskiyou National Forest. What worried Mitchell and others in the Forest Service, however, were efforts that Sabin might make to expand the monument since NPS officials had expressed the view that Oregon Caves was too small at 480 acres to warrant any large appropriation for further recreational improvements. For the time being, though, Forest Service officials wished to avoid open disputes with the NPS. It seemed a better course to simply accept the situation and continue to cooperate with promoting Oregon Caves when possible, given their overarching desire for good relations with the residents of Grants Pass and Josephine County.[86]

CHAPTER 4

Improving a Little Landscape Garden, 1934-1943

People associated caves, especially those incorporated into gardens, with contemplation and creativity in the classical world of Greece and Rome. As places where knowledge or poetic inspiration followed from encounters with the underworld, it is little wonder that some of these portals engendered their muses, oracles, and nymphs to offset the prevailing ambience of disorientation and mystery.[1] Other naturally occurring features like waterfalls, pools, springs, rock outcrops (especially if these furnished a vista), and groves of trees have also possessed intellectual and mythological significance.[2] These elements became focal points in Renaissance gardens, at a time when the rich and powerful wanted to recall the classical past while molding their domestic environment to suit their aesthetic sensibilities. The development of "taste" took a new turn in England of the eighteenth century, where the rigid lines, order, and formality that dominated Italian and French estates were cast aside for more informal landscapes imitative of wild nature. Some estate owners created their own grottos, pools, and groves in this new template, embellishing them with a greater diversity of plants than what Britain could offer—many being American species only recently described by botanists. They chose serpentine paths and carriage roads as the main circulation devices since the gardens had now fused with whole parks, the latter being formerly uncultivated and used only to enclose deer or other game.[3]

In being designed to yield individualized "scenes" alluding to classical literature or pastoral perfection, the landscape gardens became so popular among the elite that they conditioned a collective response to nature. As "pleasure grounds" such scenery furnished models for the eventual appearance of public parks during the nineteenth century, at a time when industrial capitalism increasingly pushed its workforce into rapidly growing cities.[4] Designers of the new public spaces wanted to bring the country into city life, just as the early Romans and subsequent *literati* desired, believing that "rustic" facilities in "naturalistic" landscapes best allowed the populace to enjoy fresh air, exercise, and moral improvement. The first city parks in the United States followed European precedents, but the idea of establishing public pleasuring grounds beyond city limits can be largely attributed to the opportunities presented by closing the once uncontrolled frontier. It also signaled acceptance of the idea that one should travel away from the distractions of towns and cities to experience nature, but as a cultural construction perceived as more primitive and egalitarian than urban life, and idealized in some places to be an Edenic garden.

Tourism initially developed with the rise of informal landscape gardens in the eighteenth century, since the former followed from the wealth used to create the latter. It did not take English tourists (as well as wealthy western Europeans and even Americans) long to go beyond art galleries and the pastoral landscapes of Italy to add experiencing the "sublime" as part of their itinerary. Many believed that knowledge and perhaps inspiration could be found in jagged mountains, a stormy sea, or wherever the scenery aroused feelings of awe and reverence. The sublime could even include caves, provided they were large and interesting enough to attract the few who undertook the rigors of travel. The Mammoth Cave in Kentucky, for example, could fit into any nineteenth century "grand tour" of the American sublime—one that first included the Hudson River Valley and Niagara Falls, but subsequently expanded across the continent to embrace wilder (yet also Edenic) places like Yosemite, Yellowstone, and the Grand Canyon.[5] Through a kind of perceptual lens attuned to seeing scenery as art in nature, pursuit of the sublime eventually helped link nascent regional identity with places like Oregon Caves.

FIGURE 43. Neptune's Daughter was one of many classically-based names on the tour route. Photo by Frank Patterson, 1923. (OCNM Museum and Archives Collections.)

New lights, but an old script

Pursuit of the sublime went beyond merely retaining the cave as public property and attempting to protect its components from souvenir seekers. In pitching the cave as a curiosity, both private promoters and the Forest Service guides encouraged visitors to project familiar shapes, animals, personas, and objects onto subterranean passages and formations.[6] While they might describe formation of the cave as a geological process, at least in a few places, the time required for that to occur remained distant and unknowable. The cave was thus, as in the ancient world, shrouded in mystery and distinct from the surroundings above ground, so visitors were encouraged to engage their imagination and project their fancy as they moved from room to room. Even one of the forest supervisors employed Gothic imagery drawn from the language of the sublime in early 1917 when he quoted a visitor account on his report to the district forester, one intended to justify further development of the Oregon Caves:

> "...one does indeed feel this underworld region of strange, fantastic beauty is part of a fairy story land of one's youth. For countless ages the series of galleries, passages, rooms, chimneys, and "bottomless pits" have been slowly carved from the solid limestone rock

by the dissolving effect of water. The walls are thickly studded with marvelously wrought forms of queer looking flowers and vegetables that appear as if just picked from some giant's garden. Occasionally, a huge jawbone, filled with vicious looking teeth, that one imagines belonged to some prehistoric monster, protrudes from a shadowy recess."[7]

Guides were needed in the interest of visitor safety and for deterring vandalism, but they also made the company's investments at the monument a paying proposition. None of them lasted longer or had as much effect on visitor experience at Oregon Caves than Richard W. "Dick" Rowley. Originally hired as a forest guard in 1913, Rowley hitched his wagon to the company in 1923 and then spent all his summers at the monument until his retirement in 1954. Many of the names for rooms and formations on the tour came from Rowley and were perpetuated by guides who trained under him.[8] More than that, Rowley began to personify the Oregon Caves by 1922.[9] His stories enhanced the scripted experience of a cave tour, but Rowley as a single and seemingly self-sufficient mountaineer also played the role of a hermit caretaker that eighteenth century visitors might have encountered at a garden grotto. He possessed enough practical knowledge as an ex-miner and one-time railroad worker, however, to do more than spin stories by directing the company's maintenance operation at the monument.[10]

Throughout the 1920s Rowley periodically assisted with planning for improvements like the exit tunnel and lighting system. The tunnel's completion in 1931 dictated some adjustments be made in the route that he and other guides followed, but the content of what they presented along the way largely remained within the realm of pointing out fancied creatures and telling stories that had the occasional folksy allusion to Greek and Roman mythology.[11] Electric lighting could greatly enhance story telling, given the wider range of effects possible over those conducted with carbide lamps. Its intent was communicated by a Forest Service official who quoted the electrical engineer accompanying him to the monument in 1930, writing how visitors should be "unconscious" of the lighting system so that their attention might remain "entirely focused" on the cave.[12] After cautioning against over-illumination, he then promoted the use of colored lights in Paradise Lost to create an effect known as "Dante's Inferno" on

FIGURE 44. Dick Rowley at the cave entrance, about 1938. (Oregon Caves Company photo, OCNM Museum and Archives Collections.)

the floor of the Ghost Room. Such entertaining gimmicks (which resembled, at least in spirit, those tricks once used in some of the English landscape gardens to surprise and amuse visitors) furnished a way to culminate the tour before visitors climbed out of the Ghost Room toward the exit tunnel.[13]

The first lighting system certainly had its shortcomings, since defective switches and the underpowered diesel engine intended for generating electricity at the power house in the canyon meant that some members of each tour group still carried carbide lamps. This latter type of illumination became a thing of the past in 1938, when an overhead line finally connected the monument with commercial power at Holland.[14] Rewiring inside the cave included laying armored cable and installing water tight fixtures, all at government expense.[15] Congress appropriated $20,000 for the line and rewiring, expenditures partly justified because feeder lines could be built from it to farms located at the upper end of Sucker Creek.[16]

A willingness to subsidize infrastructure that directly benefited the company's operations was not limited to that one appropriation for a utility connection, in that more improvement of the tour route took place prior to arrival of the power line through the efforts of Civilian Conservation Corps enrollees. Rowley (who at 65 years of age again found himself on the government's payroll)

FIGURE 45. Part of the connection built by CCC enrollees in the late 1930s, known as the Passageway of the Whale. (Photo by Sawyers, OCNM Museum and Archives Collections.)

supervised at least a portion of the work beginning in January 1935. This project consisted of providing more headroom in the cave (due to the increased average height of Americans) and widening the trail in places. Enrollees also built a masonry wall and seats in the Ghost Room, then installed additional pipe rail in conjunction with fashioning more than 300 marble steps in the cave.[17] In continuing with their stated aim of making the cave accessible to the "most timid tourist" while also protecting its "picturesque features," the CCC went underground again in 1937. This time they constructed an eighty-foot connecting tunnel between the crossing of a stream called the "River Styx" and a room called "The Wigwam" in order to eliminate backtracking over some six hundred feet of the tour route.[18]

The connecting tunnel essentially completed the one way trail corridor needed for tours taken by more than 40,000 visitors in 1938. With its labor inexpensive and plentiful for a time, the CCC projects in the cave accelerated what entrepreneurial effort began in the nineteenth century—the process of making the monument commercially viable as a resort. Improving the underground trail corridor constituted only one facet of the CCC contribution to improving a circulation system started by Burch and Harkness, but one that the Forest Service greatly expanded both inside the cave and above ground. The enrollees nearly finished a

IMPROVING A LITTLE LANDSCAPE GARDEN 95

resort development spread over two sites (the monument and Grayback) by the time that the CCC program was disbanded in 1942, but one whose form had fully matured into a landscape garden where the cave tour represented just one facet of what visitors could experience at the site.

Camp Oregon Caves, NM-1

In addition to providing unskilled labor in the form of enrollees who numbered between 75 and 200 at any one time, the CCC program also paid the salaries of landscape architects and engineers. The professional staff designed individual projects while skilled tradesmen (called locally experienced men or LEMs) supervised crews of enrollees. Allotments for individual projects tended to remain small (usually $8,000 or less) their number was considerably greater over the program's life (1934 to 1941) than what the Forest Service and its concessionaire had been able to undertake over the previous decade. CCC project design generally followed earlier precedents, though it also reflected how the National Park Service designed buildings, trails, walls, site features like steps or pools, as well as plantings during the 1930s. Most of these had their antecedents in earlier park design that could be traced back to landscape gardens that included model villages centered on structures built with native materials, ornamental plantings that blended with their surroundings, and circuit trails intended as the primary way to experience the site.

When the CCC arrived on the Siskiyou National Forest in 1933 they formed five camps (each being 200 men when at full strength; side or "spike" camps implied a size less than that threshold number), with no projects taking place at Oregon Caves. Most of the work during that initial six month enrollment period of May to November centered on road building and firefighting elsewhere on the forest, though new administrative structures such as the Redwood Ranger Station near the highway junction in "Caves City" received passing mention in one Forest Service accomplishment report.[19] Embellishments considered recreational by nature, like a log portal and new restrooms in the monument's lower parking area, received only brief consideration before being deferred to the future.[20] Spike camps had been difficult for the Forest Service to obtain that first period because such requests had to go through the War Department (the Army recruited and processed the enrollees) that at first experienced some difficulties in mobilizing enough officers for its command structure.[21]

By the spring of 1934, however, the problems of providing enough camp commanders and technical supervision had eased enough for a contingent of thirteen men from Camp Wineglass in Crater Lake National Park to establish a spike camp located near the confluence of Grayback and Sucker creeks for the time being. By summer the spike camp grew to roughly fifty men who made use of a messhall, washhouse, latrine, and some tent platforms.[22] The enrollees were preceded by a landscape architect funded through the program, Armin Doerner, who reported on what he believed could be accomplished by the CCC at Oregon Caves. Doerner discouraged siting even a small camp at the monument, owing to the fact that the canyon below the Chateau simply could not accommodate large numbers of enrollees housed in tents, much less withstand the impact of having to move supplies from the main parking area on a regular, if not daily, basis. The enrollees thus remained at the spike camp until a better site could be found.[23]

Much of the CCC work at the monument during the summer of 1934 was confined to reducing the fire hazard posed by debris and down fuels, but more ambitious projects could be attempted with a full camp of 200 enrollees over the following winter. The full camp resulted from a chain of events that began in September, when the Army rejected a NPS proposal to deploy enrollees stationed at Crater Lake National Park (who would otherwise be snowbound during the winter) to Lava Beds National Monument. NPS director Arno Cammerer then asked for the winter camp to be located at Grayback, assuring the Forest Service that CCC personnel not needed for work at Oregon Caves could be engaged with projects on the Siskiyou National Forest. This shift prompted funding for a camp consisting of wood frame structures to be built north of the highway, on a spot once known as Grimmett's Ranch. Carpenters followed standard plans produced by the Forest Service to erect barracks, officer quarters, an administrative building, a mess hall, and latrines that October, completing most structures prior to the arrival of another 47 men from Crater Lake at the end of the month.[24]

Camp Oregon Caves attained full strength of 200 enrollees by December, given the thinking that if snow conditions were too severe for work at the monument, careful planning might allow a

IMPROVING A LITTLE LANDSCAPE GARDEN 97

FIGURE 46. Camp Oregon Caves in 1935. (OCNM Museum and Archives Collections.)

seamless shift to Forest Service projects at a lower elevation. Despite earlier discussion of the camp being jointly administered between the two land management agencies, the NPS bore all the expenses through the CCC funds allotted to it and thus assumed charge of all work projects.[25] Heavy snowfall through the winter of 1934-35 meant about 60 percent of the manpower provided by enrollees went toward Forest Service projects. These centered on construction of a road toward French Peak and building a new campground located about one quarter mile west of the one established in 1922 at the confluence of Sucker and Grayback creeks. Clearing for "Grayback Forest Camp" started in late October and was soon joined by other CCC projects at the site, ones that had the enrollees building latrines, campground roads, a community house, and an entrance sign "motif."[26]

Development of Grayback Campground

By the time the CCC departed Camp Oregon Caves for good in November 1941, Grayback Forest Camp covered ten acres. Unlike the antecedent Sucker Creek camp, the facilities at Grayback included twenty fireplaces and tables linked to individual sites.[27] These were located along loop roads with parking for cars confined to what were called "garage spurs," defined by boulders or logs so that damage to vegetation caused by automobiles could be minimized. The so-called "Meinecke Plan" (named for the leading proponent of this type of car camping, whose ideas were quickly adopted by the Park Service and Forest Service in the early 1930s) also included planting shrubs and trees. Adding native vegetation at the site could not only enhance the campground's appearance, but also protect it from damage by confining vehicular circulation. Transplanted tree and shrubs could screen individual campsites from each other, as well as erase the view that passing motorists might otherwise obtain from the highway.

Development of the Grayback Forest Camp came as the CCC and other public works programs pushed the total number of national forest campgrounds with at least some facilities to 3,000.[28] Far fewer than that number possessed amenities equal to those at Grayback during the Great Depression, much less its proximity to a recreation center like Oregon Caves. With this in mind, the Forest Service proposed in 1939 that the CCC build an organization camp to serve groups such as the scouts, churches, and service clubs. Gust Lium, who had worked as a general construction foreman on the Siskiyou National Forest after completing the Chateau in 1934, sketched a mess hall for the camp, one to be built about half mile above Camp Oregon Caves on Grayback Creek. It was to be the initial structure in an organization camp that Forest Supervisor Edward P. Cliff envisioned as including a lodge and accommodations for a hundred or so people to be housed in eight to twelve separate dormitories.[29]

Although NPS staff in the field wanted to make the organization camp the primary CCC project for the winter of 1939-40, officials in Washington, D.C. put a damper of this undertaking by disapproving Lium's drawings.[30] The sheets supposedly did not meet NPS standards, yet the landscape architects and other agency staff did not object to Lium's drawings for a community house and restrooms at the Grayback Forest Camp in 1935, or his design used to rebuild the Cedar Guard Station and its adjacent garage in 1937.[31] The latter two projects involved moving structures originally constructed in 1933 to a new location, then revamping their interiors, re-roofing them, and sheathing both with cedar bark like the buildings at Oregon Caves.[32]

Demise of the organization camp while still in the planning stages came at a time when funding for the CCC began to decline rapidly, though this effort represented the last attempt by the Forest Service to establish a resort in the Grayback vicinity. The larger political context needed to explain why the NPS opposed a CCC project on national forest land had to do with agency leadership asserting what it saw as the Park Service's leadership role in the field of organized camping, though this was manifested more

FIGURE 47. CCC sawmill near Cave Junction, about 1937. (NPS photo by Francis G. Lange, OCNM Museum and Archives Collections.)

often in state parks of the time.[33] The Washington office of the NPS published *Park and Recreation Facilities* (1935) as well as *Park and Recreation Structures* (1938), books aimed at influencing how state parks (as well as some city parks) were designed and built with CCC funding.[34] Although the CCC also brought about a tremendous increase in the number of national forest campgrounds with facilities, the NPS (at least at the Washington level) saw the more highly developed organization camps administered by the Forest Service as competition. Since supervising the development of organized camping outside the national parks represented an expansion of NPS responsibilities, Park Service leadership did not want CCC enrollees it supervised to build organization camps for the agency's main rival. Officials closer to the ground, like those at Crater Lake, cautioned against alienating the Forest Service. Interagency cooperation appeared to them as critical in operating Camp Oregon Caves for some eight months each year, not only as a base from which to further develop the monument, but also for maintaining a sawmill which supplied lumber for CCC projects at Crater Lake and Lava Beds.[35]

CCC projects at Oregon Caves

Despite the occasionally caustic relations at the Washington office level between the Park Service and Forest Service during the 1930s, Camp Oregon Caves could generally be seen as a model of how the two agencies cooperated to their mutual benefit. Not only did enrollees undertake a number of Forest Service projects (they even built an airport several miles south of the Redwood Ranger Station) in addition to improving the Grayback Forest Camp, the CCC provided the single biggest boost in developing the monument for a growing number of visitors. Some of this came in the form of upgrades to the utility infrastructure, starting with construction of a waterline from the cave entrance area to a dam and intake on Lake Creek during the winter of 1934-35. Almost two miles of pipe were laid in conjunction with the enrollees building a storage tank reinforced with concrete and holding 38,000 gallons.[36] Other utility work at the monument included sporadic upgrading of the sewer system starting in 1934, and constructing a storm drain below the concessionaire's cabins in 1938-39.[37]

The CCC also added to the monument's building stock, though all decisions about siting and design had to go through the landscape architects supervised by the NPS. One of their first projects at Oregon Caves involved considerable excavation by hand before starting work on a ranger residence, a structure needed because the NPS intended to station one of its seasonal employees there during the summer. Once the landscape architects concluded that an entrance or "checking" station was not required in the main parking area, Francis Lange drew the final plans for a residence to be located adjacent to the company's cabins, on a site overlooking the cave entrance area.[38] He noted some uncertainty about funding the project, given the nationwide cap of $1,500 on any single CCC building project. Added costs of excavation, subflooring, and an extra bedroom intended for visiting NPS officials drove the price tag to more than $3,000 by the time enrollees completed the residence in June 1936. Other structures built or revamped by the enrollees from Camp Oregon Caves, however, averaged only $500 each. These included a new space for storing carbide lamps (replacing the "studio"), a combination garage and

IMPROVING A LITTLE LANDSCAPE GARDEN 101

FIGURE 48. Diesel house in the canyon of Cave Creek after CCC improvements, 1936. (NPS photo by Francis G. Lange, OCNM Museum and Archives Collections.)

tool house located further west from the cave entrance along the service road, and adding a roof and cedar bark sheathing to the diesel plant situated below the Chateau.[39]

A "reception center" came as the result of NPS officials reversing their decision during the summer of 1940 about the need for another structure in the main parking area. They eventually settled on a building designed by NPS architect Cecil Doty that was both ranger office and contained public restrooms. Its completion in November 1941 represented nearly the last project completed by enrollees from Camp Oregon Caves and came in response to a complaint from the concessionaire who saw a need to monitor traffic on the road linking the lower parking lot with the cave entrance area, since space for cars near the Chateau was so limited that only hotel guests could use it.[40]

Although buildings and utilities demanded periodic attention from both designers and enrollees, trail projects proved to be steadier work for the CCC. The landscape architects and engineers who worked for the NPS agreed with an initial assessment of the pedestrian circulation system at Oregon Caves that called for rebuilding all of the trails to conform with new standards set by the agency for gradient and width. In no case should grades exceed 15 percent, though the standards directed that gradient should be varied at regular intervals to avoid tiring leg muscles.

For trails attracting heavy use by hikers and horses, crews aimed to provide the frontcountry standard of four feet wide, yet they also made ten feet of vertical clearance for equestrian use. Where lighter foot traffic was expected, width could be narrowed to two feet—similar to many trails in the national forests—though the NPS at that time placed greater emphasis on designing loops and circuits (especially in a small area like Oregon Caves where the need to provide additional access for fire suppression was not great) aimed at enticing visitors into short backcountry jaunts.[41] The standards and subsequent guidance in the form of CCC project manuals emphasized that trails should be built to blend with the park landscape so well that they might be rendered invisible to anyone not on them. This aesthetic preferred water bars over the use of culverts or bridges for cross drainage, but also emphasized mitigating the effects of trail construction by taking steps to repair ragged edges at the margins of tread through raking or even rounding slopes where necessary.[42]

When the NPS and CCC arrived in 1934, only five trails existed on the monument outside the cave. These included a poorly defined path linking the main parking lot with the diesel plant located below the Chateau, as well as an unmaintained trail down Cave Creek that once served as an access route for visitors prior to the highway opening in 1922. A trail connected the exit tunnel with the cave entrance area so that visitors could make a circuit on their tour, but it was only two feet wide and slick in wet weather. The two remaining trails consisted of a steep ascent past the cave's upper entrance toward Lake Mountain that began at the Chalet, and a path leading to a large Douglas fir described as 14 feet in diameter. The latter route overtopped an older trail toward Williams for the first eight-tenths of a mile from the Chalet, but then diverged by gently climbing to cross Panther Creek where the "Big Tree" stood.[43]

Enrollees began the reconstruction effort by widening the exit trail in November 1934, realigning it slightly so that visitors returned to the cave entrance rather than having to do a steeper descent to the hotel parking southwest of the Chateau.[44] It took until the following July to finish the project, one that included hauling fill to the exit in order to provide a place for visitors to assemble and enjoy a distant prospect framed by trees at the end of their tour.[45] Another reconstruction project started during the fall of 1934, this one taking place on the trail built by the Forest

IMPROVING A LITTLE LANDSCAPE GARDEN 103

FIGURE 49. CCC enrollees rebuilding the Exit Trail, early 1935. (NPS photo by Francis G. Lange, OCNM Museum and Archives Collections.)

Service to the Big Tree. It centered on abandoning one section of old trail that would have led visitors to the new storage tank in favor of a wider route that permitted the transport of materials to the site, but also lessened the gradient. Enrollees widened other sections of the trail to four feet in making it suitable for horses, but also placed several dry laid stone benches recessed into the trail's uphill side. They built another of these benches along a rerouted trail, one largely intended for trains of pack horses which otherwise had to go through the Chalet's breezeway. This route now commenced near the monument's boundary, running above the main parking area to an intersection with the Big Tree Trail that was situated below the water storage tank.[46]

Landscape foreman Howard Buford suggested connecting the new route to Big Tree with the existing trail to Lake Mountain during the fall of 1936 in order to create a circuit. His idea came at a time when enrollees worked to improve the Lake Mountain Trail, and given how the new path to Big Tree was completed as of June 1935, a loop totaling 3.3 miles could be formed with less than a mile of new construction.[47] By the spring of 1937 the CCC had also finished building another circuit that utilized the Lake Mountain Trail, but this one included the Cliff Trail—a new route that furnished visitors an alternative to the Exit Trail when they

FIGURE 50. Picnic area in the canyon of Cave Creek, 1936. Trail connections are to the right. (NPS photo by Francis G. Lange, OCNM Museum and Archives Collections.)

finished a cave tour. The Cliff Trail allowed them to reach the cave entrance area by going above the exit tunnel and obtain views of the Illinois Valley in the distance. Enrollees built the route to cover six-tenths of a mile, but kept it two feet wide in order to limit scars. They needed to place stone steps in some sections to compensate for sudden changes in grade, something that also required the erection of retaining walls in several places. Landscape measures like bank sloping and placement of pine needles or other duff material were also included in the project since the NPS expected plenty of use.[48]

The CCC started the monument's only other trail circuit in 1935, when they abandoned a path with switchbacks that went from the main parking lot to the diesel plant situated on Cave Creek. They built a route meant to link a trailhead near the concessionaire's service station with a new picnic area built in the canyon.[49] Another year passed before another crew of enrollees constructed a short trail some two feet wide that connected No Name Creek with the end of the service road running west of the Chateau. Lange called this segment the best example of "natural trail construction" within the monument, due to the care taken to eliminate scars through bank sloping and placing duff on exposed surfaces.[50] By March 1941 this trail had been connected with the

IMPROVING A LITTLE LANDSCAPE GARDEN 105

picnic area located above Cave Creek once the CCC built a route for horses less than two miles in length, a project that included an additional connection to the picnic area and a footbridge over No Name Creek.[51]

Landscape projects followed a similar pattern to that of trails, in that the CCC began by reconstructing features that appeared when the Forest Service administered Oregon Caves. Once again, something of a template and footprint had been established under the Forest Service, so the NPS directed the enrollees to rebuild some features such as retaining walls or pools, expand planting, as well as add a number of new components. Doerner's reconnaissance report of May 1934 pointed to the need for landscaping around buildings near the cave entrance. He noted that the poor character of retaining walls marred the scene, as did a rectangular "trout pool" located at the base of a waterfall created by how Cave Creek tumbled about ten feet to the road below as it emerged from the cavern.[52]

Repair or replacement of the existing walls took place over the next five years, with most new construction not initiated until 1937. Lange commented during the summer of 1935 that many walls contained small stones that seemed out of proportion to the scale of the surroundings, something he and the enrollees attempted to counter by introducing plants into the joints of the dry laid walls.[53] Some walls simply had to be rebuilt with larger rock hauled to the site, especially if they appeared to be structurally unsound. Enrollees first undertook new construction when they replaced a rapidly failing log wall erected during the Chateau's construction with one of stone near the hotel's kitchen entrance in early 1937. That project seemed to provide the CCC crews with the experience needed for another wall constructed as part of widening the road connecting the main parking area and the Chalet.[54] By the fall of 1937 enrollees were at work building another wall for an expanded parking area west of the Chateau, a project that required 2,500 yards of fill. One section of this retaining wall gave way during the winter rains of 1939-40, but the NPS took emergency measures to limit resulting damage.[55] The CCC achieved better results with a crenulated masonry wall they built in 1940, one that defines the walkway between the Chalet and cave entrance. In conforming to specifications issued by the NPS for contracted stone masonry, however, it more resembled designed features along Rim Drive encircling Crater Lake

FIGURE 51. Masonry wall at center right with dry laid walls to left in this photo of the plaza, August 1941. Above the old Chalet are the cottages. (Photo by George Grant, National Park Service Historic Photograph Collection.)

than other dry laid rockwork at the monument.[56]

The masonry wall essentially completed landscape work around the cave entrance, an effort that began with sketches by Doerner and then Lange for how the plaza area and hotel landscape should look. Their drawings led to the first CCC plantings in the plaza, though these rhododendron and tan oak near the Chateau were limited to just a few specimens. Crews began picking rock to build retaining walls in the Chateau's courtyard once a tractor hoist became available for the heavy lifting in December 1934. They left a monument to Elijah Davidson in place near the cave entrance, but transformed the plaza's appearance with a new campfire pit and log seats located at the base of some stone steps leading to the Chalet.[57] Large logs of Port Orford-cedar served as guardrails at the road margins through the plaza, but they also separated cars from pedestrian assembly areas such as the fire pit. Enrollees also made the rectangular pool that drew a negative review from Doerner into a more naturally shaped feature flanked by transplanted trees and then added stone steps for a walkway that provided new pedestrian access between the cave entrance and the road below it.[58]

IMPROVING A LITTLE LANDSCAPE GARDEN 107

FIGURE 52. CCC enrollees working on retaining walls in the Chateau's courtyard, early 1935. (OCNM Museum and Archives Collections.)

Even more dramatic changes occurred next to the Chateau, where the CCC took an unfinished courtyard and began enlarging a pool located next to doors leading to the dining room. Enrollees employed wood blocks as a sort of flagstone paving around the pool, but also replaced log cribbing with dry laid stonework before embellishing the courtyard's appearance by transplanting trees, shrubs, and ferns in June 1935.[59] The only other landscape additions to the plaza area with CCC funding resulted from the need for outdoor lighting and fire protection. Three rustic light standards were installed near the Chateau in the spring of 1938, though recessed lights along the road between the main parking lot and hotel became more prevalent since the NPS wanted a more "restful and subdued" nighttime effect than what additional overhead standards might have produced.[60] The last CCC project in the plaza began during the winter of 1939-40, when enrollees built two concrete vaults faced with rock for fire hydrants and hose storage near the Chateau. Over the following summer they added two wooden "houses" for keeping hoses that could be attached to the hydrants located next to the concessionaire's cabins.[61]

Several of Lange's preliminary sketches done in early 1937 were aimed at how best to maximize space for parking in the main

108   IMPROVING A LITTLE LANDSCAPE GARDEN

FIGURE 53. The monument's main parking lot in 1938. (NPS photo by Francis G. Lange, OCNM Museum and Archives Collections.)

lot located near the monument boundary. They represented a start to the only other major landscape improvement implemented over the following year or so. Bank sloping done on an old landslide widened the lot in 1936 and triggered subsequent work meant to establish a vehicular circulation pattern at the site. Crews placed a long and thin island in the center of the lot, one delineated by partially buried logs treated with creosote but with individual boulders situated between them. Lange planned for the lot to accommodate more than 100 cars, most of which conveyed visitors who did not stay overnight at the monument. That meant there was a need for garbage cans, to be covered by cedar logs hollowed to fit around them. This design represented what could be the most elaborate attempt to make even small landscape features blend with their surroundings. Other CCC landscape projects at the site included plantings in the island, stone curbing placed at the base of the bank slope for purposes of delineating the lot, as well as two signs placed upright with routed letters carved into the diagonal face of treated logs.[62]

Lange also sought to separate cars from pedestrians, especially where visitors had to walk on the road linking the day use parking with the plaza and cave entrance area. He advocated widening the road to allow for building a walk parallel to the narrow driving surface, which meant laying 700 feet of stone curb on one side. Like the projects he supervised in Rim Village and along Rim Drive at Crater Lake, the walk featured asphalt paving, a component that the CCC finished by the end of June 1937. Lange was so pleased with the results that he continued to press for a similar walk on the front of the Chateau, but this project went nowhere once the superintendent at Crater Lake questioned the need for it.[63]

Internal opposition by line managers illustrated the reality that landscape architects had influence over the design and implementation of CCC projects, but were never given free reign at Oregon Caves or in any other unit administered by the NPS. They could not move immediately on a project when other NPS staff members objected, as in the case of cleaning up construction debris below the Chateau, where Lange and the landscape foremen wanted to create pools in Cave Creek by introducing additional rocks as dams that imparted what they saw as a desirable "cascading, rippling effect." Regional specialists viewed such modification of the stream as unacceptable, so this project component was dropped and the cleanup finally proceeded in 1938.[64]

Managers and staff nevertheless supported Lange's sign projects, which they recognized as a key part of design for improving the landscape's function and appearance at Oregon Caves. Although trail signs and similar devices placed in the main parking lot remained modest, the CCC built an impressive "entrance motif" at the monument's boundary along the Caves Highway in 1936. It consisted of a large redwood sign with routed letters suspended from a bollard of upright cedar logs on a stone base, with one log projected horizontally in order to suspend the sign.[65] A year later crews affixed a second sign on one side of the first, this one to indicate where motorists entered the Siskiyou National Forest from the monument. It matched the entrance signs at Crater Lake, having raised wood letters painted chrome orange against a brown stained background for visibility at night.[66]

Although perhaps more attractive than most, the motifs could not be considered uncommon. They could be seen at the boundaries of some cities and were also used to indicate the entrances of parks, as well as campgrounds in the national forests.[67] As Camp Oregon Caves began producing signs for placement along Rim Drive at Crater Lake in 1938, however, enrollees fashioned some mile markers for placement at road junctions along the Oregon Caves Highway. Not only did the five markers extend CCC signage beyond Grayback toward Cave Junction, these sported the unusual look of routed letters carved into a planed surface on one side of an upright log. Each marker indicated the number of miles remaining to be traveled until the motorist reached Oregon Caves,

FIGURE 54. Mileage sign at "Robinson's Corner" on the Oregon Caves Highway, 1938. (NPS photo by Francis G. Lange, OCNM Museum and Archives Collections.)

something Lange explained was done in support of the monument's concessionaire.[68]

Expanded concession facilities

In reinforcing how the NPS and CCC worked to continue the public-private partnership begun under Forest Service administration of the monument, the mile markers most likely contributed to

FIGURE 55. Coffeeshop in the Chateau, late 1930s. (Photo by Sawyers, OCNM Museum and Archives Collections.)

the concessionaire proposing to build an information bureau at the junction of the Caves and Redwood highways in 1943. Although not completed until the postwar years, the company's board of directors in Grants Pass had at least indicated their willingness to replace the information bureau they once operated at Grayback. Their rationale for a new structure in Cave Junction was that it might generate business from passing motorists and other casual travelers that might not otherwise be generated.[69] Private funding for further developing the monument had continued even in the midst of financial strain posed by building the Chateau, though it took the company until 1937 to open its new coffeeshop, a facility largely accessed by visitors from the hotel courtyard. An improving economy by that time no doubt helped revenue, since annual visitation at the monument almost doubled from the 32,484 in 1935 to 59,434 just two years later.

More visitors dictated the company's need to hire additional staff, but new employees faced a housing shortage. Men stayed in the guide dormitory while women slept upstairs in the Chalet, but both structures had been constructed before 1928, when annual visitation never topped 26,000. With sites for new buildings so limited at the monument, Lange opened a dialog among NPS officials in the spring of 1937 about how to guide the expansion of concession facilities. Replacing the Chalet with a new hotel came out of discussions with the concessionaire, though this came with the complication of having to find a place for a new women's dormitory.⁷⁰ Stymied for the time being, the company deferred plans for the structure and instead had an architect prepare drawings in order to expand the housing available for men in the guide dormitory.⁷¹ Work to enlarge the guide dormitory took place in 1940, a few months prior to the NPS and its concessionaire reaching an agreement on how the Chalet would be rebuilt. A new building was to contain a considerably larger dormitory for women on the two upper floors, but also housed a novelty store, restrooms, nursery, and ticket booth at ground level.⁷²

With American involvement in World War II virtually certain by the summer of 1941, and the CCC camp decommissioned by October, Lium (who had since returned to the company payroll from the Forest Service) knew to stockpile materials for the new Chalet. He and a small crew completely rebuilt the structure prior to the lean visitor season of 1942 (gas rationing and other wartime measures limited leisure travel), widening its footprint with additional excavation and adding a third story. It signified the virtual completion of planned development at the monument, but the NPS kept a relatively short list of maintenance and repair projects that the CCC had not undertaken, chief among them being the failed retaining wall near the Chateau. The number of projects expanded once a large slide in late 1942 altered the face of the main parking area, destroying the company's service station as well as the picnic area built by the CCC below it. Fixing the parking lot had to wait due to the war's effect on staffing and funding for the NPS. Both fell to less than half of what they were just a year earlier, just as travel to the parks dropped commensurately.⁷³

NPS master plans for Oregon Caves

By the middle of 1942, the Chateau and new Chalet stood squarely at the axis of a resort-cum-landscape garden and represented one of the best examples in any park of how to apply the principles of rustic architecture and naturalistic design. Not only did the development allow for day and overnight use of a small site, though the circulation systems and structures at Oregon Caves seemed to overcome the limitations imposed by steep topography and a remote location. The use of centralized planning by the NPS (where drawings from designers on the ground had to be approved at successively higher levels in the agency) is often given much of the credit for the success of park projects completed during the interwar period. To some extent this is true at Oregon Caves, where the monument's development by the concessionaire and the CCC seemed to reflect what was on the large master plan sheets that were approved by NPS officials stationed at Crater Lake, as well as those in San Francisco and Washington, D.C.[74]

At Oregon Caves and other parks during the 1930s, the sheets (often site plans) were large enough to be rolled for storage but included summaries of the work completed to that point along with projections for development anticipated over the next year or two on smaller sheets interleaved between the drawings. Lange assembled the master plans for Oregon Caves, drawing two sheets in 1936, then updating them and adding another sheet in 1938. He followed a template established for larger areas like Crater Lake, where the drawings and summary sheets were organized into sections covering road networks, trail systems, major developed areas, and minor developments. He noted in two of his reports written in 1935 how field survey allowed him to create a topographic base map, so that planned developments could then be superimposed at two different scales—one for the monument as a whole (to show circulation systems like trails), while the other needed to be twenty feet to the inch to accurately depict the main developed area around the Chateau.[75] He subsequently commented that the master plan served only as general direction at a site that did not allow for radical changes in its development.[76] Drawings for individual projects still had to be sketched, traced, finalized, checked, and then receive final approval from more than one management layer in the NPS before they could be implemented. Unforeseen circumstances often brought about changes or adjustments in the field by the CCC who functioned as day labor (direct hires) rather than contractors who bid according to advertised plans and specifications. Instead of necessarily reflecting the centralized control of development by the NPS, master plans justified the outlays made for CCC projects, as did the lengthy illustrated reports written by landscape architects, engineers, and camp foremen.

Even if the master plans were descended from how English gentry once designed their pleasure grounds, NPS control over Oregon Caves remained far from absolute. The concessionaire provided the cave tours and already occupied (on a lease basis) virtually all of the area that could be developed. To the extent that Oregon Caves somehow exemplified central planning done by the

NPS, it did so with the company firmly ensconced in central position—both physically and in regard to how the monument's clientele experienced the site. Even the two most ubiquitous characteristics of design there (cedar bark siding and dry laid retaining walls) had emerged almost spontaneously from the concessionaire, becoming so pervasive by the time NPS officials arrived in 1934 that most of what Lange and his landscape foremen did was improve the existing landscape with CCC labor rather than use another palette to create anew.[77]

Other vehicles shaping visitor experience

While the NPS tended to focus on the details of physical development at Oregon Caves during this period, most newspaper publicity and travel writing centered on how the resort facilitated visitor experience. Much of it was connected with a cave tour that often emphasized the weird or whimsical (something evident in the names of many rooms and formations), but visitors who stayed at the Chateau or in one of the cabins were also treated to a nightly program of music and entertainment. The ability to play an instrument or sing influenced how Sabin chose new hires (who were generally college students) since the company advertised this program on its promotional literature.[78] At its zenith, each program opened with a trombone and trumpet duet (the "Miserere" from "Il Trovetore"), where the players stationed themselves on opposite sides of the canyon above Cave Creek, to be followed by vocal and instrumental music that emanated from the steps below the Chalet.[79]

The musical program appealed to many of the guests who stayed in the Chateau or one of the cottages, though relatively few visitors opted for a second or third night at Oregon Caves. Guests ate their breakfast and lunch in the coffeeshop, with the evening meal served in the hotel dining room. Music from radio stations in Portland and San Francisco often played as they ate, with soft melodies occasionally heard in the evenings from the Chateau's roof speakers. Guests and employees alike enjoyed a special treat on Sunday night, when pipe organ music came over the roof speakers after the evening program. One employee remembered that hearing the sounds of Paul Carson building his "Bridge to Dreamland," inspired some couples to listen at a secluded spot on one of the nearby trails.[80]

IMPROVING A LITTLE LANDSCAPE GARDEN   115

FIGURE 56. Nightly musical entertainment for guests of the Oregon Caves Resort, about 1937. (Photo by Sawyers, OCNM Museum and Archives Collections.)

A campfire program given by the resident NPS employee constituted more regular and edifying fare during those summer evenings. Ranger-naturalists who gave the talks, however, objected to the noise from the waterfall nearest the cave, so Lange proposed to fix this distraction by diverting it for a few minutes. His landscape foreman, Ed Meola, and another man completed the project in 1939, one listed among the CCC accounts as "Silencing Waterfall." The pair blasted a ditch in order to place a corrugated metal culvert that diverted Cave Creek below the Chateau. It worked to quiet the noise of falling water, but also provided a means to avoid silting both pools when Rowley and his crew "washed down" cave formations along the tour route each spring.[81]

Promoters saw such contrivances as fitting and even "natural," because they somehow suited the setting. Even one of the ranger-naturalists at Crater Lake who taught geology at the University of Oregon echoed this point in his draft of a brochure to be issued by the NPS:

> "After his not too strenuous trip through the Caves, one can lodge for the night in one of the most attractive Chateaus in the entire Northwest and after dinner listen to a campfire program of music of unusual excellence in the shadows of a gigantic fir forest. When one drops off to sleep in his comfortable Chateau bed, he may retrace his steps through a dream forest made up of shadowy forms in part belonging to the upper groves and those of the mysterious nether regions of the Caves.[82]

The practice of issuing brochures (or "circulars" as they were often called) to promote Oregon Caves harkened back to the Forest Service that planned to print a brochure in 1921, but postponed the job until completion of the highway in June of the following year.[83] Within five years this circular grew to sixteen pages, which the Forest Service illustrated with photographs. As a device intended to shape visitor expectations of the site, this advertising medium supplied justification for efforts by the Forest Service and its concessionaire to further enhance the landscape garden that had been created at Oregon Caves. By presenting the monument as both restful and Edenic, the circular also worked to precondition how people were to view the monument upon their arrival.[84]

It could be that the concessionaire promoted the monument more effectively than the Forest Service did in having 26,000 brochures printed in 1925.[85] Information booths, service clubs, auto camps, and hotels served as distribution channels for reaching potential visitors who resided on the west coast, particularly those in California. That state routinely furnished more visitors to the monument each year than did Oregon, and with more than ten times greater population, also represented a much larger potential market.[86] The company had these facts in mind when advertising Oregon Caves in magazines, but they also tried to link the monument with the drawing power of redwood groves in California then being assembled into a chain of state parks along the coast highway leading to San Francisco. The concessionaire pitched Oregon Caves to be a northern portal to the redwoods, even though the monument was situated more than 50 miles from any such grove that a motorist might see. Its stockholders and the boosters in Grants Pass thus maintained an active role in the Redwood Empire Association, a tourism group whose membership promoted the preservation of roadside scenic attractions as a way of bringing more business to the region.[87]

Oregon Caves enjoyed a less central place in NPS promotional efforts, even though the agency had access to a national clientele and had been producing leaflets, brochures, and small booklets on the areas it administered from earliest days of its existence.[88] In contrast to the muddled place that its national monuments once occupied in the Forest Service's worldview, the NPS saw them in a fairly stratified way—as "second class sites" in relation to the national parks. In the NPS mindset of the 1930s national parks were the premier destinations for visitors within the larger system

IMPROVING A LITTLE LANDSCAPE GARDEN 117

FIGURE 57. A cave woman informs a prospect of what awaits him at the Oregon Caves Chateau while they are in the San Francisco ferry terminal, 1939. (Photo courtesy of the Josephine County Historical Society.)

of units it administered, whereas national monuments represented an enticing stopover for a few hours or more, yet one best located between jewels in the crown. As of 1934, NPS-administered Oregon Caves stood midway between Crater Lake and a future national park in the redwoods (the newly dedicated Humboldt State Redwoods Park being the top candidate), in the same way that Lava Beds was situated between Crater Lake and Lassen Volcanic, or Craters of the Moon lay between Mount Rainier and Yellowstone.[89] Even if the NPS stationed one or more of its seasonal ranger naturalists at Oregon Caves each summer (in comparison to Forest Service practice of not staffing the monument after 1921), the agency presence belied the fact that national monuments represented collateral duty for park superintendents who exercised their management authority and promotional skills from a distance. Like Lava Beds, Oregon Caves represented a satellite area of responsibility to the superintendent at Crater Lake.[90]

IMPROVING A LITTLE LANDSCAPE GARDEN

FIGURE 58. Guests at the Chateau could read about attractions located elsewhere in the Redwood Empire at the hotel's front desk. (Oregon Caves Company photo, OCNM Museum and Archives Collections.)

Although the monument might be relegated to secondary status in the hierarchy of park units administered by the NPS during the 1930s, expansion in agency responsibility during that decade indirectly enhanced the position of Oregon Caves as a tourist attraction within the region. Already a gateway to the redwoods, as well as Crater Lake and peaks located further north, visitors could also come to the monument as part of a tour centered on Oregon's renowned coastline. The NPS exercised control over the location of CCC camps in state parks, in addition to much of the work done in them, since federal funding underwrote virtually all of these projects during the Depression. Sparked by the willingness of the state to buy land for parks along the Roosevelt Highway (U.S. 101), the NPS served as the conduit for developing some of them.[91] Being somewhat analogous to state parks in the redwood region of California, this chain of spectacular parks along the coastal highway accounted for seventy percent of all state park use in Oregon during the 1930s. Not only did Oregonians use these parks, but the coast also drew visitors from California and other states. They injected a badly needed sum of $19 million into Oregon's economy in 1934, a statistic that prompted the legislature to create a travel information office within Oregon's highway department (which also managed state parks), less than two years later.[92]

As one of the best-positioned and brightest stars in Oregon's galaxy of scenic attractions, it made sense for the new travel infor-

IMPROVING A LITTLE LANDSCAPE GARDEN 119

FIGURE 59. Models pause to gaze at the River Styx, 1937. (Oregon State Highway Commission photo by Ralph Gifford, courtesy of Oregon State University Archives.)

mation office to help publicize the monument to out-of-state visitors. The office soon hired a professional photographer named Ralph Gifford to supplement news releases and travel articles with a wide range of scenic images free of impediments such as copyright. Gifford traveled around the state to secure hundreds of photos, including some at Oregon Caves. He followed in the footsteps of his father Benjamin and other pioneers of commercial scenic photography who previously adopted all the conventions of

FIGURE 60. Kiser's studio near the cave entrance, about 1927. (U.S. Forest Service photo, Siskiyou National Forest.)

another medium, landscape painting, in promoting western wonders with a camera beginning in the 1870s.[93]

Starting with Will Steel and his companions in 1888, several promoters made attempts to capitalize on the potential market for images of the cave and its setting prior to the highway's completion in 1922, but these photographs hardly put Oregon Caves anywhere near the center of a burgeoning travel industry centered on driving to experience scenic attractions. Only when road infrastructure responded to rapidly escalating automobile ownership could commercial photographers assist with fueling visitation that could, in turn, make developing a resort like Oregon Caves financially viable. Two competitors, Fred Kiser and Frank Patterson, led the way in producing large numbers of picture postcards of

Oregon Caves and its surroundings beginning in 1922, though both ended up pursuing greener pastures in California with the Great Depression's onset. Both men also sold framed scenic photographs, with most individually hand colored to imitate landscape paintings. Kiser restricted his subjects to mountain scenes of the Pacific Northwest for the most part, though he also ventured to the redwoods and the Oregon coast. Based in Portland since 1904, Kiser responded to an expanding market for scenic views during the 1920s by opening branch studios at Crater Lake, Multnomah Falls, and Oregon Caves.[94] Patterson, by contrast, operated exclusively from his headquarters in Medford, where he initially specialized in views of Crater Lake and Oregon Caves. By 1926 the Patterson Studio produced more postcards than any other such operation in the west. His stock included photos of city streets, auto camps, and scenic subjects on the Pacific Highway (U.S. 99) from Eugene to Redding, and along the Redwood Highway (U.S. 199) from Grants Pass to Ukiah.[95] In 1928 Patterson claimed that the Oregon Caves Resort could be counted as his largest dealer in postcards, though within a few years all that remained of his work were the larger hand-colored views that adorned the lobby level of the Chateau and even these were eventually outnumbered by Kiser's work displayed at the same location.[96]

The demise of Kiser and Patterson as scenic photographers by no means spelled the end of picture postcards as souvenirs, or as a device that could both shape expectations among visitors who wanted to validate their experience for friends and family. Sawyers, a Portland-based company, acquired Kiser's archive on its way to becoming one of the largest postcard manufacturers in the United States.[97] While hand colored framed enlargements of scenic views declined in popularity during the advent of color film, Sawyers brought back stereo photography in a new form by patenting View-Master in 1939. Its inventor, William Gruber, thought of placing movie film on a reel for use in a compact viewer so that full color stereo transparencies could be mass-produced. He could do little more than experiment with the stereo process until meeting Harold Graves, then president of Sawyers, in 1938. This meeting took place at Oregon Caves, after Gruber's wife supposedly rubbed a "wishing stone" on the tour, and then told her husband that she wanted something good to come of his idea.[98] He and his stereo "rig" (two cameras mounted on a tripod) came out

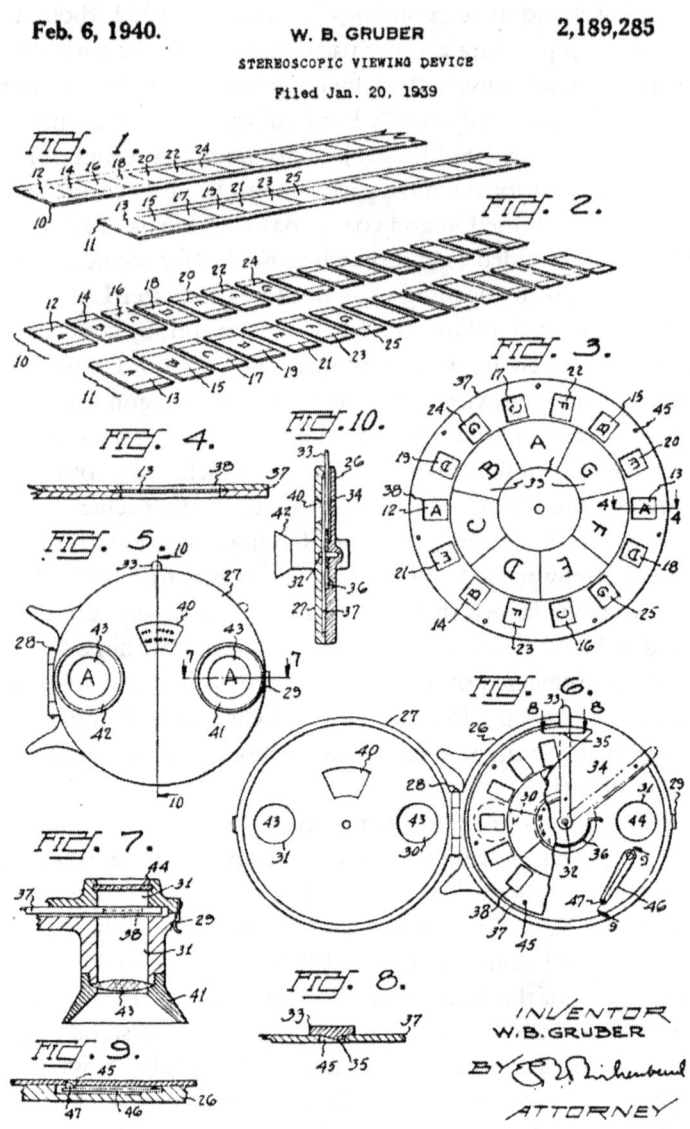

FIGURE 61. Drawing to accompany the patent application for View Master.

of the cave and directly in front of Graves, who was attempting to photograph some deer. They discussed what Gruber had in mind that night in the Chateau and subsequently made views of Oregon Caves into one of the first reels when View-Master went into production late in the following year.[99]

View-Master played an admittedly small role in promoting the monument, especially in the years prior to American entry in World War II, but the sales potential of Oregon Caves was such that it hardly lacked for promotional devices during this period. One writer published his impressions of the two-hour cave tour led by Rowley as a book in 1939, calling it "Enchanted Corridors" and included several photographs of formations from the Artcraft Studio of Grants Pass. Despite the omission of surface features like the forest trails, author Wayland Dunham reinforced the perception of the monument as landscape garden with a playful narrative of an underground journey, one with plenty in the way of allegory and mythological allusions.[100]

"Enchanted Corridors" did not possess widespread appeal judging by the small number of copies printed, but the monument featured prominently in another book devoted to Oregon's scenic attractions published in 1941. Warren D. Smith devoted all of three pages to how the monument could be experienced, leading with a bewitching cave tour. Smith then brought the reader from the cave's discovery by Davidson in 1874 through a short, but seemingly effortless progression to NPS administration that began six decades later. To justify his assessment that the concessionaire ran the top resort in Oregon, Smith cited a combination of reasons. Not only had movement through the cave been augmented by enlarged passages and dependable lights, but visitors could also enjoy quiet evenings filled with music and stories near the entrance, where all the landscaping appeared "in harmony with the wild background of this rugged country." Smith also made a point of mentioning two individuals; Rowley, who played the roles of guide and sage, and Sabin, the host who provided excellent evening entertainment as well as fine creature comforts at moderate cost.[101]

In all his praise for the development and operation at Oregon Caves, Smith failed to mention what had to be the most unique way of promoting this or any other unit in the national park system. The prospect of opening a road to the monument in 1922 led to forming the Oregon Cavemen as a booster group in Grants Pass. They bore some resemblance to organizations founded to promote other towns, such as the Craterians in Medford or the Pirates of Coos Bay, but the Cavemen quickly became known for wearing animal skins and publicity stunts that included kidnapping celebrities and inducting four U.S. presidents as members.[102] Led by a figure called "Chief Bighorn" and his associate

FIGURE 62. Members of the Oregon Cavemen posed along the tour route, late 1930s. (Sawyers photo, private collection.)

"Wingfeather," they dedicated the Caveman Bridge over the Rogue River as the northern terminus for the Redwood Highway in 1931, lent their name to Grants Pass High School, and made a point of posing for photographs at the monument each year when the Chateau opened for business. Although such promotion can be considered unusual even in show caves, it fit well with a script understood by most Americans and people of European descent that allowed for the association of both Indians and cavemen to a primitive Edenic garden. With direct connections to company stockholders and with the Grants Pass chamber of commerce, the Cavemen also functioned as an arm of the Redwood Empire Association in actively maintaining their city's link with the monument in popular imagination.[103]

Oregon Caves attracted visitors in such numbers in 1941 that the superintendent at Crater Lake told the company's attorney about carrying capacity in the cave being reached on some summer days. Not only did 1,600 visitors or more on tours each day result in unsatisfactory service, it caused a parking shortage at a national monument which could offer only a limited number of areas flat enough to accommodate vehicles. After proposing a ceiling on the number of visitors allowed through the cave each day, the superintendent also stated that Oregon Caves had almost been fully developed.[104] He noted that some other park areas faced a similar situation and this could make for some difficult choices,

FIGURE 63. Retaining walls and pools built by the CCC below the cave entrance, about 1938. (Photo by Francis G. Lange, OCNM Museum and Archives Collections.)

especially where steep topography restricted the opportunity to create more parking or build additional structures to support a larger operation. The superintendent avoided the fact that the landscape garden created at Oregon Caves consisted of more than physical features; that it also reinforced the prevailing patterns driving visitor use, such that once established, fundamental changes might lie beyond the grasp of even the most determined administrator.[105]

CHAPTER 5

Decline from a Rustic Ideal, 1944-1995

One of the most persistent, oldest, and most basic myths in all of western thought is that of a golden age. It is where human endeavors attained such heights that they were considered worthy of emulation, or at least remembrance, in a present blemished by imperfection.[1] The mountainous and picturesque district of Arcadia furnished the mythic setting in classical Greece for such an age, as an abode of a simple, pastoral people dwelling in rural happiness. Landscape gardens of the eighteenth and nineteenth centuries sought to emulate both the idyllic and heroic, though they were just as much an expression of power over nature and people. The importance of these gardens to public parks of the twentieth century, especially sites like Oregon Caves National Monument, is as a form where evolving perceptions of nature manifested themselves in a number of persistent design principles. Although the historical development of landscape gardens is a complex subject and one open to multiple interpretations, these places could be both didactic and scenic, yet they also made an overt connection between nature and personal liberty in the minds of those who created them. The best creations evoked what some called the "genius of the place," by bringing forth the emblematic or "iconic" qualities associated with each site. By responding to what nature dictated, landscapes derived from an Arcadian vision might achieve unity and harmony with circulation systems, structures, and other features built from native materials at the appropriate scale.

If the ideal of subordinating facilities by integrating them into the larger scene in American parks enjoyed a golden age, especially where landscapes were thought to allow for contact with the sublime, it had to have been during the 1930s. The so-called "rustic architecture" reigned supreme in national parks, state parks, and on many national forests of the period because it best enhanced the *genius loci* while labor and materials remained exceptionally inexpensive. Both the Forest Service and Park Service responded to an infusion of funding for infrastructure by expanding upon attempts made in the 1920s to use rustic architecture in areas they allocated for intensive recreational use. The onset of American involvement in World War II resulted in dramatically reduced budgets for recreational developments planned by both agencies, as well as the disappearance of Depression-era work relief programs like the CCC. Infrastructure needs at places like Oregon Caves had to thus stay on hold during most of the 1940s, while the few remaining landscape architects and engineers in the NPS could do little more than revise their plans and funding proposals for projects that too often remained on the shelf.

The NPS faced higher construction costs in the postwar world, something which reinforced a national trend toward "modern" design emphasizing function over form. In contrast to rustic architecture, it largely dispensed with elements or details aimed at unifying developments under one "theme" or design treatment aimed at expressing a park's individuality. Some advocates of rustic architecture had, by 1952, decried its modernistic rival as mediocre and symptomatic of decline from an ideal befitting the national parks and monuments.[2] Nevertheless, more standardized and modernistic designs dominated structures and facilities in the aftermath of World War II, especially once appropriations aimed at building up park infrastructure began to increase significantly in 1954. With the advent of a ten year program dubbed "Mission 66" (so named because of the development needed to support rising visitation in the parks, with the fiftieth anniversary of the NPS in 1966 serving as the program's sunset), some in the agency saw another golden age. Many of the same landscape architects who had directed the implementation of CCC projects oversaw Mission 66, but far more of the design and construction was contracted than had been the case two decades earlier. Once materials and labor costs had been driven upward by a booming postwar economy, rustic architecture's days as the dominant paradigm in the NPS were numbered because of it being both expensive and difficult to build.[3]

Even as the increased complexity of design and construction in the parks made both functions virtually the sole province of contractors by the 1970s, rustic architecture and its varied expressions in the parks four decades earlier acquired a new cachet. Three NPS staff members stationed in San Francisco surveyed structures located in the western parks as part of meeting the agency's responsibilities under the National Historic Preservation Act of 1966. They produced a discussion paper that made rustic architecture significant to the history of national parks in the twentieth century, and thus furnished a precursor to more expansive studies of NPS landscape design during the interwar period.[4] Not only did the number of listings on the National Register of Historic Places for these parks rise dramatically over the ensuing decade, but the authors also helped to cast rustic architecture as an antithesis to virtually all park facilities built after 1942. In divorcing postwar development from a continuum of park design that stretched over several centuries, this paper and the studies that followed it ignored what the architects of Mission 66 carried with them from the 1930s. None of them addressed the fact that master plans (which, according to these studies, furnished the epitome for all park development) had become far more detailed by the 1950s than at any time previously.[5]

Used initially to justify the appropriations needed to carry out new projects, as well as repairs to timeworn park facilities, master plans could also help the NPS deflect criticisms from those who accused the agency of overdeveloping the parks during Mission 66.[6] The full size rolls of drawings interleaved with lists of completed projects from the CCC era eventually gave way to master plans that included problem statements, staffing projections, and the desired conditions (which usually called for additional facilities) needed to serve an ever-increasing number of visitors. Master plans produced by the NPS during the postwar years for many (if not most) of the park units it administered thus called for new facilities to support added staff and expanding operations, often in conjunction with building a visitor center. At Oregon Caves, however, the NPS had to acknowledge that the monument contained virtually no suitable sites to expand park operations if the agency

FIGURE 64. Lake Creek residence, 1960. (NPS photo by James Bainbridge, OCNM Museum and Archives Collections.)

did nothing to fundamentally alter its relationship with the concessionaire. As matters stood, the company signed a succession of three 15 year contracts starting in 1940 which allowed it to conduct cave tours as well as operate the facilities that Lium had designed and built from 1926 to 1942. The monument thus gave the appearance of standing still while the postwar world changed around it; projects funded through Mission 66 at Oregon Caves understandably consisted of small undertakings that seemed largely invisible to the bulk of visitors.

Postwar park development

Seemingly content with its largely off-stage oversight role, the NPS accepted the reality that the only places that could be developed for expanding its operations at Oregon Caves lay beyond the monument's boundaries. Officials chose a site located near the highway next to Lake Creek, about 1.5 miles from the entrance sign for a future headquarters in October 1942.[7] By converting what had been used as a woodlot and garbage dump, the Crater Lake superintendent and the NPS regional director reasoned that a residence area could be erected in addition to a utility building for maintenance purposes. Not even a whiff of funding materialized for this purpose until the NPS negotiated for a special use permit from the Forest Service in June 1958, and even then a special request needed to be made to the director in Washington, D.C. It

FIGURE 65. Cover of park brochure in 1952. Oregon Caves can claim the distinction of being the first unit in the National Park System to display the new arrowhead logo.

had been triggered by the need to house a newly-funded permanent position at Oregon Caves, where a management assistant was now to be stationed all year instead of having a seasonal ranger there only during the summer.[8]

The existing ranger residence did not allow for effective winter access, so the management assistant had lived in a trailer at the main parking lot since the fall of 1956. He stayed there until early 1960, when a newly constructed house on the Lake Creek tract was ready to occupy. As a wood frame residence virtually identical to hundreds of others built in national parks during the Mission 66, it had three bedrooms and could be reached by a service road from the Oregon Caves Highway. Additional development at the site, by contrast, included some grading and utility connections that allowed several trailers to be placed below the house for seasonal employees as well as a Quonset hut for storage.

While none of the Lake Creek development could be considered even remotely rustic in appearance, it remained out of view to visitors.[9] What they might have seen at the monument for two decades after the CCC enrollees departed in 1941 could be categorized as either repair (and sometimes alteration) of existing facilities when absolutely necessary, or improvements justified by annual visitation that climbed from 61,680 in 1941 to 102,940 in 1961 and showed every indication of going still higher. The increase mirrored national trends that stemmed from a booming postwar economy, which provided more people with a middle-class income and expectations of a paid summer vacation. Many people took their families along while visiting national parks and monuments by car during the summer months; the west coast states meanwhile experienced explosive population growth, especially in already established urban areas. The concessionaire continued to advertise the charms of Oregon Caves to growing markets in California in concert with the state highway department's national campaigns to sell Oregon as a destination for vacationers.

Despite all the work aimed at promoting travel to the monument and Oregon in general, limited appropriations for the NPS during the 1940s and early 50s allowed for only a few construction and maintenance projects at Oregon Caves. The largest undertaking involved repairing the main parking lot after the slide of 1942 (something which took a decade to complete due to the complications posed by subsurface drainage problems which reemerged in late 1955), an overhaul of the cave's lighting system in 1946, and installing a new water system in 1950.[10] Having a larger reservoir allowed the concessionaire to comply with fire safety requirements at the Chateau, where automatic sprinklers were now placed throughout most of the building. Concern for visitor safety also supplied the justification for the NPS to remove the rotted wood blocks in the hotel courtyard and pave the area with

FIGURE 66. Visitors waiting for their tour at the cave entrance, 1957. Note that most wear coveralls. (Photo by Warren Fairbanks, National Park Service Historic Photograph Collection.)

asphalt in 1952, the same year that a crew reintroduced pipe rail at Oregon Caves—for use on the stone steps leading from the campfire circle to the Chalet.[11]

With their contract set to expire at the end of 1955, the concessionaire responded to postwar visitation shifting even more to the side of day use by increasing the coffee shop's seating capacity from 23 to 45. The company also reacted to a change in Oregon's liquor laws in 1954 by converting a portion of the Chateau's dining room into a cocktail lounge.[12] A rebuilt Chalet had, meanwhile, allowed them to put most supporting functions associated with the centerpiece of any visit to Oregon Caves—a tour—in that structure. They sold tickets from a registration booth located there and rented coveralls in an adjoining room until funding from Mission 66 allowed the NPS to change the wet and sometimes muddy conditions along the tour route by paving the trail with asphalt over the winter of 1957-58. Visitors waiting for cave tours also tended to cluster around the Chalet, where a soda fountain and gift shop were located across the breezeway from the registration booth, thus separating these uses from the meals and visitor accommodation provided in the Chateau.

This kind of functional separation seemed to meet with visitor approval and led to the impression among members of groups like

DECLINE FROM A RUSTIC IDEAL 133

FIGURE 67. Guide at the Beehive Room, 1963. (OCNM Museum and Archives Collections.)

the National Parks Association and the National Speleological Society that the monument was "ideal" for being under the care of a concessionaire.[13] A shortage of space near the cave entrance relegated the NPS presence at the monument to a peripheral one, but the only apparent change which occurred during Mission 66 consisted of a prefabricated office brought to the main parking lot from Crater Lake, then placed across from the "reception center" in 1964. No one seemed to notice that the most conspicuous part of NPS development which in many ways characterized Mission 66—a visitor center—had not even been requested (much less programmed) for the monument.

The company's grip on central position at Oregon Caves remained firm, though its dominance over what visitors experienced waned ever so slightly after Rowley's retirement in 1954. Guides still gave what amounted to a Rowley tour after that time, though its focus on mystery and mirth was influenced somewhat by a manual compiled by NPS staff at Crater Lake containing scientific information about cave formation.[14] With the former head guide often on site each summer until his death in 1964, all the NPS seemed to do was gently encourage the company to pursue a more thematic approach to tours, though most of the guides persisted with a scripted progression through the cave where many of the highlighted formations seemed to evoke images grounded in caricature.[15] The single most important NPS contribution to visitor understanding of the cave during this period consisted of a booklet aimed at providing a more scientific view of the cave. Written over one winter by NPS management assistant Roger Contor, it was then published in 1963 by the nonprofit cooperating association serving Oregon Caves and Crater Lake.[15]

Despite having limited power or will to alter the content of tours, the NPS nevertheless committed some funding to the cave beginning in 1956, when the lighting system was again overhauled. Lights became more reliable, but constant illumination allowed "fern gardens" and algae to become established near many of the lamps. Paving the tour route a year or so later came with some long-term impacts, in that the asphalt could leach and change water chemistry, but one realigned section of trail went through a rimstone dam called the "Atlantic Ocean" and destroyed much of a feature that took thousands of years to form. Paving continued outside in May and June of 1958 to include the full length of a widened exit trail. Over the next three years related undertakings included installation of new lights along the trail, erection of pipe railing along its margin in spots where a safety barrier seemed to be needed and construction of stone pylons to support wooden benches outside the exit tunnel.[17] Concurrent with the completed exit trail project was the installation of three gates. These came in response to problems caused by uncontrolled access to the cave by company employees and reports of vandalism that the NPS began to note in 1955, though this step was taken almost 40 years after the supervisor of the Siskiyou National Forest first recommended such devices.[18]

Changes in the forest

The gates did not correct problems caused by changes in airflow through the cave that became more apparent with the exit tunnel's completion more than a quarter century earlier. In the early 1960s, however, the NPS paid more attention to a dwarf mistletoe

DECLINE FROM A RUSTIC IDEAL 135

FIGURE 68. Patterson photo of timber stands near the highway to Oregon Caves. (OCNM Museum and Archives Collections.)

infestation in the surrounding forest. It reached such proportions by 1962 that the NPS contracted for the removal of some trees behind the Chalet, thereby altering what had once been an unbroken canopy dominated by large Douglas-fir.[19] That year the Forest Service accepted bids for three timber sale units located on Cave Creek just below the monument with the reasoning that trees killed by an insect outbreak should be salvaged. Logging of national forest land around Oregon Caves had since commenced on a commercial (rather than salvage) basis, with visual evidence of clear cutting methods becoming increasingly evident to visitors who paused at vista points on the monument's trail system. Timber sales began on Grayback Mountain in 1958 and continued in the vicinity of the monument thereafter, with one on Lake Mountain and another in upper Sucker Creek several years later.[20]

A stepped-up Forest Service timber production program worked to change the landscape around Oregon Caves over the next two decades, as it did on other national forests in the Pacific Northwest. The somewhat abrupt change from "custodial" management by the agency to one dominated by timber production started during the late 1940s, at a time when postwar demand for lumber remained high in the face of a steadily decreasing supply of old-growth trees still standing on private land.[21] Comparatively recent technological advances like chainsaws and tractors that could haul logs from steep ground made the previously inaccessi-

FIGURE 69. Mud and debris in the Chalet breezeway, December 1964. The man at left is NPS landscape architect Paul Fritz. (OCNM Museum and Archives Collections.)

ble "mountains of timber" (as photographer Frank Patterson titled one photo taken near Oregon Caves in the 1920s) commercially viable when subsidized by the Forest Service contracting to build more access roads. Consequently, these stands could now be reached from a network of roads which made truck logging triumphant over previous methods (such as railroads or streams) of delivering timber to mills located in the Illinois Valley or even further afield.[22]

At the national level, building roads in the national forests far outstripped other Forest Service program areas like grazing or recreation for more than two decades beginning in 1955. Agency officials gave the justification that a subsidized network of roads (as opposed to one funded solely from the value of timber that could be accessed from it) allowed for a variety of future uses. The increased number of roads threading the Siskiyou National Forest mirrored this trend, one that accelerated during the 1960s—a time when budget allocations for the program areas of timber and recreation in all of the national forests stood roughly equal. Recreation received its initial boost starting in 1957, one intended to "double camping and picnicking facilities in the national forests within the next five years," partly to avert an incursion by the NPS on lands under Forest Service administration.[23] The Forest Service thus launched "Operation Outdoors" to counter "Mission 66," though its effect on the Siskiyou National Forest and the Illinois Valley Ranger District in particular were not felt until 1964. In the meantime, several timber sales had taken place in the vicinity of Oregon Caves (like the one near Bigelow Lakes) which showed how quickly the forest's road network had grown.

The expanding network opened so much previously inaccessible country for logging that the Forest Service felt that it had to withdraw several sites near the monument from timber production once the Bureau of Reclamation proposed flooding a portion of the Sucker Creek drainage for an irrigation dam in 1962.[24] Flooding of Sucker Creek meant the inundation of Grayback Campground, so the Forest Service withdrew sites on the Illinois Valley Ranger District that it might develop as campgrounds to replace the sites to be lost at Grayback.[25] After making three small withdrawals on the Illinois Valley district in December 1963, the Forest Service added another in June 1965 but ended up developing only one area.[26] Contractors built Cave Creek Campground, a development below milepost 16 on the Oregon Caves Highway, in 1964. The Forest Service floated the idea of enlarging both of the Bigelow Lakes for recreational purposes as late as 1969, but settled for revamping Grayback Campground once support for the irrigation dam had dissipated.[27]

Sucker Creek flooded, though only temporarily, in December 1964 when logs and debris choked the stream near Grayback Campground. Crews salvaged much of the pile containing crisscrossed trees heaped together like a jackstraw, with the flood doing little damage to the campground.[28] This could not be said about several buildings at Oregon Caves, where a plug of debris had traveled down the usually dry "gulch," then poured through the

Chalet's breezeway and into the Chateau. Some 3,500 cubic yards of material (which included seventeen trees) hit the hotel with such force that a portion of the building had slipped from its concrete foundation. Company management feared a total loss at first, but Lium (at the time 81 years old) arrived on the scene to direct repair efforts so that the Chateau could open for the summer of 1965.[29]

Although mud and debris had filled three of the six floors in the hotel, it emerged virtually intact from the flood. The plug had so damaged the dining area that its maple floor had to be covered by carpet, but the most significant postwar change in the Chateau had occurred more than six years earlier. Winter snow loads had weakened the wooden porches, necessitating their removed in 1958. Also missing from an overnight stay by that time was the musical serenade that some guests once enjoyed from the porches. New federal labor standards issued in 1950 dictated that the musicians as concession employees had to be paid for their performances, and in some cases at an overtime rate, so the company discontinued the live entertainment.[30]

More visitors and new constituents

Annual visitation at Oregon Caves swelled to more than 150,000 in 1966 and almost crossed the 200,000 mark six years later, so the company's operation remained profitable. With commercial overnight capacity (at the Chateau and cabins) limited to what it had been before World War II, virtually all the growth in postwar visitation came through greater day use of the monument. With more visitors waiting near the Chalet for their cave tour to commence, the concessionaire responded by expanding the space allocated to their gift shop in 1972. This move came at the expense of an "employee's parlor" shown on Lium's plan for the Chalet, but the company simply relocated this function (a commons room) within an addition to their Guide Dormitory which they built at the same time. Despite all the signs of continued profitability at Oregon Caves during the early and middle 1970s, however, company stockholders voted to sell their shares to the Canteen Company of Oregon just after Canteen made a similar deal at Crater Lake.[31]

With the sale to Canteen due to become finalized by September 1977, the Oregon Cavemen made their final visit to

DECLINE FROM A RUSTIC IDEAL 139

FIGURE 70. Cavemen welcoming the Cave Junction Outlaws to Grants Pass, about 1950. (Photo courtesy of the Josephine County Historical Society.)

"open" the monument in May of that year, an annual event timed to correspond with the company starting to rent rooms in the Chateau each summer. Although they erected a giant statue of a caveman near the main freeway exit in Grants Pass as recently as 1972, the booster group's membership had begun to wane even before the sale to Canteen five years later. The organization became even more of a memory than an active force in promoting Josephine County during the 1980s (the Boatnik festivities on Memorial Day weekend had virtually upstaged them in Grants Pass by that time), though a number of businesses retained the Caveman name—as did its largest high school.[32]

These entities served as vestiges of the historic tie between Oregon Caves and Grants Pass, but the town had grown from about 6,000 in 1922 to more than 15,000 sixty years later. Along the way it diversified an economy initially dependent upon primary production (agriculture, lumber, and mining) as well as the growing sector of tourists drawn to Oregon Caves, a scenic coastline, and the redwoods.[33] As the service economy expanded in Grants Pass over the intervening decades, so did tourism in southwest Oregon. It also dispersed greater numbers of people along the lower Rogue River (which served as the setting for Boatniks) so

FIGURE 71. The monument's main parking area, July 1964. (NPS photo by R.H. Viklund, OCNM Museum and Archives Collections.)

that increasing numbers of rafts and jet boats plied the water while hikers and fishermen could be found on the banks. Funding for recreational development on the national forests that came through Operation Outdoors and the programs that followed it expanded the number of facilities like campgrounds, picnic sites, and trails in the Siskiyou National Forest as well as on other public lands that bordered the Rogue and Illinois rivers, so that Oregon Caves could no longer be considered the only visitor attraction in Josephine County that might appeal to non-residents. The monument still drew the largest day use numbers of any *single* site, even as annual visitation at Oregon Caves fell from 181,000 in 1977 to just 115,000 five years later.

Like other predominately day use park areas in the Pacific Northwest at the time, peak visitation at the monument in July and August far outstripped other times of the year. With demand at its greatest between the hours of 10 a.m. and 4 p.m. each day, parking at Oregon Caves remained at a premium through much of the summer and could sometimes involve a protracted wait. Even if visitors limited their time to just the cave tour (and these were scheduled to start every 15 minutes), waiting times could be as long as three hours for some who arrived at the monument during peak hours in mid-summer.[34] The bottleneck at the main parking lot had become egregious enough by 1978 for the NPS to request funds for land acquisition in Cave Junction, ostensibly to build an

"Oregon Caves Information Center" aimed at advising motorists during busy periods on what might lie twenty miles ahead.[35]

Cave Junction had been home to the concessionaire's kiosk promoting Oregon Caves since the close of World War II. This structure sat at the junction of highways 199 and 46, but lacked parking for trailers and other vehicles that were not recommended to go beyond Grayback Campground. The site authorized for an information center under legislation passed by Congress in 1978 fronted the south side of the Caves Highway, a hundred yards or so from its intersection with the Redwood Highway. A deconsecrated church there served as both the chamber of commerce office and "information center" for the time being while NPS staff at Oregon Caves awaited funds for building a new structure in its place, one that might hold exhibits like those of a NPS visitor center.

By the time construction of a modern, rather than rustic, center finally began in 1990, the focus on Oregon Caves had shifted to the Illinois Valley. Funding for the center came from the Oregon Lottery and was channeled through the Forest Service which oversaw construction of the facility. The Forest Service staffed it according to the terms of a partnership agreement among federal agencies and the town of Cave Junction. The NPS finally obtained a large parking lot in addition to a sales outlet for its nonprofit cooperating association (which formerly had to operate from the monument's "reception center"), but the agency lacked any real presence at the Illinois Valley Visitor Center. Annual visitation at the monument had fallen to less than 100,000 by the early 1990s largely due to an increasing number of competing attractions in southwest Oregon and a substantial hike in the price of tickets for cave tours. Concern over a shortfall of parking at Oregon Caves had thus lessened, as had the emphasis on informing visitors about conditions twenty miles away from Cave Junction. These justifications for building a facility in town had long since been superceded by key signatories to the partnership agreement expressing their desire that the center serve as a vehicle for economic development by promoting tourism throughout the valley.

If the visitor center in Cave Junction represented how the older public-private partnership to develop Oregon Caves had expanded its geographic scope, this took place at a time when many residents of the Illinois Valley were experiencing transition from what had been a timber-based economy for more than four

FIGURE 72. A small lumber mill in the Illinois Valley, 1970s. (OCNM Museum and Archives Collections.)

decades. Cave Junction became the second incorporated town in Josephine County during 1948, but the growth and infrastructure necessary to do this had largely been fueled by logging on nearby private lands which fed the operation of nearly fifty sawmills in the Illinois Valley that year.[36] Consolidation of milling capacity took place during the 1950s due to overproduction and other reasons, so that many "gyppos" (independent logging operations) washed out of the marketplace, to be replaced by larger and more capital-intensive outfits as timber supply began to shrink. Agriculture in the Illinois Valley persisted, but the service economy expanded during the 1960s and 70s to become the county's most important economic sector by the time Cave Junction's population initially exceeded 1,000 residents in 1980.

Tourism remained the most conspicuous part of the service economy, with Oregon Caves at the forefront, but local leaders wanted the visitor center to cast a wider net in promoting the valley's attractions. However, most of the more recently established publicly owned stopping points within the Redwood Highway corridor (such as the county park on Lake Selmac, Illinois River State Park, or the Rough and Ready botanical wayside) only seemed to attract local residents or those that lived no further away than the Rogue Valley.[37] An upsurge in the popularity of primitive recreation on roadless lands located away from the major road corridors of Josephine County followed a national trend beginning in the mid 1970s, so that travel to areas like Eight Dollar Mountain, Babyfoot Lake and the rugged Kalmiopsis Wilderness increased among botanists, day hikers, and backpackers.

Activists who promoted the need for more areas of national forest off limits to roads and logging fueled the interest in this type of recreation, so that southwest Oregon (and Josephine County in particular) featured prominently in political battles over extending the protections granted by the Wilderness Act passed by Congress in 1964.[38] They prevailed on two occasions, marked by passage of bills creating or expanding the legally designated wilderness on federal lands of southwest Oregon in 1978 and 1984.[39] Oregon Caves and its immediate surroundings rarely featured in the wilderness debates, mainly because what little roadless land that could be considered for inclusion under the criteria established by the Wilderness Act had been reduced by timber sales and the road network to well under the 5,000 acre minimum, though a few advocates tried to play up the possibility of the monument serving as a launch point for hiking trips to the Red Buttes area on the Oregon/California border.

Although the debate over which federal lands should remain protected from logging or other activities that could hamper the qualities associated with legally designated wilderness areas rarely touched Oregon Caves, it is worth noting that some accessible sections of the cave remained unexplored until the first attempts at mapping its extent took place in 1959. Years of subsequent effort by caving groups, however, reached a milestone in 1975, with publication of the first map showing virtually all passages as well as the location of the cave's major features.[40] The map showed that visitors saw roughly one-third of the cave system along the prescribed tour route, though what they experienced could hardly be called a subterranean wilderness. The NPS nevertheless sought a more "natural" cave during this period, if only by installing fluorescent lighting in 1975 to combat algae growth and the presence of ferns encouraged by incandescent bulbs located along the route. (Fluorescent tubes made the problem even worse by reducing the drying effect of the warmer incandescent bulbs, but also compounded the growth by illuminating more sections of the cave). The colored lights that once produced "Dante's Inferno" within the Ghost Room meanwhile disappeared, though the blue and red lights in Paradise Lost persisted for another few years. Other projects, however, served to reinforce the status quo as crews repaved the tour route in 1973 and then replaced steel stairways in the cave over the following year.

Attempts to recast the monument

The most dramatic change in what visitors experienced on the tour began in 1985, when volunteers initially organized by concession manager Chas Davis removed rubble from the entrance of one chamber. Over the next few years they re-exposed passages obscured by the "improvements" made during the 1920s and generated momentum for "cave restoration" to take hold. Building on this success, NPS staff garnered funding to replace the paving with a new surface that did not create the number of negative impacts associated with asphalt. As part of the decade-long makeover, the three gates were replaced to reduce impacts on resident bats. Crews also installed new airlock doors to lessen ice damage near the start of the tour route and airflow created by the exit tunnel. A black light in the Ghost Room, one intended to convey the phosphorescence of draperies and other formations, became symbolic of how the NPS wanted to emphasize cave processes instead of projecting anthropomorphic constructions like cartoon characters or mythic figures on to natural features. Visitors could also see the bones of a prehistoric black bear *in situ*, an exhibit they passed on their way to the exit tunnel. It and pieces of a fossilized jaguar received considerable publicity as paleontological discoveries that could illuminate how old the cave might be.[41]

Developing new interpretive devices along the tour route came at a time when the NPS attempted to give science education the preeminent role at the monument in the face of resistance from the concessionaire. Imposing thematic tours that highlighted the process of cave formation through explaining geological precepts nevertheless flew in the face of a view that visitors wanted, one company official expressed it, "strange stories and cool formations."[42] This divergence in goals between the NPS and its concessionaire could likely be traced back to the time of Rowley's retirement in 1954, at which point the chief park naturalist at Crater Lake began conducting a training course for guides. This represented a precursor to formal certification of guides by the NPS beginning in the 1970s, something that indicated their tour possessed some factual basis or at least met minimum standards set for giving an interpretive talk.

The company also opposed bestowing national historic land-

DECLINE FROM A RUSTIC IDEAL 145

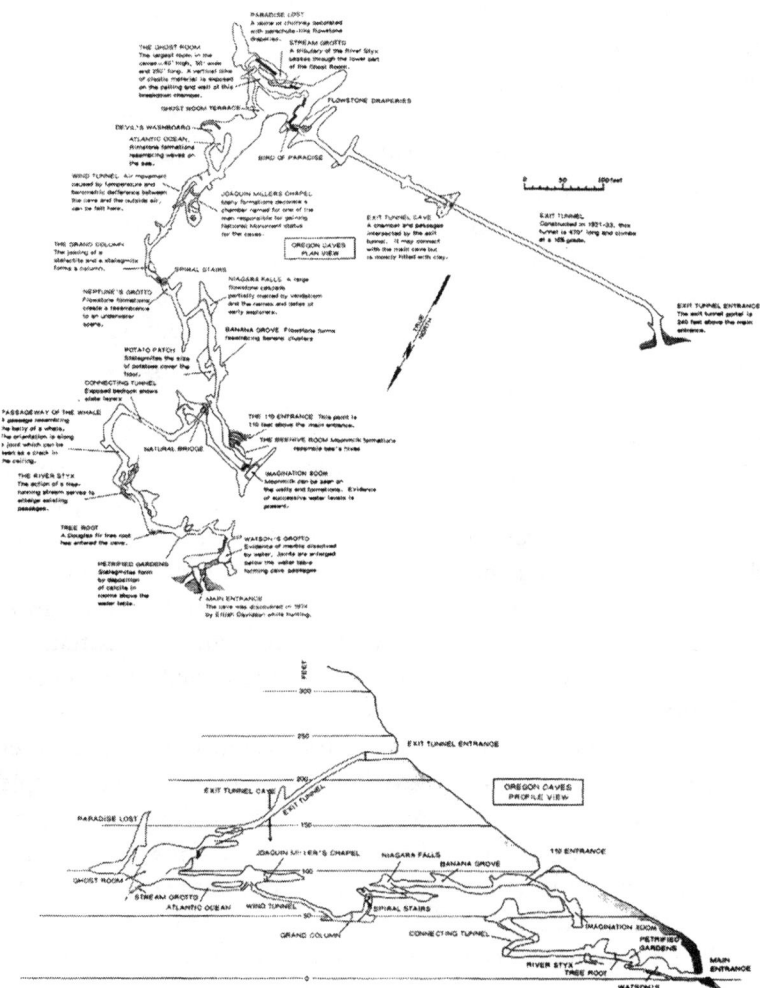

FIGURE 73. Highlighted stops on the tour route by Jim Nieland, 1974.

mark status on the Chateau, fearing that the designation (one that indicates the most significant buildings, sites, and districts in the United States) might hinder its operation. Any changes proposed to the hotel had already became subject to existing review processes conducted by the NPS, ones driven by codes for life safety and sanitation, but also by the standards of historic preservation. Using his authority under the Historic Sites Act of 1935, the Secretary of the Interior named the Chateau a national historic landmark in 1987.[43] The NPS subsequently nominated a district which included the hotel but also two other buildings where the company had a possessory interest, the Chalet and Guide Dormitory, to the National Register of Historic Places in 1992.[44] Proposed changes within the district (which also included the Ranger Residence and the "reception center" in addition to designed landscape elements) had previously been subject to an approval process conducted by the NPS, one based on standards developed from regulations following from passage of the National Historic Preservation Act (NHPA) in 1966.

Congress enacted the NHPA in response to a wave of demolition that plagued urban areas in the United States during the 1950s and 60s, so it seemed rather ironic that seven of Lium's cottages were demolished in March 1988 despite the fact that they met the requirements for listing and even predated the district's other five contributing structures. Contents from a broken pipe in one of the cottages reached the tour route one day in 1985, so the superintendent at Crater Lake pointed to the threat posed by all of the structures located above the cave and initiated the process required for removing them. It went forward with the company's concurrence, (mainly because they no longer rented the cottages to visitors) and demolition came once the prescribed documentation effort had been completed as a mitigation measure.[45] Even with much of its core missing, the district's contributing structures and adjacent features still displayed enough integrity as an example of rustic architecture to be listed on the National Register, ostensibly as a designed cultural landscape that reflected how Lium and others responded to the monument's contours and setting to develop the site as a resort.[46]

By attempting to pitch the monument as featuring something more than tours through a show cave, the NPS promoted cave restoration as an important move toward realizing the dream of pristine nature.[47] To a lesser extent, some staff members in the agency's cultural resources wing tried to call attention to the historic district as exemplifying a rustic architecture which reached its zenith during the 1930s. They made the interwar period at Oregon Caves and other parks into a kind of golden age, one where the surviving features merited preservation as long as they could be tied to architectural or site plans. Designed components like a utility line or trail segment could be included within the district as long as these fit a rectangular template derived from the National Register's emphasis on establishing distinct boundaries for historic properties. Too often, however, the underground or linear feature that contributed to how a district worked from a functional and sometimes experiential standpoint was omitted because inventory methods had not been developed to fit the models (usually based on design fields like architecture) that worked to translate nominations into listings on the National Register.

This historic district remained separate from the cave largely because the tour route supposedly lacked integrity, or the ability to convey its historic significance. The marble steps placed along the tour route by CCC enrollees, as well as earlier inscriptions left by Thomas Condon and other nineteenth century visitors, were thus not included as contributing features. Such segregation amounted to zoning, a technique long used in urban settings to differentiate uses of land, and since embraced by the NPS in order to direct future development and articulate management direction in park planning documents. This eroded the earlier rustic ideal of unifying material and experiential dimensions that reigned during the 1930s, but a tour judged on its entertainment value had now become less palatable in light of subsequent scientific knowledge about caves.

CHAPTER 6

Recommendations

Any historic resource study is essentially a site-specific context statement, with many of these works following a topical approach. This is a fairly standardized way of allowing for each topic (such as exploration, settlement, recreation, and so forth) to be summarized and related to an associated property type so that physical manifestations in a park unit that are tied to human action can be evaluated under the National Register's criteria for significance. It is a process that helps determine what historic resources are worthy of preservation. Section 110 of the National Historic Preservation Act requires the NPS and other federal agencies to inventory and evaluate those cultural resources eligible for the National Register and then nominate those properties.

Organization of historic resource studies are chronological, as it is in most historical narratives, mainly because a kind of shelf or "period of significance" can be constructed for such properties and then related to the broader regional or national context. This approach works well where a number of topics can be related to the site or park area, and the purpose is simply to support current or future nominations to the National Register. Larger meanings associated with a small place can sometimes be obscured or lost completely if a context study adheres strictly to the topical approach. To better serve the goal of interpreting the past, yet also address its material manifestations, this study makes use of bracketed time periods (beginning with 1851 to 1884) in tying

Oregon Caves to regional or national patterns.

The study still treats time horizontally rather than vertically, so that the layering of human use over a century or more is difficult to assess. Layering can run counter to judgments of integrity, since the National Register criteria for this dimension of the nomination process are most easily applied when contributing resources (buildings, structures, sites, districts, objects) reflect one period of significance, not several. This is not only expedient, but since any assessment about whether a candidate historic property can tell a story (or at least communicate its significance through physical appearance) can be defended on the basis of whether it reflects the treatment of time as horizontal; for example, does the ranger residence at Oregon Caves possess enough architectural integrity so that one could learn something about CCC workmanship? It does not, however, work so well in evaluating the cave tour route—a development which contains material manifestations of the CCC, as well as something from all of the bracketed time periods which are used as delineations to separate the previous five chapters in this study. National Register nominations can nevertheless identify important aspects of the themes presented in statements of historic context, even where time has to be seen as vertical.

Eligibility for the National Register of Historic Places

Listing of historic properties on the National Register at the monument began with designation of the Oregon Caves Chateau as a national historic landmark in 1987. Its designation by the Secretary of the Interior resulted from a theme study conducted by NPS historian Laura Soulliere Harrison called "Architecture in the Parks."[1] Listing of the Oregon Caves Historic District in 1992 expanded the National Register boundaries around the hotel and made the Chateau a centerpiece among four other contributing resources: the Chalet, Guide Dormitory, Ranger Residence, and Checking Kiosk/Comfort Station. The boundaries of this district were drawn contiguously around these five buildings, but the character-defining features went beyond the structures to include vehicular and pedestrian circulation, vegetation (plantings used to "naturalize" the area affected by construction activities as well as intensive visitor use), and small scale features such as retaining walls, steps, pools, and outdoor lighting standards. The historic district is thus a rather oddly shaped polygon.[2]

FIGURE 74. CCC enrollees doing trail work at Oregon Caves in 1935. (Photo by George F. Whitworth, OCNM Museum and Archives Collections.)

Most of the monument's trail system is potentially eligible for the National Register under criterion A (for its association with events that made significant contributions to the broad patterns of American history); and criterion C (for distinctive characteristics of a type, period or method of design). These criteria are developed more fully in regard to rustic architecture throughout the national parks by Linda McClelland in her multiple property documentation forms that were revised into a book titled *Building the National Parks: Historic Landscape Design and Construction*. In the case of Oregon Caves, the broader topics of conservation, public recreation, and landscape architecture in American history converge as a theme—naturalistic or "rustic" design practiced by the NPS. Using McClelland's work as a guide, the landscape characteristics of Oregon Caves National Monument can be organized into a general property type (National Parks, Parkways, and Monuments) and landscape sub-types such as trail systems built by the CCC from 1934 to 1941.[3]

As a pedestrian circulation system, it should have been included with the Oregon Caves Historic District nomination in 1991, though methods of documenting and evaluating such trails were arguably in their infancy at that time. With very few exceptions, the monument's trail system possesses integrity of location, design, setting, materials, workmanship, feeling, and association that still mirror the period (1935-1941) of its construction. It is thus recommended that the nomination for the Oregon Caves Historic

District be amended through a boundary increase to include most of the trail system.[4]

Properties such as the trail system must be both historically significant and possess integrity to qualify for listing on the National Register. The trails reflect design standards produced through centralized planning in the NPS instead of *ad hoc* decisions made purely at the local level, as was the case when Burch and Harkness brought the first trails at Oregon Caves into being. The Forest Service then expanded pedestrian circulation over what the private entrepreneurs started by way of access routes from Williams and the Illinois Valley, with a trail to Lake Mountain. Some of the trails on the Siskiyou National Forest have been realigned and rebuilt over time, just as those at Oregon Caves have—but the monument's trails are more directly an inheritance from the CCC, one aimed at creating a circulation system for recreational use instead of access for fire control and a variety of other purposes.[5]

The National Register also requires that historic properties eligible for listing retain a significant degree of integrity, though a property can nevertheless sustain some alteration and remain eligible as long as it retains historic character. There are trails showing changes that took place after World War II, such as the small reroutes that take hikers away from two stream crossings on the No Name loop. These adjustments do not greatly affect this trail's integrity, given how it retains a number of character-defining features (or material qualities) that are listed below:

1. *Alignment* (as built by the CCC);
2. *Width* (generally four feet, though not in all cases);
3. *Tread surface* (unpaved);
4. *Cross drainage* (mostly culverts, but also the occasional water bar);
5. *Varied gradients* (according to NPS standards issued in 1934);
6. *Banksloping* (treatments to round slopes, or use of methods like raking the trail margins back using standard ratios);
7. *Dry laid stone retaining walls* (where native rocks are stacked to support tread);
8. *Stone steps* (either carved or placed);
9. *Dry laid stone benches* (cut into hillsides and set without mortar);
10. *Overlooks, or planned views and vistas.*

FIGURE 75. Dry laid stone bench, 1935. (OCNM Museum and Archives Collections.)

The following trails thus appear to be potentially eligible for listing: a) No Name Loop; b) Cliff Nature; c) Lake Mountain (portion within the monument); d) Big Tree loop (including the spur for horses, known currently as the "Old Growth" Trail); and e) "Oregon Caves" or Williams (portion within the monument).[6] All of these trails were built (or rebuilt) to NPS standards by the CCC in accordance with location studies or drawings by engineers and landscape architects who were paid with funds provided through Emergency Conservation Work (ECW), the governing authority over the CCC.[7]

Aside from its location and setting, the Cave Exit Trail's integrity has been so badly compromised that it cannot be considered a contributing resource, or even eligible for listing on the National Register. Wooden guardrail (which recently replaced steel pipe installed during the 1950s) and asphalt paving over a widened tread surface are the major changes on this trail, one that has fewer than half of the character-defining features listed above. Its contribution to the broader CCC-built pedestrian circulation system is thus minimal. Another problem is that the exit trail constitutes a part of a loop (tour route) through the cave which starts at the main entrance across from the Chateau. Along the tour route in the cave, CCC work is largely evident only where marble steps are encountered along some parts of the route, and at the connecting tunnel.

Efforts to evaluate roads on the monument and the Caves Highway in relation to it are complicated by persistent questions about what constitutes sufficient integrity. As a "system," state highway 46 begins at the junction with U.S. 199 in Cave Junction and terminates in less than twenty miles near the cave entrance. Although a short section (measuring about 20 yards) of the original eight foot-wide "trail" built in 1922 is still intact below the Chalet (and can thus be found within the existing historic district), the other part of this linear feature leading from the main parking lot was widened when NPS landscape architect Francis Lange and the CCC added the walkway which has since vanished. The main parking lot has been widened twice, with the loss of some tree canopy and features designed by Lange having come when the NPS repaired damage stemming from the slide in 1942.

Other roads at Oregon Caves include the service route pioneered by the concessionaire in 1929 and later widened by the CCC that goes past the Chateau toward employee parking and terminates at the incinerator site. Only part of it is paved, with the unsealed portion being the most extensive, and there is damage from cross drainage failures in several places. Aside from a retaining wall supporting the employee lot, a fairly uniform gradient over its length, and two rustic lighting standards, the service road lacks integrity where a coherent design and identifiable character-defining features that go with it are clearly evident. The only other road at Oregon Caves is a segment built in 1982 to connect the Caves Highway with Forest Road 960 (and thus a network of roads on the Siskiyou National Forest) in case a forest fire or similar emergency dictates the need for secondary egress from the monument. It is not eligible for listing on the National Register even if character-defining features were present, due to not meeting the minimum age of 50 years needed for evaluating a potential historic property.

Off the monument, changes to the Caves Highway over most of its length have been minimal since the day labor project to widen it was completed in 1931. This has prompted the Oregon Department of Transportation (ODOT; formerly the Oregon State Highway Department until 1979) to have listed it as one of the few historic roads in the state's highway system.[8] What this means is questionable in light of bridge replacement over Lake

FIGURE 76. View of the highway and surroundings by Frank Patterson, about 1925. (OCNM Museum and Archives Collections.)

Creek after storm damage in 1996 weakened an earlier structure. At that point ODOT staff determined that not only was the bridge (a wooden structure patched after the 1964 flood) not eligible for the National Register, the entire Caves Highway failed to meet NRHP criteria—a finding that evidently met the concurrence of the State Historic Preservation Office.[9]

Boundaries for the existing historic district should be modified to reflect the character of physical development at Oregon Caves, in particular that which occurred from 1934 to 1942. The site boundaries shown in a cultural landscape inventory conducted in 1990 are a good start, in that the lines drawn are more in sympathy with the monument's rugged topography, even if they still exclude most of its trail system.[10] Aside from the "reception center" (Checking Kiosk/Comfort Station), however, the parking lot and picnic area have undergone such change as the result of landslides (the most recent one occurred in 1996) that both have lost integrity and do not contribute to the historic district. The trail system that radiates from the cave entrance area or plaza could be included within the existing historic district through an amended nomination, one that specifies district boundaries following trail corridors. A trail corridor is defined by the limits of original construction; in many cases this means only the width of existing tread if other character-defining features are absent. The entrance sign built by the CCC is, by contrast, a noncontiguous part of an expanded historic district, but its boundary could be drawn around the supporting structure.

RECOMMENDATIONS   155

What is presently the Oregon Caves Historic District should thus contain the five contributing resources listed in 1992, but also reflect the site boundaries recommended in the cultural landscape inventory, yet include the five trails determined eligible and the monument's entrance sign motif. All of these properties will meet the registration requirements set forth in Linda McClelland's multiple property documentation form for landscape design in national and state parks. According to this form, properties must:

1) be associated with the twentieth century movement to develop national park units for public enjoyment, and to conserve natural features and scenic areas as public parks;
2) retain several or all of the physical characteristics listed above that were developed for that area during or before the New Deal Era (1933-1942);
3) reflect the following principles and practice of park land scape design developed and used by the NPS in national parks from 1916 to 1942 and in state and national parks through ECW, CCC, the Public Works Administration (PWA), or the Works Progress Administration (WPA) projects from 1933 to 1942—
   a) protection and preservation of natural scenery and features
   b) prohibition of exotic plants and wildlife
   c) presentation of scenic vistas through the location of park facilities and development of overlooks
   d) avoidance of right angles and straight lines in the design of roads, trails, and structures
   e) use of native materials for construction and planting
   f) use of naturalistic techniques in planting and rockwork to harmonize manmade development with natural surroundings
   g) adaptation of indigenous or frontier methods of construction
   h) transplanting and planting of native trees, shrubs, and ground cover to erase the scars of construction and earlier uses of the land;
4) possess historic integrity of location, setting, design, materials, workmanship, feeling, and association, and over all reflect the physical appearance and condition of the land scape during the period of significance (1916 to 1942).[11]

Other sites related to Oregon Caves National Monument deserve further study, even if they lie outside monument boundaries. Three of them lie on the old trail to Williams, with Pepper Camp being the closest. Although it currently serves as a road junction in the national forest about two miles northeast of Oregon Caves, a number of blazed trees associated with early use can be seen there. Further away in the national forest are the Grayback Glades, in all likelihood a frequented camping spot on the old trail because it represented most of the climb from Williams. Nearer that community on the west fork of Williams Creek is Caves Camp, once the most popular trailhead for a trip to Oregon Caves, but it is located on private land. On the Illinois Valley side, the CCC site called Camp Oregon Caves is located within the national forest next to the Cedar Guard Station. Although the guard station and its adjoining garage are already listed on the National Register, an archaeological investigation could be conducted over the wider area to include the confluence of Grayback and Sucker creeks so as to discern past use as ranch property and forest camp. There are, of course, a number of other sites on the now combined Rogue River – Siskiyou National Forest such as the Bigelow Lakes, where additional information about the past as it pertains to Oregon Caves could be gleaned—though this must also be left to future studies.

Back on the monument, none of the Mission 66 era facilities are eligible for listing since they do not meet applicable National Register criteria. Under criterion A, such development would have to demonstrate the shifting focus of park concerns during the period of significance (1946 to 1972), the character of the monument's labor force and the NPS response to postwar patterns of visitation. According to a draft multiple property documentation form aimed at NPS units in the Pacific West Region (of which Oregon Caves National Monument is a part), property types associated with Mission 66 must exhibit an emphasis on: interpreting the park's resources to the public, providing for protection of the park's resources, and expanding facilities to efficiently manage the dramatic increases in visitation that parks like Oregon Caves experienced in the postwar era.[12] For the most part, Mission 66 at the monument consisted of some piecemeal changes to the facilities and infrastructure developed between 1916 and 1942. These changes have either been subsumed by subsequent alterations (as along the cave tour route), destroyed by natural hazards (such as

FIGURE 77. CCC Enrollees from Camp Oregon Caves collecting peat from one of the Bigelow Lakes in 1935.

the landslide event of 1996 that affected the main parking lot), or surrounded by newer structures (like administration building and housing at the Lake Creek site).

For Mission 66 properties at Oregon Caves to be eligible under criterion C, they would also have to be associated with the modernist design precepts and construction techniques practiced by NPS architects and landscape architects working in the Western Office of Design and Construction (WODC) in San Francisco. Stripped of excessive ornamentation (in comparison to the rustic architecture that preceded it), built of prefabricated materials, and oriented toward efficiency of visitor use, Mission 66 buildings and structures represented a distinct break with earlier naturalistic design.[13] Of the ten property types so far outlined, Oregon Caves received only three during the period of significance (1946 to 1972) and only two (the picnic area below the main parking lot and a residence at Lake Creek) are extant.[14]

In neither case, however, can the properties be considered clearly indicative of modernist trends in site planning or architectural design precipitated a shift in how an area like Oregon Caves might be characterized. The picnic area replaces the CCC built log tables and fireplaces engulfed by the landslide of 1942. It is now below the parking area (as opposed to the canyon, its location before the slide) and consists of only a few sites leveled just enough to accommodate some stout wooden tables. The Lake Creek residence resembles hundreds of others built in the national parks during Mission 66, usually as part of larger housing developments. This dwelling has undergone some interior and exterior alterations, with perhaps its only distinction being that the NPS designed and built the dwelling on national forest land under a special use permit from the Forest Service.[15]

Interpreting the Past at Oregon Caves

Nature guiding, or "interpretation" (as it came to be known), has always centered on the cave—with the vast majority of visitors experiencing the monument only through the conducted tour. Other opportunities to reach the public have nevertheless come in ranger-led campfire programs and walks, but also through non-personal services such as trail guides, wayside exhibits, indoor displays, and guidebooks. In addition to a logical focus on geology, cave life, and terrestrial biota, some aspects of the monument's social history and physical development are of interest to visitors.[17] Exploration of the topics listed below should be accompanied by application of historical method, which is centered on what the past means to the present. What visitors can verify in the realm of change and continuity at Oregon Caves can be used to bring any of these topics into their larger spatial and temporal contexts if the interpretation of the past is sufficiently thematic. Some suggested theme statements derived from this study are:

1. Indian removal in southwest Oregon is only one part in a larger process of contact and settlement that included activities like mining, commercial agriculture, and logging.
2. A "discoverer" like Elijah Davidson only becomes relevant to an industrial nation state when infrastructure like highways are extended to peripheral heritage sites like Oregon Caves.
3. Proclamation and public funding for development as a national monument can be seen as part of a larger trend of the federal government to subsidize the growth of the American west as a region in the absence of sufficient private capital.
4. Rustic architecture at Oregon Caves National Monument not only harkens back to the 1920s and 30s as a way to

unify park facilities based on the older model of a landscape garden, it also serves as a window to understanding how one culture and its progenitors perceive nature.
5. While rustic architecture can be linked with a desire to make earth into a vision of heaven, more standardized types of park facilities have, by contrast, been seen in a negative light, as intrusions on a scene that do little to evoke the "genius" of the place.

Most people learn to value the past through concepts or patterns only when they can literally see them assume physical form. The foregoing theme statements can be used as organizing devices to illustrate how the past at Oregon Caves with all its incongruities relates to the present, but only in concert with tangible objects or the experience of specific places. What follows are some suggestions about how to approach the theme statements as reflected in corresponding chapters of this study:

Contact and settlement. This is perhaps best illustrated away from the monument, in the wider Illinois Valley, though a program given below the Chalet or at the visitor center in Cave Junction. It could use an oak tree to illustrate how the survival of indigenous peoples was tied to the availability of local food resources like acorns. There is a reconstructed dwelling at the Kerbyville Museum on the Redwood Highway, but Indian removal is a difficult topic to convey without traveling to places much more distant—like Fort Hoskins in Benton County or what remains of the Siletz Reservation in Lincoln County.[18] Signs of mining activity are plentiful throughout the Illinois River basin, though few are located where visitors will congregate. Still, the best interpretive device that pertains to hydraulic mining is undoubtedly the Gin Lin Trail next to Flumet Flat Campground on the Rogue River National Forest south of Ruch (in Jackson County), though the results can still be seen in the landscape around Waldo.

Commercial viability. Remnants of wagon roads persist throughout southwest Oregon, though the old stage route (which is still maintained for travel by BLM) between Selma and Williams provides a sense of how the rugged topography affected early travelers. At least one of the Davidson homesteads can be seen from a distance around Williams, not too far from Elijah's grave in the Sparlin Cemetery. These could be linked with the commemorative stone next to the entrance of Oregon Caves, as might the signa-

160 RECOMMENDATIONS

FIGURE 78. Carter Davidson's signature of July 10, 1878 can be seen at the bottom of this image taken in 1931. (U.S. Forest Service photo, Siskiyou National Forest).

ture of his brother Carter on one of the formations. A small piece of the trail blazed by Burch from Williams can be followed for a short distance before it disappears into a brush field in the Siskiyou National Forest, but perhaps more evocative of early attempts to promote a show cave are the discolored rooms and broken formations left by early visitors. Exactly what can be attributed to the smoking torches and souvenir hunting associated with expeditions like the *Examiner* party is nearly impossible, however. A trail linking the monument with Cave Creek Campground corresponds with the route taken by many visitors before the Oregon Caves Highway was completed in 1922. It provides an acute sense of how remote the possibility of a commercially viable show cave was without an automobile road.

Federal aid for infrastructure. Roads and development of recreational facilities are only two ways in which governments have subsidized infrastructure in the west. They did so for geopolitical and economic reasons, with roads serving as an example of how the quickly evolving technology associated with automobiles dictated centralized authority in federal and state governments that had to prevail over county jurisdiction or local initiative in building roads. The earliest iteration of the Oregon Caves Highway can be seen in two locations: one being a short section of roadway below the Chalet; the other is below a concrete bridge spanning Sucker Creek near the realigned section of highway at Grayback. Subsequent widening produced the Oregon Caves Highway as seen above Grayback since 1931, where major alterations have been limited to a flood-damaged section where the road crosses Lake Creek. Aside from some small sections of dry laid wall that blend together with later work and some fragments of the diesel house and studio, there are precious few reminders of facility development at the monument which pre-date transfer of Oregon Caves to the NPS in 1934.[19]

Rustic architecture. The existing historic district is configured to emphasize naturalistic landscape design and the rustic architecture that still characterize what visitors see around the cave entrance and to some extent on the trail system. Many of the high points about culturally-contrived perceptions of nature can be covered on a tour of the Chateau (see Appendix 1). Readers are urged to consult the district nomination and cultural landscape report, as well as Historic American Buildings Survey documentation and the historic structure report on the Chateau for background and specifics.[20] Understanding how the Civilian Conservation Corps shaped the monument requires some acquaintance with the area around Cedar Guard Station, as the site of Camp Oregon Caves is located between the highway and a road going up Grayback Creek. The camp's influence goes beyond the NPS and USFS projects undertaken throughout this part of the Illinois Valley, since its sawmill allowed enrollees to produce lumber for CCC projects like picnic tables, furniture, and rustic signs shipped to other park sites.[21]

Postwar changes. Some writers have cast rustic architecture as the antithesis to park facilities built after 1942, but most development above ground remained somewhat subtle and small in scope. This reinforced the perception that the resort created before World War II ended had largely stood still, even if changes on the tour route or in the main parking lot came with measurable impacts. Most of the inadvertent damage to the cave has been reversed, or at least mitigated to some extent, but there is an opportunity for interpreters to combine a "natural" topic with its "cultural" overlays. This is true in the cave (where the effect of asphalt paving, for example, could be discussed) or above ground, whether one highlights changes in forest composition due to fire suppression or wants to make natural hazards like landslides relevant to visitors standing in the main parking lot. Relating how the monument is positioned in a scenic "hierarchy" of units administered by the NPS or among the region's visitor attractions is more elusive, however, since the conceptualization needed will be better suited to a written, rather than an oral, presentation.

Additional research

Any study of this type can raise more questions than it answers. New lines of inquiry open from locating materials that support broad themes, especially those that have physical manifestations that are clearly or even subtly evident at a site like Oregon Caves National Monument. Chapters three and four form the heart of this study, yet they also could serve as the launching point to pursue further development of the following topics, especially in a comparative context:

1. There must be parallels in the way this cave has been developed and perceived with others in the United States or elsewhere (see Appendix 2). These patterns could support a model that might be used to organize and present an administrative history of Oregon Caves National Monument.

2. The relationship of the federal government to its concessionaires has never received broad enough treatment for comparisons between sites so as to explain the relationship of regulator to the regulated. Oregon Caves represents an engaging case study, one that could be presented in some form through an administrative history, of how concession operations dominated the concerns of both NPS and USFS managers for more than 75 years.

3. Development of roads and trails in or around the monument needs to be set against a background of how transportation infrastructure in the surrounding area developed from decisions made by engineers or other key officials acting through federal and state authorities.

4. The effects of promoting the monument as a show cave needs to be better understood, especially where constituent groups like the Grants Pass Chamber of Commerce and its offshoot, the Oregon Cavemen, exerted their influence on early managers of the monument. These promotional efforts need to be understood in context of other civic boosters in Oregon and perhaps elsewhere, especially as they relate to commercial advertising by concessionaires and institutional efforts like those of the Oregon State

RECOMMENDATIONS   163

FIGURE 79. Joaquin Miller's Chapel served as the venue for this wedding in 1944. (OCNM Museum and Archives Collections.)

Highway Commission or the NPS.

5. Gust Lium's role as designer and contractor at Oregon Caves should be placed in context to his work for the Forest Service and in Grants Pass for private parties. Some additional biographical information might also be useful.

6. More information about how the Civilian Conservation Corps operated at Camp Oregon Caves could not only yield important information about their projects at the monument and on the Siskiyou National Forest, but also how enrollees at this camp provided lumber from its sawmill for other park units, or made custom furniture and rustic signs. The camp also interacted with NPS administration at Crater Lake, as well as CCC detachments at Lava Beds and sites under the jurisdiction of the Oregon state parks superintendent Samuel Boardman.

7. A chronology of timber sales near Oregon Caves, particularly those that occurred within the area proposed for expansion of the monument, could be compiled to determine whether activities on adjacent lands come with an impact on a small national monument. This question and the perceptions that come with it might be addressed within an administrative history of the park.

Available funding for this study did not permit a visit to the National Archives II in College Park, Maryland, where early records pertaining to the proclamation and management of Oregon Caves are likely housed in record groups 95 (U.S. Forest

FIGURE 80. The Oregon Caves Company's kiosk and billboard at Cave Junction in June 1958. (OCNM Museum and Archives Collections.)

Service) and 49 (General Land Office). This repository could be the ideal spot to also investigate RG 79 (National Park Service) as part of comparative work that involves other federally-administered caves and concession operations (topics 1 and 2).

A more systematic search for records pertaining to road construction might be conducted, beginning in RG 30 (Bureau of Public Roads) at the National Archives branch in Seattle, but a search for possible BPR materials may prove rewarding at the Federal Highway Administration office in Vancouver, Washington (topic 3). The Oregon State Archives in Salem also houses records relating to the construction of state highways in southwest Oregon, but use of the finding aids that can be obtained from the Oregon Department of Transportation's History Center is recommended before visiting the archives. More information about trail construction, especially the early routes on the Siskiyou National Forest, might be available through RG 95 in the Seattle branch of the National Archives; alternatively, a visit to the Illinois Valley Ranger District in Cave Junction may prove to be just as fruitful.

Promotion as a show cave might be better understood if boosterism could be put in statewide context and even regional perspective (topic 4). On a publicly supported basis, organized boosterism began tied to the rise of commercial clubs (or chambers of commerce, as they became known); material held at the Oregon Historical Society in Portland could doubtless illuminate the wider patterns. As for the role of individual promoters tied to the Oregon Caves, more information about the concession company stockholders and their employees such as Gust Lium (topic 5) could be gathered in repositories like the Southern Oregon Historical Society (Medford) and the Josephine County Historical Society (Grants Pass).

Some additional material related to Camp Oregon Caves (topic 6) has been collected from RG 35 (CCC) and RG 79 (NPS) from the NARA II facility at College Park. To adequately put the CCC at the monument into context, however, a special study of the program as it operated at four national park units (Oregon Caves, Crater Lake, Lava Beds, and Lassen Volcanic) within the larger Western Region of the NPS is recommended. Surprisingly little work has been done to assess the full impact of this work relief program on the development of these parks, let alone differentiate projects funded from other sources like the Public Works Administration. A multi-park study would involve visits to the National Archives branch in San Bruno, California, to review material housed in both of the aforementioned record groups (35 and 79), but also should include some tracking of CCC companies as they moved to spike camps and/or work sites away from the four parks.

Notes

Preface

1. Stephen R. Mark, Oregon Caves Historic District, nomination to the National Register of Historic Places, June 1991, section 10.

2. USDI-NPS, *Guidelines for Completing National Register of Historic Places Forms*, National Register Bulletin 16, Part B (Washington, DC: Government Printing Office, 1991), 1.

3. The version called *History and Prehistory in the National Park System and the National Historic Landmarks Program* (Washington, DC: GPO, 1987) contains a framework in the form of an extended outline that aims to list every major facet of American history, whereas the "Themes and Concepts" document of 1994 is broad and open-ended in its revised framework; see http://www.cr.nps.gov/history/

Introduction

1. Even if rarely expressed, only the deepest, oldest and strongest beliefs are likely to have structured space and time in caves and parks developed as "Edenic," or those which express the desire to make earth into a vision of heaven. Newer constructs such as the frontier, science, the sublime, and capitalism can be considered an outgrowth of older beliefs, if only because some type of technological development is necessary as a precondition, but they follow from more archetypal concepts which link them to the Edenic vision. Examples are mystery (where landscapes pro-

vide the impression that new information by traveling deeper into them) legibility (which allows for exploration in an environment that can be discerned if one travels further into it), prospect (gaining information by seeing outward), and refuge (gaining information without giving any away, or seeing without being seen) which can be used to manipulate a person's surroundings—as in a garden.

2. It could be that the more technologically powerful and wealthy a society becomes, it is more interested in its own past than that of myths or archetypes which transcend individual nation states. In this study, for example, myths are reinterpreted through a cultural lens which melds the archetype (such as an Edenic garden) with newer concepts (like the frontier) to make the composite seem uniquely American. Widespread belief by Americans in this "composited construction" has profoundly affected the course of events in places like Oregon Caves. This study, however, is not historiographical critique, though it does make use of some myths affecting the monument as organizing devices. Causal connections among major ideas that extend backwards into prehistory tend to be speculative for purposes of historical narrative because such "meta-text" is not explicitly stated in written source material.

3. No. 876, July 12, 1909, 36 Stat. 2497.

4. Ibid. The proclamation's use of "scientific interest and importance" as a justification for the monument's establishment is significant by virtue of its rarity in enabling legislation for national park units until the 1960s, as well as the fact that virtually nothing scientific was known about Oregon Caves at the time.

5. USDA-Forest Service, *An Ideal Vacation Land: the National Forests of Oregon* (Washington, DC: Government Printing Office, 1923), 28.

6. USDA-Forest Service, *The Oregon Caves: a National Monument* (Washington, DC: GPO, ca. 1925], 3. The names of cave formations and rooms at the time, however, did not suggest random or truly varied resemblances. Some names, such as "paradise," "Eden," "garden," and "grotto" with allusions to Indians or to Greek and Roman lore reinforce how the cave was considered to be part of an idealized landscape—and could be made more so by using such appellations.

7. Toll to the NPS director (Horace Albright), February 6, 1932, 4-5.

8. Narrative on pages 1-3 of the master plan, attached to a memorandum from Ernest P. Leavitt, superintendent of Crater Lake National Park, to the Regional Director of Region 4, February, 16, 1945.

9. USDI-NPS, Master Plan Development Outline, Oregon Caves National Monument, March 1952, 1-2.

10. Thomas Williams to NPS Director (Conrad Wirth), April 7, 1955, 3.

11. USDI-NPS, Prospectus No. 1, Mission 66, OCNM, July 29, 1955, 1.

12. USDI-NPS, Mission 66 Prospectus, OCNM, November 15, 1957, 1; Paul Fritz, Master Plan of OCNM, Chapter 2, Area Objectives, August 23, 1964, 1.

13. USDI-NPS, *Master Plan, Oregon Caves National Monument, Oregon* (Washington, DC: GPO, 1975), 8. Calcite deposition at what is now the monument and in much of the Far West was most likely on seamounts (a submarine mountain rising more than 500 fathoms above the ocean floor) or on the edge of volcanic island arcs amid mostly deeper water not conducive to calcite deposition. This and the subsequent splitting apart of limestone or marble masses through extensive faulting resulted in small and medium-size caves in much of the region. Although such processes resulted in less intriguing caves due to small sizes, they also resulted in caves of medium dimension (like Oregon Caves) being relatively rare and thus appealing as a tourist attraction.

14. See, for example, a statement for management written by Superintendent John Miele dated June 2, 1983 where the significance appears verbatim on page 2.

15. Statement for Management, OCNM, August 1994, 9-10. The structures are mentioned, however, in the monument's resource management plan of the time. They appear in a section which identifies resource values; Resource Management Plan, OCNM, approved September 8, 1994, 4-5. This was also the first time that some of the animals found only at Oregon Caves were mentioned. Although they have been singled out by a few scientists as nationally significant, it is not generally known that an entire family of soil millipedes is endemic to the monument.

16. USDI-NPS, Draft General Management Plan and Environmental Impact Statement, OCNM, December 1997, 5.

17. USDI-NPS, General Management Plan, OCNM, August 1999, volume 1, 4-5.1

1. Locked in a Colonial Hinterland

1. Manufacturing and distribution centers in large retail markets create added value for products and are hence the secondary part of the economy. This value added is generally lacking at the primary tier, partly because farmers, loggers, and miners lack the investment capital necessary for what is called vertical integration—where the extraction, manufacture, and distribution of the product is controlled by the same entity.

2. George McKinley and Doug Frank, Stories on the Land: An Environmental History of the Applegate and Upper Illinois Valleys, report to the Medford District, Bureau of Land Management, September 1995.

3. Ibid., 30. The loss of game has repeatedly resulted wherever farming cultures moved into areas held by hunter gatherers, though there are exceptions to this—such as the bison extinction in southeast Oregon made possible by hunter gatherers who acquired horses; Vernon Bailey, *The Mammals and Life Zones of Oregon*. North American Fauna 55, USDA-Bureau of Biological Survey, June 1936, 57-61.

4. Jeff LaLande, *First Over the Siskiyous: Peter Skene Ogden's 1826-1827 Journey Through the Oregon – California Borderlands* (Portland: Oregon Historical Society Press, 1987), 108; cited in McKinley and Frank, 18. A shorter account of Ogden's travels appeared in Elizabeth Heckert's *The People and the River* (Ashland: Aquarius Press, 1977), 121-122.

5. Stephen Dow Beckham, Cultural Resource Overview of the Siskiyou National Forest, report to USDA Forest Service (1978), 62.

6. Beckham, *Requiem for a People: the Rogue Indians and the Frontiersmen* (Corvallis: Oregon State University Press, 1998), 47-52.

7. For a map showing the areas and duration of disease outbreaks in Oregon, see William G. Loy (ed.) *Atlas of Oregon* (Eugene: University of Oregon Press, 2001), 16-17.

8. Speakers of Karok, for example, are estimated to have numbered between 1,500 and 2,000 prior to contact; William F. Shipley, "Native Languages of California," in *Handbook of North American Indians volume 8, California* (Washington DC: Smithsonian Institution Press, 1978), 85. Other accounts substantiate the idea that this part of California had a higher ratio of Indian population in relation to whites than about any other part of the state; Shelburn F. Cook, "Historical Demography," op cit., 91. In the Rogue River Basin, by contrast, an 1852 estimate of indigenous population puts fourteen bands of Indians at only 1,136 in number. Of these fourteen, only one group was placed in the Illinois Valley, whereas three lived in the Applegate drainage; Nathan Douthit, *Uncertain Encounters: Indians and Whites at Peace and War in Southern Oregon, 1820s-1860s* (Corvallis: Oregon State University Press, 2002), 227 (n27).

9. Beckham, Cultural Resources Overview, 80. The limited ethnographic record for southwest Oregon groups is reflected in the entries which appear in the *Handbook of North American Indians, volume 7, Northwest Coast* (Washington, DC: Smithsonian Institution Press, 1990), 580-592, and the previously cited volume 8 of that series, 211-224.

10. Francis Paul Prucha, "U.S. Indian Policies, 1815-1860," *Handbook of North American Indians, volume 4, History of Indian-White Relations*, (Washington, DC: Smithsonian Institution Press, 1988), 43-49.

11. The federal Supreme Court decision in *Johnson vs. McIntosh* ruled that Indian nations held aboriginal use and occupancy rights on their lands, meaning that tribes could live on their lands until their lands were purchased by the United States Government. Indian title, however, had to be formally recognized by treaty or statute, and only the federal government could purchase and convey Indian lands. Congress created a problem in Oregon by disregarding Indian property rights with passage of the Donation Land Act on September 27, 1850 which permitted taking of some 2.5 million acres of Indian lands prior to any treaty ratification; Jeff Zucker, et al., *Oregon Indians: Culture, History and Current Affairs* (Portland: Oregon Historical Society Press, 1987), 81-82; William G. Robbins, "Extinguishing Indian Land Title in Western Oregon," *The Indian Historian* (Spring 1974), 12-15.

12. The treaties of interest in reference to Oregon Caves are the one of September 10, 1853 at Table Rock, as well as one on November 18, 1854, at the mouth of Applegate Creek on the Rogue River; also the traditional affiliation study on Oregon Caves by Douglas Deur.

13. Zucker, et al., *Oregon Indians*, 85.

14. Most of the archival records relating to the conflicts that took place between 1850 and 1856 focus on the Rogue Valley and southern Oregon coast; see Beckham's Requiem for a People and Douthit's *Uncertain Encounters* for more context and detail. Francis Fuller Victor's 1891 account in Dorothy and Jack Sutton (eds.), *Indian Wars of the Rogue River* (Grants Pass: Josephine County Historical Society, 2003) is also useful. The Illinois Valley and upper Applegate were largely peripheral to most of the trouble, but troops under the command of Captain Robert Williams skirmished with Indians in 1853 on the creek later named for him. At approximately the same time, Indians attacked miners on the Illinois, an action that led to a pitched battle in the mountains. Soldiers believed these natives were Tolowas from the mouth of the Smith River in California; Victor noted that miners in the Illinois Valley had been annoyed by depredations they attributed to coastal Indians forced inland by warfare in October of that year (see Beckham, *Requiem for a People*, 126-127). Miners and Indians had meanwhile negotiated an informal treaty to limit hostilities in the valley, though this served only to postpone the violence until May 1855; Beckham, *Requiem for a People*, 104, 149.

15. Beckham, Cultural Resources Overview, 80-83.

16. Zucker, Oregon Indians, 112-113.

17. Quoted from Edward Sapir (1907) in Dennis J. Gray, *The Takelma and their Athapascan Neighbors*, anthropological papers 37 (Eugene: University of Oregon, 1987), 13.

18. In 1861 a group of Takelma appeared in the Table Rock vicinity, demanding that white Americans comply with the terms of their 1853 treaty, but this group was quickly sent back to the Siletz Reservation; Jacksonville *Table Rock Sentinel* microfilm, Southern Oregon Historical Society.

19. McKinley and Frank, Stories on the Land, 30-32.

20. McKinley and Frank, Stories on the Land, 33. These food sources are listed by Jeff Lalande, Cultural Resources Overview for the North Siskiyou Planning Unit, May 1977, 11. Most of the agricultural potential in the Illinois Valley lies within a "triangle" which has the communities of Kerby, O'Brien, and Holland at its corners; Samuel N. Dicken, *Oregon Geography: the People, the Place, and the Times* (Eugene: University of Oregon Bookstore, 1965), 83-84.

21. Jackson County was bounded by Douglas County to the north, Coos to the west, and Wasco to the east; Loy, et al., *Atlas of Oregon*, 21.

22. Russell Working, "Name that Town," in Etc. Magazine, Grants Pass *Courier* (December 1989), 27-28; see also Lewis McArthur, *Oregon Geographic Names* (Portland: Oregon Historical Society Press, 1974), 397-398.

23. Willard and Elsie Street, *Sailors' Diggings* (Wilderville, Ore.: Wilderville Press, 1973), 11. The authors note that the number of Chinese was derived from mining licenses granted, not an actual count made from the county census.

24. See George Kramer, Mining in Southwestern Oregon: A Historic Context Statement, Heritage Research Associates Report 234, Eugene, December 1999.

25. Catherine Noah, "Where's Waldo," *Table Rock Sentinel* 12:6 (November/December 1992), 23.

26. McKinley and Frank, Stories on the Land, 28.

27. Kramer, Mining in Southwestern Oregon, 7-8. This is also true in California, though the scale is different. The population there peaked at 500,000 between 1852 and 1857, largely as the result of the gold mining boom. California's non-Indian population fell to 310,000 by 1860, a figure that reflected how the placer mining period had passed; Kenneth N. Owens, Historic Trails and Roads in California: A Cultural Resources Study. Volume 1: Historic Context and Typology. Report prepared for the California Department of Transportation, March 1990, 51 (note 34).

28. William H. Brewer, *Up and Down California* in 1860-1864

(Berkeley: University of California Press, 1966), 483. The earliest figures for gold production in Oregon were not generated until 1866; Kramer, Mining in Southwestern Oregon, 7.

29. Kramer, Mining in Southwestern Oregon, 42-44.

30. Kramer, Mining in Southwestern Oregon, 45; Brewer, Up and Down California, 484.

31. Walling, *History of Southern Oregon* (1884) quoted in Kramer, Mining in Southwestern Oregon, 21. By 1855 there seemed to be little opportunity for the independent miner at places like Sailors Diggings (Waldo) if they lacked the capital needed for a long sluice, a situation repeated during the placer phase throughout the west. Although the prospects for finding and processing viable lodes remained somewhat limited in southwest Oregon, all of the sub-basins between Althouse and Jacksonville saw some placer mining activity during the 1850s and 60s; McKinley and Frank, Stories on the Land, 28-29.

32. Kramer, Mining in Southwestern Oregon, 36.

33. Kramer, Mining in Southwestern Oregon, 65. From the sketchy data available, gold production for both Jackson and Josephine counties for the period between 1855 and 1863 amounted to $1.5 million, falling to $1.2 million between 1864 and 1896 (these figures are based on the standardized price for gold of $20.87 per ounce set by the U.S. Treasury in 1837, one effective until 1933). By comparison, gold production in California (most coming from the Sacramento drainage and/or Sierra foothills) amounted to $41 million for 1850 alone. The strikes in southern Oregon during the 1850s were simply a small portion of a larger tripling of worldwide gold production during that decade, with much of it attributed to opening of the new western American goldfields. Gold mining in the United States, however, did not begin in California, since gold worth some $60 million had been extracted in North Carolina from 1799 to 1860; Tony L. Crumbley, "America's First Gold Rush," *American Philatelist* 118:6 (June 2004), 511.

34. Loy, et al., *The Atlas of Oregon*, 26-27.

35. Modeled somewhat after earlier legislation that brought white Americans to Texas, the DLCA had several aims. First, it legitimized claims made by Oregon Trail "emigrants" who had reached the Willamette Valley in the 1840s. The act also made all future claims correspond to a rectangular grid established by the Pacific Coast Survey created by this legislation. Third, the DLCA provided settlers with incentive to stay in Oregon rather than moving to the California goldfields, as many had in the aftermath of the "rush" that commenced in 1848. Much of the land claimed in Oregon, however, had not been divested of Indian title at

the time of initial white settlement.

36. McKinley and Frank, Stories on the Land, 36-37.

37. Under the first donation land law in effect from 1850 to 1852, a male settler could claim and assume ownership of 320 acres of unsurveyed land if he resided on the land for four consecutive years. If married before December 1, 1851, his wife could also claim 320 acres. By 1853, however, the allowable claim had been reduced to 160 acres for each spouse, but the required occupancy went down to two years. The Homestead Act provided 160 acres to any settler paying the filing fee and who could reside on his property and improve it for five years. If they wished to buy the land for $1.25 an acre after six months, the settler could do so. Various "preemption" (squatting) acts were passed to facilitate settlement of the west starting in the 1830s, though the settler had to have the cash to pay for the land when it came up for sale.

38. Edna May Hill, *Josephine County Historical Highlights I* (Grants Pass: Josephine County Historical Society, 1980). The route is described in more detail by Stephen Dow Beckham, Cultural Resources Overview, 95, and Ruth Pfefferle, *Golden Days and Pioneer Ways* (Grants Pass: Josephine County Historical Society, 1977), 83-84.

39. McKinley and Frank, Stories on the Land, 64-65.

40. McKinley and Frank, Stories on the Land, 85.

41. Walling, *History of Southern Oregon* (1884), 350, quoted in McKinley and Frank, Stories on the Land, 91.

42. McKinley and Frank, Stories on the Land, 77-78.

43. McKinley and Frank, Stories on the Land, 33.

44. "Note on Williams Valley Recall Early Settlers, Important Events," Grants Pass *Courier*, April 2, 1960.

45. Oregon Mining Journal for 1897, cited in Kramer, Mining in Southwestern Oregon, 106.

46. McKinley and Frank, Stories on the Land, 34.

47. This interpretation of western America is still debated with much fervor among historians; see, for example, Richard W. Etulain, *Does the Frontier Experience Make America Exceptional?* (Boston: St. Martins, 1999).

48. David Hackett Fischer, *Albion's Seed: Four British Folkways in America* (New York: Oxford University Press, 1989).

49. Olga Weydemeyer Johnson, *They Settled in Applegate Country* (Grants Pass: Josephine County Historical Society, 1969), 52.

50. Ibid. The move to Nome completed a move across the North American continent in three generations. It began with Davidson's grandfather, Elijah Barton Davidson, Sr., who went from his birthplace of

Rutherford, North Carolina, to Warren, Kentucky. He then went west with his son, Elijah Barton Davidson, Jr., to Monmouth, Oregon; pedigree chart attached to a letter from Chuck White to John Roth, May 1991.

51. E.J. Davidson, "History of the Discovery of the Marble Halls of Oregon," *Oregon Historical Quarterly* 23:3 (September 1922), 274-276.

52. William W. Fidler, "An Account of the First Attempt at Exploration of the "Oregon Caves," *Oregon Historical Quarterly* 23:3 (September 1922), 270-273; this version retitled from initial version that appeared in the Portland *Oregonian* on August 1, 1887.

53. Davidson, "History of the Discovery," 276. There is speculation that the bear may have been a grizzly; Larry McLane, remarks at Oregon Caves history seminar, OCNM, June 5, 1992.

54. Thomas Atwood to General Superintendent (Don Spalding), July 6, 1979, H1415, Davidson file, OCNM.

55. Visitation in 1921, for example, was 1,133 but only 363 in 1910.

56. Fidler, "An Account of the First Attempt," 273.

57. Eighteenth century Romantics incorporated wild and deep caves (as opposed to the shallow grottoes in contrived landscapes) into the construct of Edenic garden through their concept of the sublime. Animals served as intermediaries between people and caves by prompting their discovery—as in this case and many others, including Mammoth and Carlsbad. More on the practical side, Davidson logically opted for a bear over the deer because the former supplied a bigger hide, meat, and more especially tallow for boots, grease, and cooking. If the bear was a grizzly, it may well have been one of the few in Oregon at the time. The last grizzly on the western side of the Cascade Range was reported killed in 1877; McKinley and Frank, Stories on the Land, 78.

58. Fidler, "An Account of the First Attempt," 270-273; see also Frank Walsh, "Excerpts from the Robert A. Miller Journal [trip of August 14-16, 1878], *The Speolograph* 31:11 (November 1995), 144; George Dunn, A Trip to Josephine County Caves, 1883, in Southern Oregon Historical Society manuscripts collection [references a trip made by Thomas Condon and University of Oregon students]. These parties and others of the time also left inscriptions in the cave which place the Condon trip in August 1884 rather than 11 months earlier; Denise M. Heald, Historical Graffitti of Oregon Caves National Monument, A Limited Survey, compiled in 1987, OCNM files.

59. Dunn manuscript, 2-3.

60. Burch, Oregon Caves as they were in the '80s, manuscript c. 1925, Josephine County Historical Society, Grants Pass, Oregon Caves file.

2. The Closing of a Frontier

1. Richard White, *It's Your Misfortune and None of My Own: A New History of the American West* (Norman: University of Oklahoma Press, 1991), 243-246. White makes the point that this export economy resulted from rapid world population growth during the nineteenth century, increased urbanization, improved transportation links, and European imperialism. These factors produced an escalating demand for basic commodities in Europe and the United States.

2. Jack Sutton, *110 Years with Josephine: The History of Josephine County, Oregon, 1856-1966* (Grants Pass: Josephine County Historical Society, 1966), 18. Prior to 1885, the closest rail connection to Josephine County was at Roseburg, where the Oregon and California Railroad (recipient of a land grant from Congress in 1866) arrived in 1873. Once the O&C fell into bankruptcy, some refinancing allowed the Southern Pacific to build the line to Grants Pass.

3. Ibid.

4. McKinley and Frank, Stories on the Land, 68-69. Both were on the same stage route, one which utilized Deer Creek from Selma to reach the Applegate drainage.

5. See Ruth Pfefferle, *Golden Days and Pioneer Ways* (Grants Pass: Bulletin Publishing Company, 1995), 81-84, for a description of travel through the Illinois Valley using both stage and freight wagon. See also Sutton, *110 Years with* Josephine, 86.

6. Much of this was done speculatively, with the principal being Jonathon Bourne, a Portland attorney who later became a United States senator from Oregon. Sol Abrams, who eventually returned to Roseburg, held the Grants Pass townsite that Bourne sought to control; McLane, Oregon Caves history seminar, June 5, 1992.

7. Harkness owned the Grove Creek Ranch in Sunny Valley and married Cassie Burch of Canyonville. He worked for Bourne and bought up lots as an agent, an activity that made him unpopular with some Grants Pass residents. Copy of mining entry recorded by Charles Hughes, Josephine County Clerk, May 19, 1885; location notice dated May 2, 1885; Oregon Caves pre-1900 file, OCNM.

8. Burch, Oregon Caves as they were in the '80s, 1. McLane has stated that Burch and Harkness could have obtained title at least one other way under the land laws (a declaratory statement allowed under the pre-emption act of 1841), though this would probably have reduced the patented acreage given that payment for land was expected at the time of survey. A location notice was probably sufficient to stifle any potential

competitors, yet also served as a way to avoid taxes while the pair improved the claim and determined whether they could afford to hold the land in fee simple.

9. Ibid. Roughly 420 feet of ladders had been built by the end of the following year.

10. Ibid. See also Frank K. Walsh and William R. Halliday, *Oregon Caves, Discovery and Exploration* (Coos Bay: Te-Cum-Tom, 1982), 7. Admission to the cave was set at $1; advertisement in the Rogue River *Courier*, July 9, 1886.

11. Virtually all the publicity on the cave up to that time had been generated locally, with seemingly little effect, even when feature articles appeared in the Grants Pass paper throughout the summer of 1886; see, for example, "Limestone Caves of Josephine County, Rogue River *Courier*, July 1 and July 8, 1886, and "The Greatest Natural Curiosities of Oregon," Rogue River *Courier*, September 3, 1886. The literary magazines generally commanded audiences over a greater geographic area than newspapers of the time; in this instance, see "The Caves of Southern Oregon," *The West Shore*, January 1888, 31-32.

12. S.S. Nicolini, "Explorers Return from a Visit to the Ice Caves of Josephine County," Portland *Daily News*, September 10, 1888, and Nicolini, "Crater Lake: A Visit to that Picturesque Body of Water," Portland *Daily News*, September 11, 1888. Similarly, Steel wrote articles titled "In the Josephine Caves," Portland *Oregonian*, September 10, 1888, and "Visit to Crater Lake," Portland *Oregonian*, September 11, 1888.

13. Frances Fuller Victor, *Atlantis Arisen: Talks of a Tourist about Oregon and Washington* (Philadelphia: J.B. Lippincott, 1891), 136-137.

14. The Mining Law of 1872 dictates how claims made on public can become private property or "patented." Although this is a way of avoiding the stipulation of a survey requirement that generally limit how a homestead or other types of claims could be acquired, there was little incentive to pay property taxes on such property until the claim could pay either in extracted ore, as a tourist attraction, or possibly a speculative holding.

15. Charles Michelson, "Another Western Marvel," San Francisco *Examiner*, July 11, 1891, and "Our Splendid Caverns," July 12, 1891. Two refutations appeared in Portland papers; W.W. Fidler, "Oregon's Great Caves," Portland *Oregonian*, July 21, 1891, and George Moffett, "Oregon's Great Cavern," Portland *Evening Telegram*, July 21, 1891.

16. During that period separate rooms were often referred to as a single cave, hence the aggregate became "caves" or "caverns," as at Carlsbad in New Mexico or Cumberland in Tennessee.

17. Walsh and Halliday, *Oregon Caves, Discovery and Exploration*, 7.

18. "Oregon's Mammoth Cave," Grants Pass *Oregon Observer*, December 28, 1893. The hyperbole is reminiscent of the earliest Euro-American account fantasizing about Yellowstone's "petrified birds singing on petrified trees," an exaggeration common enough in the promotion of tourist attractions at the time.

19. Ibid. Not that westerners hadn't seen such grandiose plans before; the same page of the *Observer* carried a story about the collapse and sale of the Oregon Pacific Railroad, a scheme whose promoters claimed would connect Boise with Corvallis and make Newport a major shipping terminus.

20. Ibid. He even wanted to build a large hotel at the cave and connect it with Crescent City by railroad through the Illinois Valley.

21. Letter from A.B. Smith, January 2, 1894, transcribed by Veda Thomas with e-mail message sent to OCNM, August 21, 2004; articles in the *Oregon Observer*, "The Great Caves," February 3, 1894, and "Oregon's Great Cave," February 24, 1894.

22. Walsh and Halliday, *Oregon Caves, Discovery and Exploration*, 8.

23. "The Josephine County Caves," *Oregon Observer*, April 28, 1894.

24. "Unexpected Reception," *Oregon Observer*, May 19, 1894.

25. F.B. Millard, "Down in the Underland," San Francisco *Examiner*, June 3, 1894.

26. Millard, "Monte Cristo's Treasures," San Francisco *Examiner*, June 10, 1894. They apparently surmised the paths taken by previous visitors through evidence of breakage and the discoloration left by the use of coal oil on torches.

27. Ibid.

28. "Notice to the Public," *Oregon Observer*, June 23, 1894. The assessment notice appeared again a week later, also announcing that all unpaid stock was to be auctioned by the end of August.

29. Walsh and Halliday, *Oregon Caves, Discovery and Exploration*, 8. A sheriff's sale of the company's movable property in October 1894 netted only $60. Its collapse is also mentioned in "The Caves of Oregon," *Oregon Observer*, September 19, 1906.

30. As an example, "Into the Cave," Roseburg *Review*, June 10, 1894, announced two additional expeditions to the cave had formed on the heels of what the *Examiner* reported. One was to start from Portland about July 1 and explore the Cascade Range before arriving at the cave, while another organized in San Francisco had the same object. Such prospects quickly evaporated in the wake of the company's potential demise, but the writer for the Roseburg paper made the overt connection

between exploration and money needed to make the cave accessible to the "average tourist" who preferred "walking erect in search of the curious and rare in nature."

31. John H. Mitchell, "The Oregon Caves," *National Geographic* 590, April 20, 1895, 275; editorial in Jacksonville *Semi-Weekly Times*, October 3, 1895; "A Great Honey-Combed Mountain Forty Miles from Grants Pass," *Oregon Observer*, December 21, 1895; H.R., "A trip from Grants Pass to the Limestone Caves of Josephine County – the Greatest Natural Curiosities of Oregon," Grants Pass *Courier*, September 3, 1896; article by Amos Voorhies in the *Courier*, August 19, 1897, as referenced in the same newspaper on October 25, 1977. Virtually all of the writers made reference to a bottomless pit and other such features.

32. This type of writing continued to appear until 1915 or so; see, for example, a piece by one of Smith's business associates, F.M. Nickerson, "The Oregon Caves," *Oregon Teachers Monthly* 19 (September 1914), 2.

33. "Josephine County Caves" section of a circular printed on April 1, 1896 by the Mazamas group in Portland that promoted their excursion set for August that year to Crater Lake and other points in southern Oregon.

34. Kramer, Mining in Southwestern Oregon, 60.

35. Cameron Jenks, Development of Government Forest Control, 109.

36. The most prominent advocate for the reserves in Oregon was John B. Waldo, a former chief justice of the state supreme court, who began his efforts to establish reserves in the 1880s; for the complete text of such debates, see Gerald W. Williams and Stephen R. Mark (comps.), Establishing and Defending the Cascade Range Forest Reserve: as found in letters, newspapers, magazines, and official reports. USDA-Forest Service, Pacific Northwest Region, September 30, 1995. For more about the idea of a frontier commons, see Mark, "Closing Down the Commons: Conflict between Sheep Grazing and Forestry in Oregon's Cascade Range, 1865-1915," *Journal of the Shaw Historical Library* 18 (2004), 63-74.

37. Quoted from Walling, *History of Southern Oregon* (1884), 455, in McKinley and Frank, Stories on the Land, 152. A single mill located two miles below Williams served local needs in the upper Applegate Valley at that time; Walling, *History of Southern Oregon*, 458, in Beckham, Cultural Resources Overview, 131. Small mills were operated either by water power or hand-pulled whipsaws.

38. McKinley and Frank, Stories on the Land, 153; the "light growth" characterization is in Henry Gannett, *The Forests of Oregon*,

USGS Professional Paper No. 4 (Washington, DC: Government Printing Office, 1902), 23. Some operations in Grants Pass prospered, however. Robert Booth, for example, became the principal contractor supplying bridge and tunnel timbers for a portion of the Southern Pacific Railroad and became the leading lumberman in his county between 1886 and 1898. He then relocated to Springfield to form the Booth-Kelly Lumber Company, one of the longest-lived timber enterprises in Oregon; Beckham, Cultural Resources Overview, 131.

39. It should be noted that Hermann, a former Oregon congressman from Douglas County, had been implicated in the land fraud scandals of the time.

40. Freida F. Glicemae, Forestry Legislation in the History of Forest Reserves in Oregon, MA thesis, University of Oregon, 1940, 30-32. Langille had earlier reported on the Cascade Range reserve and had served there in an administrative capacity. He supported the Rogue River withdrawal to conserve timber from destructive fires and to keep it from the machinations of land syndicates.

41. Portland *Oregonian*, October 8, 1903, cited by Glicemae, Forestry Legislation, 39. A map of the withdrawal appeared in the *Oregon Observer*, May 30, 1903.

42. Glicemae, Forestry Legislation, 63-65; see also L.J. Cooper, History of the Siskiyou National Forest, Section III, in A History of the Siskiyou National Forest (1939), 1-2.

43. Within a year Fulton had been implicated in the land fraud scandal that enveloped Oregon and other western states. Although so reticent about the need for reform of the land laws that he opposed repeal of the Timber and Stone Act of 1878, Fulton proposed an idea that was eventually adopted, in that he proposed that 25 percent of revenues generated on reserved forest lands (called national forests after 1907) be returned to counties as partial compensation to counties for the loss of potentially alienable land from their tax rolls; see Glicemae, 64.

44. These include the first monument, Devils Tower (1906) and many that immediately followed: Petrified Forest (1906), Lassen Peak (1907), Muir Woods (1908), Pinnacles (1908), the Grand Canyon (1908), and Jewel Cave (1908).

45. Ashland *Tidings*, August 1, 1907. Watson pursued varied interests and several career paths throughout his life before practicing law in Ashland. There is precious little published information about him, though his short-lived vocation as a timber cruiser in the Klamath River country is instructive; Watson, "War on the Forest Primeval: Recollections of a Western Timber Locator," *Overland Monthly* 75 (June 1920), 506-508,

553-556. He also produced reminiscences for the Ashland *Tidings* which appeared on October 25, 29, and 30 of 1923, and then May 28, June 8, July 2, and 8 of 1924.

46. Miller, "The Sea of Silence," *Sunset* 13:5 (September, 1904), 395-404.

47. Anderson to the Forester (Gifford Pinchot), August 3, 1907, as transcribed from J.H. Billingslea, Forest Supervisor (of the Siskiyou NF) to Regional Forester, January 27, 1931, Boundaries (L) file, copy in OCNM archives. It is unclear as to whether Veach could have succeeded in gaining control of the cave as Harkness and Burch had with a location notice, given how a patent could not be issued without a survey and that the Forest Service had orders from Pinchot to stop such subterfuge of the land laws.

48. Fred Bennett, Acting Commissioner (of the GLO) to Registrar and Receiver (of the Land Office), Roseburg, Oregon, August 12, 1907, transcribed as Exhibit A of a memorandum from C. Richard Neely, USDI assistant regional solicitor to NPS regional director, May 26, 1976.

49. Draft special use permit attached to a letter from Anderson to Pinchot, December 16, 1907. This represented something of a response to Pinchot's request on October 30 for a full report on Oregon Caves.

50. L.J. Cooper, History of the Siskiyou National Forest, Section III, 5. Their work centered on claims made under the Timber and Stone Act of 1878, most of which Cooper described as fraudulent, as well as claims resulting from the Forest Homestead Act of 1906.

51. Anderson to the Forester, January 1, 1908, referencing Pinchot's letter to Anderson dated October 30, 1907. In the latest request for a permit, Oium proposed an entry fee to be set by the Forest Service which the permittees could collect in exchange for a lease of ten acres and the improvements outlined in 1907; Oium to Anderson, October 13, 1908.

52. Dean ran a convenient measure of 60 chains by 80 chains within the parcel withdrawn in 1907, something that could be overlain on the U.S. Geological Survey map of the Grants Pass quadrangle printed in 1908. Acreage was calculated on the basis of a square chain being one-tenth of an acre. For more on the conventions of surveying and the implications of using the Gunter chain in such work, see Arno Linklater, *Measuring America: How the United States was Shaped by the Greatest Land Sale in American History* (New York: Plume, 2003).

53. Dean, Report on Proposed National Monument and Description of Survey with map sheet, October 23, 1908.

54. Anderson to Pinchot, October 29, 1908.

55. "The Caves of Oregon," Grants Pass *Oregon Observer*, September

19, 1906. Such vandalism is certainly implied in one article about Walter Burch's plans for a return to Josephine County on a projected trip in which he intended to obtain "a lot" of specimens to exhibit at the World's Fair held over the summer of 1905 in Portland; Glendale (Ore.) *News*, July 28, 1905. Vandalism was mentioned in one article that during Miller's visit; "Oregon Caves in National Park," Portland *Oregon Journal*, August 16, 1907. In this article Anderson had worked with Jefferson Myers (one of Miller's companions who hailed from Portland) for "several days" to locate the boundary lines of the "new park" (the four sections withdrawn) prior to the excursion.

56. Anderson, "Oregon Caves National Monument," report of February 1909 attached to transmittal by E.T. Allen, District Forester, who wrote to the Forester (Henry S. Graves), June 19, 1909.

57. It remains the smallest area that is predominately "natural" within the National Park System, save for Timpanogas Cave National Monument in Utah.

58. Anderson to the District Forester (E.T. Allen), February 10, 1909.

59. Gilbert Thompson, Map of the State of Oregon showing the Classification of Lands and Forests [1900], included with Gannett, *The Forests of Oregon*.

60. Section 2, An Act for the preservation of American antiquities, June 8, 1906 (34 Stat. 225).

61. A draft proclamation was submitted by H.O. Stabler on February 16, 1909, presumably to the district forester; C.J. Buck to the Forester, January 13, 1931. This and other papers were then conveyed to Washington; E.T. Allen to the Forester, March 1, 1909.

62. Pinchot quoted by David A. Clary, *Timber and the Forest Service* (Lawrence, KS: University Press of Kansas, 1986), 22.

63. For more about Pinchot's publicity campaign, see Jeff LaLande, "The 'Forest Ranger' in Popular Fiction," *Forest History Today* (Spring/Fall 2003), 2-28.

64. William G. Robbins, *The Oregon Environment: Development vs. Preservation, 1905-1950* (Corvallis: Oregon State University Press, 1975), 8-9. A shortened version of this discussion is in Robbins, *Landscapes of Promise: the Oregon Story, 1900-1940* (Seattle: University of Washington Press, 1997), 240.

65. Teal to Pinchot, June 21, 1909.

66. Overton W. Price to Teal, July 6, 1909.

67. E.T. Allen to Pinchot, June 19, 1909. Watson wrote a self-published regional travelogue that included Oregon Caves which put forth the case for a prehistoric Siskiyou "island" somewhat in line with what

Thomas Condon had taught about the state's geology, whereby the Blue Mountains and the Siskiyou Mountains had roughly similar orogenies but had been separated by as yet little understood forces. Watson's book appeared in January 1909 and may have helped justify the proclamation's description of the cave as being of "unusual scientific interest and importance," though little in the way of references had yet appeared in contemporary scientific literature; Watson, *Prehistoric Siskiyou Island and the Marble Halls of Oregon*. Reports from the Oregon Conservation Commission did not mention the Oregon Caves until 1911, when it provided a short acknowledgment of Watson's role in the proclamation; see *Oregon Historical Quarterly* 20 (1919), 400.

68. Anderson to E.T. Allen, June 18, 1909.

69. Miller, "Oregon's Marble Halls," *Sunset* 23:3 (September 1909), 227-235. His nickname for the cave, "The Marble Halls of Oregon" had already been pitched, starting with news accounts of the excursion in 1907; "Oregon Cave is wonderful place," Portland *Oregonian*, August 15, 1907, and "The Wonderful Cave of Oregon," Jacksonville *Times*, August 24, 1907. The nickname was also used by W.L. Grissley in "Oregon Caves Rivals the Mammoth Cave of Kentucky, Portland *Oregonian*, July 19, 1908, and again in "The Marble Halls of Oregon," *Pacific Outlook*, August 1, 1908. The trip in 1907 was entirely aimed at generating publicity, as Watson and Miller were accompanied by Jefferson Myers, a man Miller credited with being the leading organizer of the Lewis & Clark Exposition (World's Fair) of 1905 held in Portland. Their guides, Frank Nickerson and John Kincaid, harkened back to earlier attempts to develop the cave. Nickerson, however, actively disassociated himself from Smith's enterprise in the 1890s; Watson, *Prehistoric Siskiyou Island and the Marble Halls of Oregon*, 134.

70. Taft, proclamation 876, July 12, 1909.

71. Frank Bond, chief clerk at the GLO, wrote all 28 proclamations according to Hal Rothman in *Preserving Different Pasts: The American National Monuments* (Chicago and Urbana: University of Illinois Press, 1989), 81. In this case, however, Bond must have simply revised the existing Forest Service draft.

72. "Marble Halls are Reserved," Portland *Oregon Journal*, July 15, 1909. Accounts of the Ellis tragedy are notable for being melodramatic; "Frank Ellis shoots himself," Grants Pass *Oregon Observer*, August 4, 1909; "Widow Mourns beside her Dead," Portland *Oregonian*, August 4, 1909; "A Terrible Tragedy in Depths of Oregon Caves," Grants Pass *Courier*, August 6, 1909; and Cornelia Templeton Jewett, "Woman's Bravery put to Awful Test," *The Woman's National Daily*, September 25, 1909, 9-10.

73. Guides were usually obtained at either Williams or Kerby, depending upon which route was selected. Some Josephine County residents like those in the Ellis Party, however, chose to bring their own gear over the trails improved by the Forest Service that led to the cave.

74. C.J. Buck, acting chief of operations, to Anderson, July 13, 1909.

75. Cooper, History of the Siskiyou National Forest, 4.

76. R.L. Glisan, a prominent Portland dentist and member of the Mazamas (a climbing group started by Steel) wrote to the commission's chairman, J.N. Teal, about the cave in September 1910. Teal, who had earlier contacted Pinchot with Watson's endorsement of the monument proclamation, forwarded a letter about what Glisan saw during his visit. One formation had been badly splintered by souvenir hunters who left pieces of it on the floor, an observation later reported by the state's largest newspaper along with the Forest Service intention to hire someone to protect the monument; Glisan to Teal, September 24, 1910; Teal to District Forester, September 26, 1910; Charles H. Flory, Acting District Forester, to R.L. Fromme, Forest Supervisor, October 27, 1910; C.S. Chapman, District Forester, to Teal, November 26, 1910; "Siskiyou Caves to be Protected," Portland *Oregonian*, December 4, 1910.

77. This may well constitute the first instance of "interpretation" in a national park or monument funded through Congressional appropriation, but due to the fact it came through the Forest Service does not appear to be considered a precedent by those affiliated with the NPS; C. Frank Brockman, "Park Naturalists and the Evolution of National Park Service Interpretation through World War II," *Journal of Forest History* 22:1 (January 1978), 24-43.

78. Fromme to District Forester, August 29, 1911.

79. See Clary, *Timber and the Forest Service*, 3-28.

80. Beckham, Cultural Resource Overview, 96.

81. "Caves line is planned," Portland *Oregonian*, February 2, 1911; "Caves line is aided," Portland *Oregonian*, February 4, 1911.

82. A photo of the terminus at Waters Creek is in Len Ramp and Norman Peterson, *Geological and Mineral Resources of Josephine County, Oregon*, Bulletin 100, Department of Geology and Mineral Industries (Salem: State Printer, 1979), 32.

83. Anderson to Fromme, February 9, 1912; Fromme to Anderson, February 13, 1912. The application was in the name of T. H. Johnson of Portland; Henry S. Graves (chief forester) to Rep. William C. Hawley, April 1, 1912.

84. George H. Cecil, District Forester, to Graves, March 1, 1912; "Tourist Hotel may soon rise at the Josephine Caves," Grants Pass

Courier, March 21, 1912; James B. Adams, Assistant Forester, to Cecil, April 2, 1912; "Desire fee to enter caves," Grants Pass *Courier*, April 8, 1912. In a somewhat conciliatory move, Fromme appointed Richard Sowell as the forest guard at the cave for 1912, also granting a special use permit for his wife to furnish tent lodgings and meals on national forest land just outside the monument; "Welcome Visitors to the Oregon Caves," Grants Pass *Courier*, June 13, 1912.

85. "National Park Projected," Portland *Oregonian*, July 8, 1912; Fromme to District Forester, July 9, 1912.

86. These were Saddle Mountain in Clatsop County and Humbug Mountain in Curry County. Neither successfully garnered that designation, though both later became units in the state park system; for Saddle Mountain, see "Formation of National Park," Astoria *Budget*, January 23, 1912; "Amended Bill Passes," Astoria *Astorian*, March 23, 1912.

87. For the text of these bills see Catherine Franks, et al (comps.), Legislative History of Oregon Caves National Monument, NPS regional library, Seattle, 1986, volume 1, 11-16. The rationale is described in "Oregon Caves National Park," Grants Pass *Courier*, January 17, 1913.

88. Cecil to MacDuff, January 13, 1913; MacDuff to Cecil, January 16, 1913. Only 250 people visited the monument during the 1912 season.

89. C.J. Buck to MacDuff, January 17, 1913; MacDuff to Cecil, January 18, 1913.

90. *The Josephine County Caves: A Magnificent Labyrinth of Halls Located Near Grants Pass, Oregon* [1913], booklet on file at the Southern Oregon Historical Society, Jacksonville.

91. "Mazamas off to Marble Caves," Grants Pass *Courier*, May 30, 1913; "Mazamas Return from Caves," Grants Pass *Courier*, June 6, 1913; "Mazamas Resolve," Grants Pass *Courier*, July 18, 1913. A summary of the trip is in Mary Henthorne, "The Oregon Caves," *Mazama* 4:2 (December 1913), 57-60. The Cave Day event was summarized by Cleaveland Hilson, "Celebrate Josephine Cave Day: First Annual Observance is a Success," Grants Pass *Courier*, June 21, 1914.

92. Graves saw facilities at Oregon Caves as the needed precursor to future development of the Siskiyou National Forest; Graves to District Forester, September 4, 1913; "Resolution" by the GPCC, October 15, 1913; C.J. Buck to Graves, October 22, 1913.

93. This began in earnest with an endorsement prior to introduction of the park bills; "Hotel Men Want Road to Caves," Grants Pass *Courier*, November 22, 1912.

94. "Caves to be exploited," Portland *Oregonian*, February 13, 1914.

95. Joseph N. Teal, et al., *Third Annual Report of the Oregon*

Conservation Commission (Salem: State Printer, 1910), 35.

96. One example among the many contemporary proposals that failed was a proposed road to Mount Ashland from the Rogue Valley, where a congressman from Oregon asked for $13,500; "A Highway for Mt. Ashland," Ashland *Tidings*, January 22, 1912.

97. Work began that summer under the direction of the Army Corps of Engineers, who used a specifically earmarked portion of a much larger appropriation aimed at Yellowstone for their work at Crater Lake. Steel supported national park status for Oregon Caves, citing the need for facilities and development there; "Crater Lake National Park," Grants Pass *Courier*, June 13, 1913.

98. "State cannot build road to Crater Lake," Portland *Oregon Journal*, February 15, 1910; "The Crater Lake Decision," Medford *Mail Tribune*, February 13, 1910. Supporters in Jackson County then raised funds for construction through private subscriptions, but the small amount of seed money meant that Medford still looked to the state for additional funds. By 1911 the governor assigned convicts to construction work in order for the project to continue with county funds. An editorial in the Medford paper supported national park status for Oregon Caves, but made mention of the "local affair" ruling in its appeal for state aid in building a road to the cave; "A new national park," Medford *Mail Tribune*, January 14, 1913.

99. Robert W. Hadlow, Columbia River Highway National Historic Landmark nomination, Oregon Department of Transportation, February 4, 2000, 59-60. The number of cars cited is something of a midpoint during a five-year surge; in 1910 the number totaled only 2,500, but increased to 23,585 by 1915; George Kramer, "The Pacific Highway in Oregon," *Oregon Heritage* 1:4 (Winter/Spring 1995), 5.

100. Hadlow, Columbia River Highway nomination, 60. The highway served as impetus because it originated in Multnomah County, where the state's largest city, Portland, grew from 46,000 in 1890 to 207,000 residents by 1910. Railroad tycoon and good roads advocate Sam Hill provided the spark for a highway commission by inviting the entire legislature to his estate on the Washington side of the Columbia), where he built demonstration roads complete with hard surfacing.

101. Kramer, "The Pacific Highway in Oregon," 5-7. Josephine County had some of the worst sections, one being the route over Sexton Mountain, something not lost on the boosters who promoted bonds; "Pacific Highway and Better Roads," Grants Pass *Courier*, May 16, 1913.

102. "Plan road to caves from Illinois Valley," Medford *Mail Tribune*, June 25, 1914.

103. The Josephine County tax levy in 1908 was some 14 mills, with roads receiving 2 mills; Grants Pass *Courier*, January 10, 1908; "National Forests as aid in the building of roads," Portland *Oregon Journal*, October 11, 1914. A subsequent news article made note that Graves estimated in 1914 that roads adjacent to timber greatly affected the stumpage value of "ripe" trees, as that time estimated to be some 31 billion board feet on the national forests of northern California and southern Oregon.

104. The Caves Camp Company built a tent "city" at the confluence of Sucker, Cave, and Grayback creeks as of July 31, 1914 and competed with the Three Creeks Camp on Sucker Creek, Grants Pass *Courier*, July 31 1914. By 1915 a furnished camp on the Williams side had appeared, one with wood floor tents and beds. Horses could also be furnished at "Caves Camp" for the trip; Grants Pass Courier, July 16, 1915.

105. "Hawley working for Oregon Caves," Medford *Mail Tribune*, December 29, 1915.

3. Boosterism's Public-Private Partnership

1. Most famously articulated by Frederick J. Turner, "The Significance of the Frontier to American History," *Annual Report of the American Historical Association for the Year 1893* (Washington, D.C.: Government Printing Office, 1894), 189-227. Turner's thesis has fueled more debate among historians in the United States than any other single piece of writing in American historiography; see, for example, Richard W. Etulain (comp.), *Does the Frontier Experience make America Exceptional?* (Boston: Bedford/ St. Martins, 1999).

2. LaLande, "The 'Forest Ranger' in Popular Fiction," 2-28.

3. Stephen J. Pyne, *Tending Fires: Coping with America's Wildland Fires* (Washington, D.C.: Island Press, 2004), 88-90.

4. Cover inscription of *American Motorist* magazine (4:8, August 1912) used to illustrate an article by David Cole, "Magazines for Early Motorists," *Society for Commercial Archeology Journal* (Spring 1996), 6-11.

5. Marguerite S. Shaffer, *See America First: Tourism and National Identity, 1880-1940* (Washington, D.C.: Smithsonian Institution Press, 2001), 138-140.

6. The act was passed on July 11, 1916; Program Management Function, State of California, Department of Public Works, Some Historical Information Concerning Federal Aid for Highways, June 1972, 1-2. In addition to triggering the creation of the Oregon State Highway Department, the legislation also led to the transformation of the Portland

Auto Club (organized in 1905) into the Oregon State Motor Association as of December 16, 1916 so that the entity might produce the first signs and maps for automobilists; History of Automobile Club of Oregon, January 1977, typescript, 2.

7. B.J. Finch, Acting District Engineer, to J.S. Bright, Senior Highway Engineer, September 18, 1917.

8. "Building of the Highway to the Josephine Caves has been ordered," Grants Pass *Courier*, November 21, 1919. The legislation became known as the Post Office Act of February 28, 1919. Figures are in David G. Havlick, "Behind the Wheel: A look back at public land roads," *Forest History Today* (Spring 2002), 12.

9. The job required 95,000 cubic yards of excavation (much of it side hill) and 100,000 pounds of dynamite to remove rocks. Funding for the $126,000 grading contract was split between the state highway commission and the Forest Service, with entire job coming to roughly $152,000; J.A. Elliott, Senior Highway Engineer to the BPR district engineer, September 9, 1921. This figure differs from the total of $205,000 cited in the state highway commission's biennial report for 1921-22 (p. 339) which also mentions that separate contracts were awarded to C. Frank Rhodes and White Brown & Leahy Company. The funding formula dictated that two units of road be constructed; one between Robinson's Corner and the forest boundary (roughly MP 6 and MP11), whereas the other was completely within the Siskiyou National Forest.

10. "Opening road to marble cave celebrated," Medford *Mail Tribune*, June 21, 1922. Actual completion did not come until October 2. The visitation figure for the 1922 season is from the biennial report of the Oregon State Highway Commission (Salem: State Printer, 1922), 341. District Forester C.J. Buck gave the visitation figure for 1921 in an article published a decade later as 1,100. Buck also made the point that the Oregon Caves Highway was funded as "recreation road" funded by an appropriation that stipulated a cooperative effort with the state highway department; Buck, "Forest Recreation in Oregon and Washington," *The Oregon Motorist* (August 1931), 15.

11. Oregon State Highway Commission, *Fifth Biennial Report* (1921-22), 340.

12. O.S. Blanchard to C.H. Pursell, BPR, May 31, 1924; Roy A. Klein, OSHD, to Pursell, June 7, 1924. Boosters in California had previously dubbed what is now U.S. 101 from San Francisco to Crescent City "the Redwood Highway" and agreed with compatriots in Oregon on the desirability of extending that designation to Grants Pass; John Robinson, "The Redwood Highway," *California Highways and Public Works* 43

(June-July 1964), 2-11. Federal aid monies continued to increase during this period, with major legislation passed in 1921 and 1925.

13. The Oregon Caves post office in Caves City was created on July 30, 1924; Maynard C. Drowson, "Oregon's Own Marble Halls," Salem *Capital Journal*, June 15, 1968, 1. The importance of Oregon's gasoline tax in financing the state's highways is described in Lawrence C. Merriam, Jr., *Oregon's Highway Park System* (Salem: State Printer, 1992), 262.

14. "Caves Highway Widening Necessary," Grants Pass *Courier*, September 9, 1926; "Caravan Urges Widening for Caves Highway," Grants Pass *Courier*, October 14, 1926. Surfacing with gravel took place on the Oregon Caves Highway in 1925 over the first 12 miles, at about the time that contractors graded the Redwood Highway between its junction with the Caves Highway and Waldo; S.H. Probert, State Highway Work in Southern Oregon, December 9, 1925, in OSHD, 76A-90, AD-1 General Correspondence 1925, Box 29, Oregon State Archives, Salem.

15. Unlike the earlier project, this was done by day labor instead of a contract due to relatively small yearly allotments of around $15,000; H.D. Farmer to A.B. Lewellen, February 2, 1927, and W.H. Lynch to L.I. Hewes, January 30, 1929. This work also included straightening the most dangerous curves, especially as more funding became available; "Caves Road Shovel Progressing Rapidly," Grants Pass *Courier*, April 6, 1928.

16. "Traveling Oregon's Highways and By-ways," *Oregon Highways*, March 12, 1927. Some boosters such as Grants Pass attorney O.S. Blanchard stressed the road's importance in lowering freight rates to San Francisco, especially if work in the Illinois Valley was completed; Blanchard to Roy Klein, State Highway Engineer, April 1, 1926, with attachment from the Grants Pass *Courier*, "Freight Rates to S.F. Cut Via Redwood Route," OSHD, 76A-90, AD-1 General Correspondence 1926, Box 29, File 100-05, Oregon State Archives, Salem.

17. "Caves attraction to receive much needed attention," Medford *Mail Tribune*, March 1, 1929; H.D. Farmer to files, March 28, 1929. By the end of 1929 most of the road had been widened to 16 feet; Oregon Caves Forest Road Project 13-A3B2 completion report, 1.

18. "Work on Caves Road Complete," Grants Pass *Bulletin*, August 21, 1931, and "Paving to Caves now Completed, Dustless," Grants Pass *Bulletin*, September 11, 1931. Reports differ as to how wide the completed road was, with some suggesting that the paved surface was as much as 18 feet; E.P. Leavitt to [NPS] Regional Director, May 26, 1945.

19. A campaign conducted largely in Jackson County from 1926 to 1929 clamored for a road to link the Oregon Caves with Medford via Williams, an effort that failed in the face of reluctant local taxpayers (who

voted against forming a road district) and the Forest Service; "Caves Route to be voted upon," Jackson County *News*, January 8, 1926, February 5, 1926, and February 19, 1926; "Caves Road in under eye of Forest Bureau," Medford *Mail Tribune*, September 30, 1927; "Meeting called for Caves Road Advocacy," Medford *Mail Tribune*, January 30, 1929; "Caves Road will be discussed at Medford Meeting," Medford *Mail Tribune*, February 14, 1929.

20. "Honey Combed Mountain of Southern Oregon Filled with Marvels of Nature's Art," Grants Pass *Courier*, Travelogue, June 1931.

21. Most hotels, originally cited in city centers next to rail stations, did not possess their own parking lots until World War II or later. Parking on the street was generally prohibited, so garages (often located some distance from a hotel) were a requirement for travelers using automobiles. For more about the evolution toward auto camping in southwest Oregon, see Steve Mark, "Save the Auto Camps!" *Southern Oregon Heritage* 3:4 (1998), 29-32.

22. Warren James Belasco, *Americans on the Road: from Auto Camp to Motel, 1910-1945* (Cambridge, Mass.: MIT Press, 1979), 77.

23. The demand for camping directly corresponded to increases in automobile ownership. One million Americans owned cars in 1912, a figure that increased 15 fold in eleven years. It jumped another four million in 1924, a year when five million automobiles took their occupants to campgrounds. Such surges placed demands on the system most states used, where motorists had to register their cars when they crossed state lines, but also increased the potential for privately run campgrounds with or without cabins; "More Time Urged for Auto Permits," Portland *Oregonian*, February 21, 1926.

24. Attendance at the Grants Pass Auto Camp, which was located adjacent to Riverside Park, reached 5,200 cars that year; Jack Sutton, *110 Years with Josephine*, 205.

25. Norman Hayner, "Auto Camps in the Evergreen Playground," *Social Forces* 9:1 (October 1930), 256-266.

26. Cabins in commercial camps were generally kept small (12 feet wide and from 12 to 16 feet long), separated from other cabins compartments for cars, though this was not always the case. Although "kitchenettes" could sometimes be found in the early cabins, showers and toilets were usually located in a central bath house. Resort cabins, by contrast, generally featured more amenities and had plumbing; Mark, "Save the Auto Camps!"

27. William C. Tweed, *Recreational Site Planning and Improvement in National Forests, 1891-1942,* Publication FS-354 (Washington, DC:

Government Printing Office, 1980), 4. The park encompassed waterfalls on the Oregon side and administered by the Forest Service in conjunction with parks established by the city of Portland. The secretary's declaration appeared to be a way of blunting a national park proposal centered on Mount Hood, a bill that if enacted would have resulted in a land transfer to the Department of the Interior.

28. Tweed, *Recreational Site Planning*, 13.

29. Siskiyou National Forest, Oregon Caves Recreation Area, survey map of December 1922. The map shows a camp area with notation indicating the Congressional authorization, OCNM map files. The urgency for such legislation was evidently provided by the highway which vastly increased visitation at Oregon Caves. One writer suggested that at least some of the area was already in use as an auto camp during the summer of 1922; this appears as a glancing reference in "The Mystic Caves of Oregon," *The Oregon Motorist* 3:3 (August 1923), 6.

30. E.H. MacDaniels to District Forester, September 11, 1923, 2. Supervisor MacDaniels characterized demand as so heavy that a septic tank and possibly flush toilets were needed, in addition to a larger campground and more roadwork at the site. Initial construction, according to an earlier estimate, was to cost $1,830, almost one-third of the entire campground appropriation.

31. C.J. Buck, "Forest Recreation in Oregon and Washington," *The Oregon Motorist* (August 1931), 7-19.

32. USDA-Forest Service, North Pacific District, *Road and Information Map for the National Forests of Oregon* (GPO: 1923). These maps continued to be printed on an annual basis through the 1930s.

33. USDA-Forest Service, North Pacific District, *An Ideal Vacationland: the National Forests in Oregon* (GPO: 1923).

34. Steve Mark, "Thinking Like a Park," *Wilderness Journal* 1:1 (September 1989), 8-11. By the end of Greeley's tenure as chief in 1928, the wilderness argument in conjunction with a conscious effort to improve public relations had resulted in the Forest Service fending off about three-quarters of the proposals for land transfers to the NPS.

35. The Forest Service promoted a "purer" form of Edenic landscape for other reasons, not least because the inheritors of eighteenth century romanticism (the prose and poetry that gave rise to the wilderness aesthetic) abhorred what they perceived as commercialism in the national parks; Thomas R. Dunlap, *Faith in Nature: Environmentalism as Religious Quest* (Seattle: University of Washington Press, 2004).

36. C.J. Buck, "Oregon's Highway Park System," undated manuscript [c. 1927], in the A.L. Peck Papers, Highway folder, Oregon State

University archives, Corvallis; also quoted by Chester Armstrong, *Oregon State Parks History* (Salem: State Printer, 1965), 10.

37. V.L. Sexton, Oregon's Wildlife Resource, study by the Oregon State Planning Board, November 1936. There were a number of refuges in Oregon, as was also the case in California, where state wildlife officials thought that game species could be protected by keeping them in one area where prohibitions on hunting and fishing remained in effect. By the early 1950s, however, managers in both states had found that regulations in all areas proved more effective in protecting game populations, so all but the national wildlife refuges were disbanded; Gay Halland Berrien, "Trinity Game Refuge," *Trinity 1997* (Weaverville, California: Trinity County Historical Society, 1997), 34-39.

38. "Game Refuge," Grants Pass *Courier*, April 10, 1926. One writer linked a deer which ate candy provided by visitors to the refuge, where carrying a gun was not allowed; Sandy Grant, "Jimmie Deer," Philadelphia *Queen's Gardens*, January 22, 1927. A tame deer fit the Edenic ideal exemplified by the landscape gardens, as did the role of Dick Rowley as solitary hermit and gardener, who also supposedly allowed deer to sleep on his bed.

39. Forest Service officials stressed publicly that national forest facilities were not intended to compete with those in national and state parks, but rather supplement what was available within a state or region; Buck, "Forest Recreation in Oregon and Washington," 18.

40. Munger was accompanied by one of the potential applicants for a permit on the inspection trip; Munger to Cecil, May 2, 1917, 9. The solicitor's opinion was referenced in a letter from E.A. Sherman to Cecil, January 15, 1917, 1. The Term Occupancy Act served as an impetus for recreational developments elsewhere in the national forests; Tweed, *Recreational Site Planning*, 3-4.

41. N.F. MacDuff to District Forester, January 25, 1917, 1. Additional details are in "Old Attire Needed for Visit to Caves," Portland *Oregonian*, July 15, 1917, 10. Another source is Hamilton M. Laing, "By Motor and Mule to the Marble Halls," *Sunset* (November 1917), 74-80. The author's great aunt rode a horse to Oregon Caves that summer on one of her weekends when employed as the home extension agent for Jackson and Josephine counties; Dawna Curler, "Anne McCormick: A Modern Lady for Modern Times—One Woman's Influence on Southern Oregon's Home Extension," *Southern Oregon Heritage Today* 8:4 (Autumn 2005), 8-10.

42. E.H. MacDaniels, Report on Oregon Caves, February 14, 1920, 1; "Information for Tourists who desire to visit Oregon Caves," Grants

Pass *Courier*, July 30, 1919. Many of the campers used the terrace sometimes called "Government Camp," now the site of the Chalet.

43. Buck to MacDaniels, February 20, 1920; P.G. Guthrie Memorandum, October 15, 1921, 2.

44. Buck to MacDaniels, October 21, 1921; January 14, 1922; April 24, 1922.

45. MacDaniels to District Forester, April 27, 1922; "Caves Camp ready in June," Grants Pass *Courier*, May 10, 1922; Buck to MacDaniels, September 21, 1922; O.S. Blanchard, Grants Pass Chamber of Commerce, to Buck, December 18, 1922.

46. MacDaniels to District Forester, January 19, 1922; Buck to MacDaniels, March 16, 1923. The seven stockholders were O.S. Blanchard, Frank Mashburn, Ed W. Miller, Wilford Allen, S.H. Baker, John Hampshire, and A.E. Voorhies. Sabin was to manage the resort operation.

47. USFS Special Use Permit [January 1923], 2.

48. "Forest Men Visit Oregon Caves," Portland *Oregon Journal*, June 24, 1917. Waugh did more in the way of advocacy than actual design for the Forest Service; Waugh, "Landscape Architecture in the Forests," *American Forests* 27:327 (March 1921), 143-146.

49. These styles were "picturesque and distinctive" in accordance with the Edenic ideal celebrated in American landscape architecture during that period, though they can be found in the work of Andrew Jackson Downing that served as the basis for later pattern books; Downing, *The Theory and Practice of Landscape Gardening* (New York: Orange Judd, 1841).

50. Fred Lockley, "Impressions and Observations of the Journal Man," [interview with George Sabin], Portland *Oregon Journal*, August 17, 1936.

51. MacDaniels to District Forester, April 9, 1923, 1-2. Some sources credited Peck with the entire architectural scheme; "Construction to start soon," Grants Pass *Courier*, April 22, 1923, and E.T. Reed, "Oregon Caves are of major interest," Corvallis *Gazette-Times*, August 4, 1924, 2.

52. MacDaniels to District Forester, December 22, 1923, 2.

53. McDaniels to Buck, September 11, 1923; Buck to McDaniels, September 19, 1923, 1-2. The company's reluctance seemed to center on the unknown market for such a hotel, especially one built within a mile of where an existing hostelry, the Lind Home Resort, already represented competition.

54. A.H. Wright, Forest Supervisor, to Sabin, October 9, 1924, 4; "The Oregon Caves are now open," *The Pacific Northwest Home* [1926].

55. The lamp house/studio was placed on a small terrace that had been previously leveled over the objections of the forest supervisor, who related how the superintendent of Crater Lake National Park did not like the idea of a detached building being so conspicuous near the cave entrance; Wright to Sabin, February 11, 1924.

56. Wright to District Forester, December 17, 1926, 1.

57. The beginning of softening the Forest Service position on developing Grayback came, ironically enough, from Buck making an allowance for replacing some of the tent houses with cottages as early as the spring of 1922; Buck to Forest Supervisor, April 24, 1922, 2. The guide dormitory was listed as being 28 feet by 16 feet with flush toilet, large enough to house 14 guides; F.W. Cleator memorandum for Lands, July 9, 1927, 1.

58. J.H. Billingslea, Forest Supervisor, to District Forester, February 28, 1928, 1.

59. Buck to Forest Supervisor, April 29, 1922, 1.

60. Wright to District Forester, December 10, 1925, 2.

61. Ladder replacement occurred during the seasons of 1921 and 1922; Cecil to Chief Forester, January 13, 1923, 2; L.J. Cooper, History of the Siskiyou National Forest, IV-25, 29. Work to widen passageways was ongoing, though a newspaper article from early 1920 mentioned that material removed from floors or ceilings was often dumped into "pits" within the cave. These areas were judged to have "no scenic value," and served to obviate the need to take the "waste" outside; "Forestry officials make winter trip to Josephine Caves and Plan Improvements," Oregon *Observer*, January 21, 1920. Improvements to the trails within and to the monument were also counted, though the forest supervisor stated that they would have been made irregardless due to the necessity for fire control access; Wright to District Forester, December 10, 1925, 1.

62. The effects of candle drippings were mentioned by Buck in a letter to Forest Supervisor MacDaniels, October 26, 1921. Some vandals preferred to scratch their initials on formations then "smoke" them with carbide lanterns, a practice that the Forest Service wanted to halt by installing electric lights; "Defacing the Oregon Caves," Coquille *Sentinel*, September 8, 1922.

63. A.M. Swartley, Oregon Bureau of Mines, and E.H. MacDaniels, Lighting Plan, Oregon Caves, November 20, 1920; Swartley to Henry M. Parks, Oregon Bureau of Mines, April 19, 1921; MacDaniels to the Chief Forester, July 14, 1921; MacDaniels, Memorandum for the Grants Pass Chamber of Commerce, January 25, 1922.

64. Henry C. Wallace, Secretary of Agriculture, to George W. Norris, Chairman of the Senate Committee on Agriculture, February 18, 1924.

65. "Deficiency Bill provides $35,000 for Oregon Caves," Portland *Oregonian*, February 18, 1930. The legislation simply authorized the appropriation which was later attached to a bill enacted in March 1930; "All of funds for scrubbing Oregon Caves," Medford *Mail Tribune*, April 7, 1930. The Forest Service logic resembled the reasoning behind reclamation projects, though the agency's interest in self-supporting national monuments went back to at least 1925; L.F. Kneipp, Assistant Forester, to District Forester, December 1, 1925. Passage of the bill could also be attributed to the Hoover Administration being more amenable to special appropriations for national parks and monuments than previous Republican administrations; Kneipp to District Forester, October 8, 1929. Wording of the act was attached to a letter form Kneipp to the District Forester, March 13, 1929. The company immediately objected to the "pass through" provision, fearing that the six percent of tour fees charged might endanger profitability given how the country had since slipped into the Great Depression; Sam H. Baker to McNary, October 14, 1930; R.Y. Stuart, Chief Forester, to McNary, November 26, 1930.

Officials in the Forest Service noted that the well-publicized report by an independent "Mount Hood Committee" (a group commissioned by the Secretary of Agriculture to recommend ways for recreational development could proceed in the national forest surrounding Oregon's highest peak) backed the idea of imposing fees on users based on the amount of money invested by the government; John D. Guthrie, Acting District Forester, to the Chief Forester, November 21, 1930. He referenced F.L. Olmsted, Jr., et al., *Public Values of the Mount Hood Area*, Senate Document 164 (Washington, DC: Government Printing Office, 1930). As something of a postscript, McNary opposed requiring the concession to maintain improvements financed by the appropriation and felt that fees for guide service should be lowered so as to not allow the concession to "profit unduly by reason of the outlays of federal funds." The concession was not required to pay for the cave lighting financed by the federal government (nor were guide fees lowered), in part because Sabin told McNary that work toward building a $50,000 hotel (the Chateau) would necessarily cease if the company had to pay back the $35,000 appropriation for lights.

66. F.V. Horton, Assistant District Forester, to District Forester, April 26, 1930, 1. Forest Service support for this project arose in 1927, when the company's head guide, Dick Rowley, pointed out a need to wash mud from the cave; J.H. Billingslea, Memorandum of Inspection, July 14, 1927. This concern was likely based on how the Edenic ideal did not include dirty formations and inconvenience to visitors.

67. H.J. Weil, Memorandum for the Assistant to the Solicitor, April 10, 1930. Building another structure seemed least desirable to the Forest Service at the time, but later proved useful as a backup generator during power outages. Adding transformer near the Chalet was part of building the power plant; Charles W. Gowan to James Franklin, June 14, 1930.

68. The earliest survey somewhat approximated the chosen route; Wright to R.W. Rowley, September 16, 1926. A need for the tunnel to accommodate 400 people per day was mentioned in the memorandum of inspection by Billingslea, July 19, 1927. Billingslea mentioned this number again in a letter to the district forester, July 3, 1929.

69. "Forest Service makes survey of Oregon Caves," Grants Pass *Bulletin*, March 21, 1930; [Siskiyou National Forest Lands Division], Proposed Improvements – Oregon Caves, March 28, 1930. The profile was titled "Oregon Caves Exit Tunnel," [1930], one sheet.

70. Some officials in the Forest Service preferred day labor over contracts because of the uncertainties that could be encountered underground; Buck to the Chief Forester, May 24, 1930, 2. Details about the tunnel's construction are in Bruce Muirhead, The History of Oregon Caves Exit Tunnel Construction, October 1985, and are based on an extended interview with one of the Forest Service engineers, Keith Wells.

71. Cleator, Memorandum for Lands, July 9, 1927, 2.

72. The Forest Service seemed to give up on the company making any additional investments at Grayback in 1925. Sabin, however, waited another three years to bring up the subject of a hotel at the monument; Sabin to Buck, December 1, 1928. What appears to have prompted the meeting with Billingslea was a letter from company president Sam Baker to District Forester C.M. Granger, August 6, 1929.

73. Billingslea to District Forester, September 3, 1929, 1. Billingslea also mentioned that Peck suggested additional cabins might be built at two new sites: above the service road to No Name Creek and above the road connecting the main parking area with the Chalet.

74. Forest Service officials expressed concern about the intertwining of permits beginning in October 1929; Buck to Forest Supervisor, October 2, 1929, and Granger to the Chief Forester, October 3, 1929. C.J. Buck subsequently indicated that the hotel would not have been built without the substantial public subsidy made under the auspices of the Forest Service; Buck to the Chief Forester, January 9, 1931. Most of the terms on the 20 year permit had been drafted by June 1, 1931, so the stockholders felt confident in paying for construction materials delivered to the monument so that work could begin in October; "Oregon Caves visited by 28,000 this year," Grants Pass *Bulletin*, October 23, 1931.

75. Sabin to Billingslea, February 12, 1931; Billingslea to Regional Forester, March 9, 1931; F.V. Horton to Forest Supervisor, April 2, 1931. The Forest Supervisor also noted that gas station attendants could prevent auto theft and police the grounds, especially when heavy visitation demanded economizing with parking space; Billingslea, Report on Special Use Application, [1931], 1.

76. "Oregon Caves Elect Officers, Offer Stock," Grants Pass *Bulletin*, January 15, 1932; G.E. Mitchell, Forest Supervisor, to Regional Forester, March 2, 1932, 2, and June 23, 1932, 1-2.

77. Oregon Caves National Monument Development Outline, Utilities, January 1945, 3; the full dimension are in Estimated Cost of Water System, OCNM, September 1949, 1, but the dates of construction are incorrect.

78. Ernest W. Peterson, "New Chalet planned at state cave," Portland *Oregon Journal*, July 31, 1931, Section 6, 1; "Beautiful New Lodge at Caves Near Completion," Medford *Mail Tribune*, August 19, 1932; "Builds Fireplace at Caves Resort," Crescent City *Del Norte Triplicate*, [summer] 1932. As part of publicizing their venture, the company eagerly furnished Lium's perspective drawing which overlaid a photographic backdrop to newspapers and prospective investors; Lium, Perspective Oregon Caves "Chateau," Now Under Construction, [1931].

79. Mitchell to Regional Forester, June 13, 1932; F.V. Horton to Mitchell, June 24, 1932.

80. Albright to Newton B. Drury, Save-the-Redwoods League, September 21, 1931. This may have been prompted by Albright's mother and brother visiting Oregon Caves earlier in the summer; Albright to Sabin, May 2, 1933.

81. Toll to Albright, February 6, 1932, attached to inspection report of visit made on October 19, 1931. Sabin to Buck, April 15, 1933.

82. Albright to Sabin, May 2, 1933; Sabin to Albright, May 8, 1933.

83. Executive Order 6166, June 10, 1933; text is in USDI-NPS, *Laws Related to the National Park Service* (Washington, DC: Government Printing Office, 1944), 203-205.

84. The only record of the conference is in an oral history interview with Leon Kneipp conducted by Amelia Fry and others from the Regional Oral History Office at the Bancroft Library in Berkeley during 1964-65. Apparently Kneipp felt he reached an agreement with Arno Cammerer and Arthur Demaray that the NPS would take only three or four of the 16, a position subsequently overruled by Albright—though the director did not inform chief forester R.Y. Stuart of this. According to Kneipp, Stuart did not object to the executive order's provision about national

monuments because he thought a gentleman's agreement had been reached; Kneipp interview, "Land Planning and Acquisition, U.S. Forest Service," 78. For additional background about the interaction between the two agencies during this period, see Hal K. Rothman, "A Regular Ding – Dong Fight," Agency Culture and Evolution in the NPS – USFS Dispute, 1916-1937, *Western Historical Quarterly* 20:2 (May 1989), 141-161.

85. The 16 national monuments included Chiricahuya (Arizona), Devil's Postpile (California), Gila Cliff Dwelling (New Mexico), Holy Cross (Colorado), Jewel Cave (South Dakota), Lava Beds (California), Lehman Cave (Nevada), Mount Olympus (Washington), Old Kasaan (Alaska), Saguaro (Arizona), Sunset Crater (Arizona), Timpanogos Cave (Utah), Tonto (Arizona), Walnut Canyon (Arizona), Wheeler (Colorado) and Oregon Caves: USDI press release, April 1, 1934.

86. Mitchell to Regional Forester, September 5, 1934, with attachment titled "Administrative Statistics, Oregon Caves National Monument in Siskiyou National Forest, same date: Kneipp to Regional Forester, October 1, 1934; F.V. Horton to Mitchell, October 8, 1934.

4. Improving a Little Landscape Garden

1. Stephanie Ross, *What Gardens Mean* (Chicago: University of Chicago Press, 2000), 57.

2. These landscape features naturally had a place in classical gardens; see John Dixon Hunt, *Garden and Grove: The Italian Renaissance Garden in the English Imagination, 1600-1750* (Philadelphia: University of Pennsylvania Press, 1986), 11-14.

3. There is a rich literature about the cultural perception of nature and how it developed during this period; see, for example, Paul Shepard, *Man in the Landscape: A Historic View of the Esthetics of Nature* (New York: Knopf, 1967); and Denis Cosgrove, *Social Formation and Symbolic Landscape* (Madison: University of Wisconsin Press, 1998).

4. Susan Lasdun, *The English Park: Royal, Private, and Public* (New York: Vendome Press, 1992), 135-186.

5. John F. Sears, *Sacred Places: American Tourist Attractions in the Nineteenth Century* (New York: Oxford University Press, 1989), 31-48.

6. Examples include the Petrified Gardens, Banana Grove, Paradise Lost, Neptune's Grotto, Niagara Falls, Bird of Paradise, and many more.

7. Nelson Macduff, Forest Supervisor, to District Forester, January 26, 1917, 7.

8 Bruce Muirhead, Names "Created" by Dick Rowley, and A History

of the Names Used in the Past and Present Along the Present Tour Route, both September 1985, OCNM files.

9. "Dick Rowley – Original Cave Man," Grants Pass *Courier*, June 23, 1922.

10. The "practical hermit" persona came across in a number of news articles about Rowley and information distributed by the concessionaire; see, for example, Oregon Caves Resort, Dick Rowley and the Oregon Caves [1936], Rowley file, OCNM.

11. Transcription of Rowley's tour dated August 1934 with notes by Bruce Muirhead, July 1984. For more about how the route changed once the exit tunnel was completed, see Muirhead, A History of the Development of the Oregon Caves Tour Route, September 1985, OCNM files.

12. F.V. Horton, Memorandum for the District Forester, April 20, 1930, 2.

13. Horton memorandum, 3. Planning for colored lights started in 1927, when the company first expressed its desire for such effects; F.W. Cleator, Memorandum for Lands, July 9, 1927, 1. Some guides during the 1930s and 40s chose to provide the lighting effect of Dante's Inferno at the "balcony" above the Ghost Room, prior to their tour party entering the exit tunnel; Bud Breitmayer to the author, April 29, 2006, 2.

14. Seatic wax candles were used in caves and elsewhere for illumination from 1860 or so until roughly 1917, when carbide lamps superceded them. Carbide lamps (or acetylene lanterns, as they were sometimes called) went into commercial production about two decades after their invention in 1897.

15. Ernest W. Peterson, "Underground Caverns Made More Beautiful by Scientific Lighting," Portland *Oregon Journal*, March 13, 1938, 6; Francis G. Lange, Resident Landscape Architect, to [NPS] Chief Architect, September 25 to October 25, 1937, 1-2.

16. "Oregon Caves Floodlighting Plan Complete," Portland *Oregon Journal*, November 19, 1937.

17. George Whitworth, CCC project superintendent, report to Crater Lake National Park superintendent, February 9, 1935; additional detail is in Lange's reports of January 9 and March 12, 1935. The count of steps is derived from NPS documentation of the trail: Oregon Caves National Monument, The Cave Tour, April 2, 1969, 2.

18. Ernest W. Peterson, "Major Improvement Made at Oregon Caves," Portland *Oregon Journal*, April 24, 1938. For more detail about construction, see notes titled "CCC connecting tunnel" attached to a letter from John Miele, Superintendent, to John A. Ulrich, October 7, 1982. Additional detail is in the report by Lange to the Chief Architect,

April 24 to May 24, 1937, 15.

19. L.J. Cooper, History of the Siskiyou National Forest [1939], part IV, 6. The camps consisted largely of tents and were located at Selma, Agness, Mount Reuben, Rand, and Williams. Building a new ranger station on the Redwood Highway represented a permanent move for the ranger and staff of the Page Creek District. New guard stations were begun at Store Gulch and Grayback that year, though it is unclear whether these were erected with CCC funding.

20. F.V. Horton to G.E. Mitchell, April 21, 1933; Mitchell to Horton, April 23, 1933.

21. Mitchell to Regional Forester, September 5, 1934, 2. The shortage of command personnel also prevented the Forest Service from responding to Sabin's request for cleaning up debris around buildings at the monument.

22. [USDI-NPS], Justification, Spike Camp, Oregon Caves, May 1, 1934, 1.

23. Lange, Report on ECW camp nos. 1 and 2, June 1, 1934, 1-2. Doerner, Report on Oregon Caves National Monument, May 4, 1934, 6. Other NPS staff members concurred, including chief landscape architect Thomas Vint; Doerner, Monthly Report, September 25, 1934, 1.

24. Whitworth, Report for first half of fourth enrollment period, OCNM, January 18, 1935.

25. Ibid.

26. Table I, Analysis of Work Projects, Camp Oregon Caves NM-1, Fourth Enrollment Period [Spring 1935], 13-16.

27. USDI-NPS, OCNM, Development Outline: Operator Sites, Leases, Permits, January 1945, 3-4.

28 L.F. Kneipp, "Public Campgrounds in the National Forests," *American Civic Annual* 5 (1934), 61-62.

29. G.E. Mitchell, Forest Supervisor, to Regional Forester, February 8 and March 3, 1939; Cliff to Regional Forester, August 19, 1937.

30. M.M. Nelson, District Ranger, to Cliff, August 29, 1939; Cliff to Regional Forester, March 21, 1940.

31. Ernest P. Leavitt, Superintendent (of Crater Lake National Park), to Regional Director, January 15, 1940, 1-2; "Caves Camp Notes," Medford *News*, February 20, 1935. Lium's work for the Forest Service is briefly noted by B. Sam Taylor in Glenn Howell's *C.C.C. Boys Remember* (Medford: Klocker Printery, 1976), 85.

32. Projects noted in Abstract of CCC Projects, Siskiyou National Forest, by Oregon Caves CCC Camp, May 1, 1945. There is some uncertainty over the date of original construction; Stephen Dow Beckham, An

Inventory and Evaluation of the Historical Significance of the Civilian Conservation Corps buildings on the Siskiyou National Forest, 1979, 53-63; Terry West, Inventory sheet for the Cedar Guard Station, September 29, 1983. Construction of the station was noted by L.J. Cooper in 1939 as part of his compilation for the Siskiyou National Forest. There is a note about the original roof being rather flat in an analysis of CCC work during the winter of 1934-35; shoveling the station's roof was necessary to prevent the building's collapse; Table 1, Analysis of Work Projects, Camp Oregon Caves, Fourth Enrollment Period, 17.

33. This is evident in a mimeographed booklet titled "The National Park Service in the Field of Organized Camping" extracted from the 1937 yearbook of the National Conference of State Parks, *Park and Recreation Progress*, 7-9. Recreation Demonstration Areas, such as the one at Silver Falls State Park near Salem, are the clearest expressions of NPS design intent during the 1930s.

34. This effort actually started in early 1934 with assembling a booklet titled *Portfolio of Privies and Comfort Stations* as well as drawings with floor plans of selected structures built by NPS crews in the national parks. A copy of the former is lodged in the ODOT History Center, Salem, while the latter is part of the Francis G. Lange Collection in the Crater Lake National Park Museum and Archives Collections.

35. Leavitt to Regional Director, January 15, 1940. Abundant snowfall at Crater Lake usually kept enrollees there only four months, with the remaining eight to be spent at Oregon Caves. The mill site was located 1.5 miles from Cave Junction, on the Oregon Caves Highway. It was also the source of wood for signs made by the CCC at all three parks and allowed the enrollees a way to produce furniture like a conference table and benches intended for use by the NPS at Crater Lake.

36. "Water System is being installed at Oregon Caves," Medford *News*, February 12, 1935. Some of the pipe was laid along the trail to Williams, by that time known as the Oregon Caves Trail.

37. Record of Improvements, OCNM, May 1, 1945, 2-3.

38. One of the landscape architects, Armin Doerner, initially believed such a structure should be located just inside the monument boundary, above the road and accessible by a short trail; Doerner, Report on Oregon Caves National Monument, May 4, 1934, 7. Doerner, Lange, and two others subsequently decided on the other site because a residence in the parking area would have formed a monotonous line in combination with the concessionaire's service station; Lange, Report for the Month of April 1934 to the Chief, Western Division, Item IX.

39. Record of Improvements, OCNM, May 1, 1945, 1. The design

intent of all three projects is noted in Lange's field trip reports of December 17, 1935, 1-2, and March 13, 1936, 1-2.

40. Leavitt to the Director, September 13, 1940, 2; Record of Improvements, OCNM, 1. Its construction was noted in the Portland *Oregonian*, August 12, 1941, 11. Despite the moniker of "checking station," no fees were collected there.

41. The utilitarian Forest Service, by contrast, usually placed fire prevention needs over recreational pursuits, so trails tended to be more linear (and thus steeper) to reach ridge tops and other places not accessible by road. Both agencies adopted similar standards for recreational trails by the 1940s, though it took the Forest Service several decades to rebuild and realign many of its trails originally constructed for fire patrol access.

42. Frank Kittredge, Standards of Trail Construction, Office of Chief Engineer [San Francisco], October 1934. A "best practices" guide appeared in February 1937; Guy B. Arthur, *Construction of Trails* (CCC Project Training Series no. 7), Emergency Conservation Work Project Training Manual 95570.

43. Doerner, Report on Oregon Caves National Monument, May 4, 1934, 2-3.

44. Map of projects for Camp Oregon Caves, First half, Fourth Enrollment Period, in Whitworth, Narrative Report of ECW Activities, January 18, 1935.

45. Lange, Report to the Deputy Chief Architect, May 1938, 2. The project also included adding a log guardrail and some stonework; Lange, Report to the Chief Architect, July 1, 1935, 1-2.

46. Table I, Analysis of Work Projects, Fourth Enrollment Period, 5-6; Lange, Report to the Deputy Chief Architect, June 13, 1935, 2.

47. Lange, Report to the Deputy Chief Architect, June 1935, 2. The attribution to Buford is from Mark J. Pike, Forestry Comment, OCNM, November 14, 1936, 1. This link differs from the trails it connects with by being only two feet wide, something mentioned by Lange in his report to the Chief Architect, October 25 to November 25, 1937, 2.

48. Lange, report to the Chief Architect, April 17 to April 24, 1937, 4.

49. Lange, report to the Chief Architect, field trip of December 17, 1935, 2.

50. Lange, report to Chief Architect, April 24 to May 24, 1937, 3. Lange credited the chief park naturalist at Crater Lake, John Doerr, with both the Cliff Trail and No Name loop; Lange interview, February 1, 1991, 2.

51. Record of Improvements, OCNM, 1. Horses rarely, if ever, traversed this route—one whose stated intent was to provide another alterna-

tive aimed at keeping pack trains and equestrians away from the Chalet. Evidently the original intent behind the trail from the service road to No Name Creek was to provide part of a circuit where hikers could take the Lake Mountain Trail to its junction with the Limestone Trail, then descend by way of a 1.5 mile trail completed in 1938 (now abandoned) that linked the Limestone Trail with No Name Creek; Abstract of CCC Projects on the Siskiyou National Forest by the Oregon Caves CCC Camp (attached to Record of Improvements, OCNM), May 1, 1945, 1.

52. Doerner, Report on Oregon Caves National Monument, May 4, 1934, 4-5.

53. Lange to the Chief Architect, report for fourth period projects, July 25, 1935, 2.

54. Lange to the Chief Architect, report for April 24 to May 24, 1937, 2.

55. Lange to the Chief Architect, report for October 25 to November 25, 1937, 2, and report for April 8 to April 25, 1938, 2.

56. Lange, Walk and Curb, New Chateau Area, drawing 2055A, January 25, 1938, one sheet; Lange, Stone Walls, Chateau Area, drawing 2014, April 6, 1940, one sheet.

57. Sketches are referenced in Doerner, Monthly Report, August 25, 1934, 1, and Lange, Memorandum to Mr. Carnes, October 31, 1934, 1. Progress in the early landscape projects is described by: Lange to Chief, Western Division, December 13, 1934, 4; Lange to Chief Architect, January 31, 1935, 1. Detail concerning the Davidson monument hauled to Oregon Caves by one of his neighbors in Williams is in J.H. Billingslea to George Grobbin, October 21, 1929.

58. Lange to the Deputy Chief Architect, report for May 1935, 1; Lange to the Chief Architect, July 1, 1935, 1. Howard Buford, Stone Steps, Exit Trail, drawing 3003, November 14, 1934, one sheet.

59. Lange to the Deputy Chief Architect, June 13, 1935, 2; Lange to the Chief Architect, final report of July 25, 1935, 12. What species were planted is unknown, though there are photographs; Cathy Gilbert and Marsha Tolon, Cultural Landscape Report: Cultural Landscape Inventory of Oregon Caves National Monument, Winter 1992, USDI-NPS, Cultural Resources Division, Pacific Northwest Region, 38. Lange mentioned that the enrollees planted ferns around both pools; Lange interview, February 1, 1991, 3.

Douglas fir blocks were promoted as imitation paving early in the twentieth century as in "Field for Wood Blocks," *Motorland* (October 1915), 20.

60. Lange to the Chief Architect, report for April 8 to April 25,

1938, 3; Lange to the Chief Architect, report for May 25 to June 25, 1938, 6-7. He and others quickly found the recessed light less subject to damage from snow than a bracket type originally installed along the exit trail. Any such lighting was, of course, made possible by the connection with the power line from the Illinois Valley in 1938.

61. Jack B. Dodd to the Regional Director, August 5, 1940, 1; B.F. Manley to the Superintendent of Crater Lake National Park, August 9, 1940.

62. Lange to the Chief Architect, report for April 8 to April 25, 1938, 1-2; Lange to the Chief Architect, report for May 25 to June 25, 1938, 1-4. One sign was placed in the island to indicate the direction of vehicular circulation, while the other showed visitors how to reach the trail to a picnic area built by the CCC in 1936. The three Port Orford-cedar tables placed in the picnic area proved to be quite attractive so that others were made at Camp Oregon Caves and placed at Grayback Forest Camp. Some of the tables built by the CCC went as far as Crater Lake National Park and Lava Beds National Monument.

63. Lange to the Regional Landscape Architect, report for January 15-16, 1937, 2-3; Lange to the Chief Architect, report for April 17 to 24, 1937. Rationale for the Chateau walk is in Lange to the Chief Architect, report for October 25 to November 25, 1937, 2. Crater Lake superintendent Ernest Leavitt raised doubts about how feasible the walk adjacent to the Chateau might be; Leavitt to the Regional Director, January 12, 1938, 1-2.

64. E.A. Davidson to the Regional Director, September 29, 1937; E. Lowell Sumner to the Regional Director, October 1, 1937.

65. Lange to the Chief Architect, March 13, 1936, 2.

66. Lange to the Chief Architect, report for April 17 to 24, 1937, 2; Lange to the Chief Architect, report for April 24 to May 24, 1937, 4-5.

67. Motifs were not universally popular, as indicated by an editorial by Robert W. Sawyer in the Bend *Bulletin* of August 25, 1936, criticizing two built by the CCC at Crater Lake. He saw them as heavy and incongruous, like those in Bend; Sawyer to David H. Canfield, Superintendent, November 7, 1936; a letter from John C. Merriam to Sawyer on October 7, 1936, references the editorial. Sawyer was a key supporter of parks in Oregon at the time, having been a former state highway commissioner and friend of Stephen T. Mather, the first director of the NPS.

68. Lange to the Chief Architect, report for April 8 to 25, 1938, 2; Lange to the Chief Architect, report for May 25 to June 25, 1938, 2.

69. Richard L. Sabin, Assistant Secretary of Oregon Caves Resort, to Ernest P. Leavitt, Superintendent, August 16, 1943; Leavitt to Sabin, August 28, 1943.

70. The new hotel evolved from discussions with the concessionaire, where the company had originally wanted to build more cabins—a prospect that the NPS believed would lead to overcrowding on the hillside. Lange to E.A. Davidson, August 23, 1937; Lange to the Chief Architect, report for April 8 to April 25, 1938, 4; Lange to the Chief Architect, report for July 25 to August 25, 1938, 1; Lange to the Chief of Planning, July 25 to August 25, 1939; Leavitt to the Regional Director, April 3, 1940.

71. Robert J. Keeney, "Addition to Guides Cabin, Oregon Caves National Monument," no drawing number, June 1, 1938, four sheets.

72. G.A. Lium, New Chalet, revised drawing 8001, November 4, 1941, seven sheets; Cecil Doty, New Chalet, to be filed with drawing 8001, September 13, 1941, one sheet showing perspective of breezeway. The largest change made during construction stemmed from Lange's successor, Lester Anderson, recommending that Lium pull the Chalet ten feet further back (a move that required more excavation) to provide a larger assembly area in front of the building; Leavitt to the Regional Director, March 26, 1942, 1.

73. This is reflected in the NPS section of the department's annual report for the year; *Annual Report of the Secretary of the Interior* (Washington, DC: Government Printing Office 1942), 159-184.

74. For a detailed overview of how the NPS planning process evolved during the 1930s, see Linda McClelland, *Building the National Parks: Historic Landscape Design and Construction* (Baltimore: Johns Hopkins University Press, 1998), 300-312.

75. Lange to the Chief Architect, January 9, 1935, 1, and January 31, 1935, 1.

76. Lange interview, February 1, 1991, 2.

77. The use of cedar bark siding as a design feature caught on to the extent that it spread to Grayback (where it can still be seen at the guard station and garage) but elsewhere on the Siskiyou National Forest. It sheathed the guard station at Store Gulch on the Illinois River and a work center at Ferris Ford near Powers; Elizabeth Gail Throop, Utterly Visionary and Chimerical: A Federal Response to the Depression, MA thesis, Portland State University, 1979, 184-185. No matter how Lange and others disliked the walls so sporadically built by Rowley and other company employees, they dismantled very few of them, choosing to hide or at least obscure the joints with plantings; Lange to the Chief Architect, July 25, 1935, 2.

78. Oregon Caves Resort, *Oregon Caves Chateau* (Grants Pass: Courier Printing, 1935); later reprinted with different photographs.

79. Fred Lockley, "Impressions and Observations of the Journal Man," Portland *Oregon Journal*, August 17, 1936. The music program was initiated even before the Chateau's construction; "At the Ghost Chamber," Portland *Oregon Journal*, August 24, 1927; "Cave Attendance Showing Boom," Medford *Mail Tribune*, June 24, 1931. By 1938 every employee was expected to join in the medley of college songs that marked the program's conclusion. The final numbers were "Good Night Ladies" and Taps; Bud Breitmeyer to Steve Mark, November 26, 2005, 1.

80. Bud Breitmayer to the author, April 29, 2006, 2.

81. Lange to the Chief Architect, October 25 to November 25, 1938, 2; Lange to the Regional Director, November 5, 1938; Bud Breitmayer to Steve Mark, July 18, 2005; 1-2. Breitmayer later recalled that Meola used only a quarter stick of dynamite each time and never cracked a single window; Breitmayer to the author, April 29, 2006, 1.

82. "The Marble Halls of Oregon," Warren D. Smith to David Canfield, September 13, 1935, extract from attachment, 2.

83. Amos B. Guthrie, in charge [USFS] public relations, memorandum of October 15, 1921, 3.

84. USDA-Forest Service, *The Oregon Caves, Siskiyou National Forest* (Washington, D.C.: Government Printing Office, c. 1926).

85. "Cave folders out," Grants Pass *Courier*, May 15, 1925. The company titled its early brochure "Oregon Caves: A National Monument," then revised and retitled it in 1934 as "Oregon Caves Chateau."

86. "California Tourists Lead," Oakland *Tribune*, [February] 1938, though a comment about tourism at Oregon Caves appeared in the Portland *Oregon Journal*, February 16, 1938.

87. Rationale for the group and its link to preservation efforts is briefly stated in Mark, *Preserving the Living Past*, 89-90.

88. In contrast to the booklets produced by the agency at the time for national parks like Crater Lake, the NPS brochure for Oregon Caves during the late 1930s consisted of a single sheet. On one side of it the map depicted much of the landscape garden (cave entrance area) in plan view, with highlighted features like "Joaquin Miller's Chapel" and the Big Tree drawn as insets; USDI-NPS, *Oregon Caves National Monument*, February 1939, OCNM museum collection.

89. For additional detail see Hal Rothman, *Preserving Different Pasts: The American National Monuments* (Urbana and Chicago: University of Illinois Press, 1989), 89-118, and David Louter, *Administrative History, Craters of the Moon National Monument* (Seattle: USDI-NPS, 1992), 69-89.

90. This was the implied direction of the NPS even before transfer of the 16 national monuments managed by the Forest Service occurred, as

indicated by a booklet issued by the agency titled *Our National Monuments* (Washington, DC: Government Printing Office, 1932).

91. Lawrence C. Merriam, Jr., *Oregon's Highway Park System, 1921-1989: An Administrative History* (Salem: State Printer, 1992), 25-30.

92. "Tourist Harvest Said $19,000,000," Portland *Oregonian*, February 10, 1935. The figure was derived from information gathered after a letter and questionnaire had been sent to 5,000 motorists who had registered as visitors to Oregon in 1934. This was during a period that out of state vehicles were still required to register their vehicles at offices located near the state's borders.

93. For more on this point, see two articles on photographers and Crater Lake; Sharon M. Howe, "Photography and the Making of Crater Lake," *Oregon Historical Quarterly* 103:1 (Spring 2002), 76-97, and Lee Juillerat, "Peter Britt and Fred Kiser: Pioneer Photographers and the Promotion of Crater Lake," *Journal of the Shaw Historical Library* 15 (2001), 56-66.

94. Kiser's studio at Oregon Caves lasted only a few years, with the merchandise long since removed in favor of storing carbide lamps until the CCC removed the building in 1936; "CCC will erect new buildings in area near caves," Grants Pass *Courier*, January 20, 1936.

95. Stephen Boyd, "Picture Windows: How Picture Postcards Portray and Promote our Paradise," *Lithiagraph* 10:8 (October 1992), 1, 6-7.

96. Patterson was quoted in "Patterson Pictures," Medford *Mail Tribune*, January 1, 1928.

97. Paul Luartz, "Photo Finish was only beginning for Portland Concern," Portland *Oregonian*, May 25, 1946, magazine section, 5, in Thomas Robinson, *Oregon Photographers: Biographical History and Dictionary* (Portland: the author, 1992), entry for Sawyer's.

98. Also called the "Wishing Rock," it was handled by thousands who the guide told to rub it three times in order to make the wish come true; Portland *Oregonian*, August 9, 1936, section 2, 2.

99. John Dennis, "View-Master Then and Now," *Stereo World* (March-April 1984), reprint edition [1989]; Mary Ann and Wolfgang Sell, "The Man behind the magic: the inventor William Gruber," [undated article in employee newsletter], 2-4.

100. Wayland A. Dunham, *Enchanted Corridors* (Portland: Dunham Printing, 1939).

101. Warren D. Smith, *The Scenic Treasure House of Oregon* (Portland: Binford and Mort, 1941), 108-109.

102. Russell Working, "Clan of the Cavemen," *Table Rock Sentinel* 12:3 (Summer 1992), 2-13. The Cavemen founded the Pirates as a

branch organization on the coast, though the latter never adopted the audaciousness of their progenitors; "Turn to Cave-Men and Cave-Women Once Every Year," *American Weekly* [June?] 1935.

103. The linkage began as the road to the monument opened; "Cavemen make trip to upper valley towns," Grants Pass *Courier*, September 21, 1922, 1. The Cavemen even petitioned Congress and government officials for funding to improve the monument; Oregon Cavemen, Inc., Mandate to Congress, attached to letter from Charles A. Hansen, Chief Bighorn, to C.H. Purcell, Bureau of Public Roads, January 27, 1928. Their link to the Redwood Empire Association is evident in a newspaper editorial titled "What makes the Redwood Empire "Tick," Grants Pass *Courier*, December 8, 1931. They opened the new Chateau in May 1934 after some of them several years earlier dangled from the unfinished building; "New structure at Oregon Caves ready to open, Oregon Cavemen, Inc. to check fitness of Lodge to Operate in Domain," Grants Pass *Courier*, May 11, 1934. The tripartite union among Grants Pass, Oregon Caves, and the Redwood Empire became evident to all passing motorists when all three parties funded a sign erected at the Caveman bridge in 1939; "To Erect Big Grants Pass neon road sign," Grants Pass *Courier*, January 30, 1939. The Cavemen even helped the Redwood Empire Association stage an "Indian marathon" in 1927, where native runners traveled by foot from San Francisco to Grants Pass.

104. E.P. Leavitt, Superintendent, to Neil R. Allen, Attorney [for the Oregon Caves Resort], April 21, 1944; Allen to Leavitt, June 9, 1944; Leavitt to Allen, June 16, 1944, 2-3.

105. In terms of size and level of development, the only comparable site in Oregon might be Honeyman Memorial State Park, though this 522 acre area is situated on the Oregon coast around two freshwater lakes confined by sand dunes. For detail about the CCC role there, see Nancy Ann Niedernhofer, Reconnecting Nature and Design: The Civilian Conservation Corps in Oregon State Parks, 1933-1942, M.A. thesis, George Washington University, 2004.

5. Decline from a Rustic Ideal

1. Many writers have contrasted the decay and misery of their present with a golden past despite there being little historical or scientific evidence for such an inclination; Jared Diamond, "The Golden Age That Never Was," *Discover Magazine* (December 1988), 71-79.

2. Devereaux Butcher, "For a Return to Harmony in Park

Architecture," *National Parks Magazine* 26:111 (October – December 1952), 150-157. Butcher's opposition to the "urban commonplace" reflected a desire for visitors to sense they were in a new kind of environment; Butcher to Robert P. Darlington, *National Parks Magazine* 28:116 (January – March 1954), 31-32.

    3. Sarah Allaback, *Mission 66 Visitor Centers: The History of a Building Type* (USDI-NPS: on-line book, 2000), Introduction: The Origins of Mission 66; www.cr.nps.gov/history/online_books/allaback.

    4. William C. Tweed, et al., National Park Service Rustic Architecture: 1916-1942. Typescript dated February 1977, Division of Cultural Resources Management, NPS Western Regional Office.

    5. Two NPS studies published in 1998 are subject to the same criticism, though the "period of significance" usually established for NPS rustic architecture (1916-1942) is a byproduct of the National Register process which requires setting what often amounts to a sometimes arbitrary timeframe for properties nominated and then listed. The studies, which reflect assumptions driving the documentation of rustic architecture since 1980 or so, are: Ethan Carr, *Wilderness by Design: Landscape Architecture and the National Park Service* (Lincoln: University of Nebraska Press, 1998); Linda Flint McClelland, *Building the National Parks: Historic Landscape Design and Construction* (Baltimore: Johns Hopkins University Press, 1998).

    6. Even though Mission 66 completion reports carried the words "Preservation through Planning," such slogans did not stem the rising tide of discontent with the NPS; see Ronald Foresta, *America's National Parks and their Keepers* (Washington, DC: Resources for the Future, 1984), 52-57.

    7. Sheet titled "Oregon Caves, Future Government Administrative Area," October 21, 1942.

    8. Memorandum of Understanding between the Forest Service, U.S. Department of Agriculture, and the National Park Service, U.S. Department of the Interior, for use of lands within the Siskiyou National Forest for construction and maintenance of a permanent park ranger residence and related facilities, signed by H.C. Obye, Forest Supervisor, June 12, 1958, and Thomas J. Williams, Superintendent, June 28, 1958. The plea to house the permanent ranger stemmed from Lawrence C. Merriam, Regional Director, to the Director, January 17, 1957.

    9. The special use permit from the Forest Service specified that all construction, to the extent possible, be screened from the view of passing motorists traveling the Caves Highway.

    10. Ernest P. Leavitt, et al., to the NPS Director, May 12, 1942, and

H.F. Cameron to Regional Engineer, August 8, 1949; the natural hazard affecting the lot was summarized in the wake of a flood event in 1955; Emergency Estimates of Storm Damage, Narrative Statement [January 1956], 2-4. The cave lighting system overhaul was not noted in the Superintendent's Monthly Reports at Crater Lake for 1946. Building a new water system was predicated on contemporary needs, with estimated capacity based on calculations from cave visits, overnight stays, and monument totals; NPS, Estimated Cost of Water System, OCNM, September 1949.

11. W.J. Westley, Acting Regional Landscape Architect, to the Superintendent, June 9, 1952. Pipe railing had been used during the 1920s on the tour route and in front of the cave entrance but the latter was replaced by logs a decade later.

12. Stephen R. Mark, Historic American Buildings Survey documentation for Oregon Caves Chateau, HABS no. OR-145, [1990], 13.

13. William J. Stephenson, "Caves of the National Parks," *National Parks Magazine* 26:110 (July – September 1952), 104. Stephenson served as chairman of the National Speological Society's Conservation Committee; photographs for the article were taken by Devereaux Butcher, who in most ways led the NPA until 1957. NPA became the National Parks and Conservation Association (NPCA) in 1970; John C. Miles, *Guardians of the National Parks: A History of the National Parks and Conservation Association* (Washington, DC: Taylor and Francis, 1995), 241.

14. As one contemporary account put it, "The labyrinth now has colored lights in it, the vaults are named, bridges lead over chasms in the subterranean trail and visitors are supposed to see likenesses of people and other things in the stalactites and stalagmites—which are, of course, interesting enough in themselves without looking like anything else." Ron Fish, *This is Oregon: The Northwest Adventure Series.* Book Four, Volume 1 (Caldwell: Caxton Printing, 1957), 44.

15. One example was what Rowley called the "Wigwam Room," where guides pointed out a formation called "Chief Rain in the Face," where dripping water struck a suggestive likeness; the name of that chamber was summarily changed to the "Imagination Room" in 1974 and the formation no longer highlighted on the tour.

16. Roger J. Contor, *The Underground World of Oregon Caves* (Crater Lake: Crater Lake Natural History Association, 1963).

17. Marvin L. Nelson, Completion Report, Cave Exit Trail Improvements, 1959.

18. Inspection of the gates (which were placed at the main entrance, the upper [or 110'] entrance, and at the end of the exit tunnel) came on June 3; Superintendent's Monthly Report [for Crater Lake and Oregon

Caves], July 13, 1958, 10. The recommendation for gates was made by E.H. MacDaniels, Report on Oregon Caves, February 14, 1920, 3.

19. This part of the monument is hardly a monoculture, since the surrounding plant community type contains ten tree species—the largest number in any community thus far identified; James K. Agee, et al., Oregon Caves Forest and Fire History, report CPSU/UW 90-1, Winter 1990, 20-25. Mistletoe had likely increased because of fire suppression leading to greater density of trees in the forest.

20. Jeff LaLande, Cultural Resources Overview for the North Siskiyou Planning Unit (Rogue River NF, Siskiyou NF, and Klamath NF), CR Job RR-15, May 1977, 40.

21. Two works substantiate this point in much greater depth: David A. Clary, *Timber and the Forest Service* (Lawrence: University Press of Kansas, 1986), and Paul Hirt, *A Conspiracy of Optimism: Management of the National Forests since World War II* (Lincoln: University of Nebraska Press, 1994).

22. George McKinley and Doug Frank in their environmental history called "Stories on the Land" make the point that timber access roads began with the "truck trails" built by the CCC. One was the road along Grayback Creek started by enrollees from Camp Oregon Caves during the 1930s which became the route connecting the Illinois Valley with Williams, but used mainly by log trucks in the 1950s; Eric Allen, "Trip Made from Oregon Caves into Applegate Area Described," Medford *Mail Tribune*, October 7, 1956. The truck trail was included in a NPS document called the Work Program Outline [for the CCC camp] from October 1, 1939 to June 30, 1940.

23. Hirt, *A Conspiracy of Optimism*, 157-159.

24. W. Ward Yeager, Crater Lake superintendent, to Chief, Columbia River Recreational Survey Branch, March 14, 1962.

25. The total loss due to inundation was projected to be 110 acres; Neal G. Guse, assistant superintendent, to Yeager, August 9, 1962.

26. The sites listed as possible campgrounds in the withdrawals of 1963 were on Cave Creek and at Bigelow Lakes and Tannen Lake. A site called "Monument Campground" (so named because of its proximity, being near the Big Tree Trail, to the lands administered by the NPS) joined them in 1965; Public Land Order 013667 (December 3, 1963), 1, and Public Land Order 3671 (June 10, 1965).

27. "Plans for more recreation areas outlined at meet," Medford *Mail Tribune*, February 26, 1969.

28. "Grayback area now open to the public," Medford *Mail Tribune*, May 3, 1965.

29. Christine Barnes, *Great Lodges of the National Parks* (Bend: W.W. West, 2002), 80-81.

30. "New Park Concessioner Labor Regulations Issued," USDI-NPS news release, May 3, 1950.

31. In both cases a smaller local concern was swallowed by an Oregon-based corporation later known as the Estey Corporation. The sale at Crater Lake was prompted by a "water crisis" in 1975, during which the park was ordered closed after employees and visitors became ill from contaminated drinking water.

32. Russell Working, "70 Years of Club-Wielding," Grants Pass *Courier*, May 23, 1992, 14A. The Cavemen did, however, recall their past in sponsoring six Grants Pass High School alumni who re-enacted the Redwood Empire Indian Marathon of 1927 sixty years later; "Redwood Empire Run Run Again," *Grants Pass High School 100 Year Centennial Newsletter*, January 1988, 1-2. The Boatnik festivities began in 1959.

33. The population figure given for 1922 appeared on the Grants Pass Chamber of Commerce folder for that year, which shows, among other things, Grants Pass and Oregon Caves at the center of a regional map depicting an 80 mile radius. City population figures by decade are in William G. Loy, et al., *The Atlas of Oregon* (Eugene: University of Oregon Press, 2001), 28-31.

34. This figure is based on the experience of the writer, who in the summer of 1973 arrived at Oregon Caves in company with family members. The time given has also been substantiated by a former NPS superintendent there; John Miele interview, November 30, 1999.

35. Funds to purchase eight acres came through omnibus legislation enacted on November 10, 1978 as P.L. 95-625. See section 301, subsection 14 in Dorothy J. Whitehead (comp.), *Laws Relating to the National Park Service*, Supplement IV (Washington, D.C.: Government Printing Office, 1980), 425. This acquisition was later reduced by half through sale of four acres.

36. Cave Junction *Illinois Valley News*, "City of Cave Junction 50th Anniversary, 1948-1998," 7.

37. In chronological order, the Rough and Ready site north of O'Brien came first through a lease of 70 acres by the state parks obtained in 1937, though they did not acquire a deed on 30 acres (what became the wayside) of that tract from the Bureau of Land Management until 1962. Acquisition of what became Illinois River State Park located south of Cave Junction began in 1961, but the present total of 368 acres did not come until 1977. The county park at Lake Selmac, a reservoir near Selma, originated in the 1960s.

38. This began with publication of a nationally-distributed book focusing on hikes in roadless areas of southwest Oregon and northwest California which the author considered eligible for inclusion in the National Wilderness Preservation System; John Hart, *Hiking the Bigfoot Country* (San Francisco: Sierra Club Books, 1975).

39. These were the Endangered American Wilderness Act which formally designated additions to the Kalmiopsis Wilderness Area and the Wild Rogue Wilderness in 1978. The Oregon Wilderness Act of 1984 came as one of several bills aimed at resolving what was to be protected under the terms of the Wilderness Act of 1964; it designated three new wilderness areas on the Siskiyou National Forest: Grassy Knob, Red Buttes (Oregon portion), and Siskiyou (in conjuction with the Klamath and Six Rivers national forests).

40. Steve Knutson, *Oregon Caves* survey map (Crater Lake: Crater Lake Natural History Association, 1975).

41. John Roth, "Fossil Finds and the Age of Oregon Caves," *Nature Notes from Crater Lake* 27 (1996), 29-32.

42. Mike Romick, Manager, to Craig Ackerman, Superintedent, July 27, 1998, 2. Records indicate that as early as 1952, the NPS wanted more natural history content, especially geology, to be included on the cave tour; Lawrence C. Merriam, Regional Director, to Superintendent, Crater Lake, December 11, 1952, and Harry C. Parker, Chief Park Naturalist, to Superintendent, Crater Lake, November 11, 1952.

43. The nomination form is in Laura Souillere Harrison, *Architecture in the Parks: National Historic Landmark Theme Study* (Washington, DC: Government Printing Office, 1987), 383-395. Harrison visited the Chateau in 1985, as part of a field visit to this and other buildings nominated in the study.

44. Stephen R. Mark, Oregon Caves Historic District, National Park Service nomination to the National Register of Historic Places, June 1991.

45. Gretchen Luxenberg, Historic American Buildings Survey documentation for Oregon Caves Concession Cottages (narrative and photographs), HABS no. OR-147, 1988.

46. Mark's nomination used a format developed from a cultural landscape report for Rim Village at Crater Lake to describe the district's character and significance. Initial inventory and documentation of the site came about through the efforts of Cheryl Martin at the University of Oregon in 1984, though her work was largely baseline information centered on architectural significance.

47. Erasure or reduction of impacts associated with the linear tour route through Oregon Caves could be achieved only through restoration

of the original air flow (something which hinged on restricting air in the connecting and exit tunnels) and continued removal of organic matter brought underground by visitors and staff.

6. Recommendations

1. Laura Souillere Harrison, *Architecture in the Parks: National Historic Landmark Theme Study* (Washington, DC: Government Printing Office, 1986), 383-395.

2. The authors of a subsequent cultural landscape inventory for the monument made a convincing argument for adjusting the district's boundaries based on topographic considerations and original design intent; see Cathy Gilbert and Marsha Tolon, Cultural Landscape Report: Cultural Landscape Inventory of Oregon Caves National Monument (Seattle: USDI-NPS, Cultural Resources Division, 1992).

3. Linda Flint McClelland, Historic Park Landscapes in National and State Parks, NPS multiple property documentation form, August 8, 1995, 176-182.

4. For additional detail on how integrity has been assessed at the monument, see Cathy Gilbert and Marsha Tolon, Cultural Landscape Report: Cultural Landscape Inventory at Oregon Caves National Monument, Winter 1992, USDI-NPS, Cultural Resources Division, Pacific Northwest Region, 50.

5. For the distinction in the design and construction of recreational trails, as opposed to trails primarily built for other uses, see McClelland, Historic Park Landscapes in National and State Parks, multiple property documentation form (1995), 85-88; or for more detail, *Building the National Parks*, 233-242.

6. This route follows the Big Tree Trail as it leaves the Chalet and then diverges from the loop in eight tenths of a mile, to where hikers (who astutely step around the brush piles made to obscure it) follow a path made for access along the water line to Lake Creek. This trail disappears into a brush field (clear cut area) once it leaves the monument.

7. George F. ("Fred") Whitworth was probably the most influential engineer, whereas Francis Lange, Edwin Meola, and Howard Buford as landscape architects all had some effect on the trail projects.

8. Oregon Department of Transportation, Highway Division, Planning Section, Systems Studies Unit, *Oregon Historic and Scenic Highway Program* (Salem: State Printer, n.d.), 28.

9. Oregon Department of Transportation, Technical Advisory Committee, Lake Creek Bridge Project (Key No. 03895), August 18,

1994, 1.

10. Gilbert and Tolon, Cultural Landscape Report, 6.

11. McClelland, Historic Park Landscapes in National and State Parks, 194-195. Two sites should be further studied in order to determine whether they meet the eligibility criteria. Both are remnants of earlier water systems serving the monument, with the first being a surface diversion dating from the early 1920s on Cave Creek, situated across the stream before it disappears underground in the cave system. The second is what remains of a subsequently constructed concrete reservoir located above the Chalet at roughly the 4,300 foot contour. The writer is grateful to long-time seasonal ranger Ron Reed for information on how to reach this latter site.

12. A portion of the old Caves Creek Trail blazed by Walter Burch appears to be intact near a waterfall about a mile below the campground. It can be accessed from the highway near milepost 15, where a small road has been punched into a flat area that allows for vehicle parking. Follow an older bulldozed road on foot until two distinct sections of trail (one with blazes) can be identified near the waterfall.

13. Elaine Jackson-Retondo and Len Warner, Pacific West Region Mission 66 Resources, draft multiple property documentation form, August 10, 2004, 38.

14. Ibid.

15. The other was a portable ranger station brought from Crater Lake in 1964. It was renovated and expanded in 1982 and then removed in 1996. The property types identified include: visitor centers, administration buildings, campgrounds, ranger stations, school houses, comfort stations, maintenance and utility buildings, residences, roads, and miscellaneous developments (such as picnic areas).

16. It should also be noted that rubble from a mining operation can be found near the residence. The claim dates from the early twentieth century, but virtually all the disturbance stems from one "Jiggs" Morris who extracted a limited amount of calcite from the site between the late 1960s until his operation was shut down in 1971.

17. See the Long Range (comprehensive) Interpretive Plan for Oregon Caves National Monument completed in 2003 for further justification.

18. Janice Tiland, "The Siletz Indians: forgotten but not gone," and Marilyn Maurais, "Hoskins: a fort," *Pioneers!* (Philomath: Benton County Historical Society, 1975), 16-22. The Grand Ronde Reservation in Yamhill County is perhaps just as suggestive in illustrating the challenges posed by removal.

19. Other vestiges of this period (1916-1933) consist mainly of pri-

vate property developed in response to federal and state outlays for roads. The Lind Home, located near the forest boundary below Grayback and abutting the state highway, continues to furnish a striking example of an early, but modest, resort complete with several cabins. Later and more typical auto camps can be seen south of Cave Junction on the Redwood Highway, though these remain in private hands as well. By contrast, the site of Grayback Park (alternately called the Oregon Caves or Sucker Creek forest camp) is on federal land but is now the parking area and start of an interpretive trail leading to Grayback Campground.

20. Stephen R. Mark, Oregon Caves Historic District, NPS nomination to the National Register of Historic Places, June 1991 (listed February 1992); Cathy Gilbert and Marsha Tolon, Cultural Landscape Report: Cultural Landscape Inventory of Oregon Caves National Monument, Winter 1992 (Seattle: USDI-NPS, Cultural Resouces Division); Gretchen Luxenberg, Historic American Buildings Survey document of Oregon Caves Concession Cottages, HABS No. OR-147, 1988; Stephen R. Mark, Historic American Buildings Survey documentation of the Oregon Caves Chateau, Oregon Caves Chalet, and Oregon Caves Ranger Residence, HABS No. OR-145, OR-146, and OR-149, 1990; Alex McMurry, Historic Structure Report, Oregon Caves Chateau, Oregon Caves National Monument, terminal project, Historic Preservation Program, School of Architecture and Allied Arts, University of Oregon, June 1999.

21. Examples are the Port Orford-cedar tables still extant at Lava Beds National Monument, where particularly nice examples can be found at Fleener Chimneys and Indian Well. Crater Lake National Park still has four benches and a conference table produced by the camp, as well as several wooden signs with raised lettering made by enrollees.

Bibliography

Books

Contor, Roger J. *The Underground World of Oregon Caves.* Crater Lake: Crater Lake Natural History Association, 1963.

Dunham, Wayland A. *Enchanted Corridors.* Portland: Dunham Printing, 1939.

Gray, Dennis J. *The Takelma and their Athapascan Neighbors.* University of Oregon Anthropology Papers 37. Eugene: University of Oregon Department of Anthropology, 1987.

Pfefferle, Ruth. *Golden Days and Pioneer Ways.* Grants Pass: Bulletin Publishing Company, 1995.

Walsh, Frank K. and Halliday, William R. *Oregon Caves, Discovery and Exploration.* Coos Bay: Te-Cum-Tom, 1982.

Periodicals

Davidson, E.J. "History of the Discovery of the Marble Halls of Oregon," *Oregon Historical Quarterly* 23:3 (September 1922), 274-276.

Dennis, John. "View Master Then and Now," *Stereo World* (March-April 1984), 1989 reprint edition.

Fidler, William W. "An Account of the First Attempt at Exploration of the 'Oregon Caves,'" *Oregon Historical Quarterly* 23:3 (September 1922), 270-273.

Forst, Jim. "Sixty Years at the Oregon Caves Chateau: The Inn Place to Be," *Oregon Parks* 1:5 (March – April 1994), 39-45.

Mark, Steve. "Where Art Imitates Nature," *Nature Notes from Crater Lake* 31 (2000), 22-24.

Miller, Joaquin. "Oregon's Marble Halls," *Sunset* 18:5 (September 1909), 227-235.

Roth, John. "Fossil Finds and the Age of Oregon Caves," *Nature Notes from Crater Lake* 27 (1996), 29-31.

Working, Russell. "Clan of the Cavemen," *Table Rock Sentinel* 12:3 (Summer 1992), 2-13.

Government Reports

Agee, James K., et al. Oregon Caves Forest and Fire History, report CPSU/UW 90-1 to USDI-National Park Service, Winter 1990.

Beckham, Stephen Dow. Cultural Resources Overview of the Siskiyou National Forest, report to the USDA-Forest Service, 1978.

Gilbert, Cathy and Tolon, Marsha. Cultural Landscape Report, Cultural Landscape Inventory of Oregon Caves National Monument, USDI-National Park Service, Cultural Resources Division, Pacific Northwest Region, Winter 1992.

Kramer, George. Mining in Southwestern Oregon: A Historic Context Statement, Heritage Research Associates Report 234 to Medford District, USDI-Bureau of Land Management, December 1999.

Luxenberg, Gretchen. Historic American Buildings Survey documentation, HABS No. OR-147, (Oregon Caves Concession Cottages), 1988.

McKinley, George and Frank, Doug. Stories on the Land: An Environmental History of the Applegate and Upper Illinois Valleys, report to the Medford District, USDI-Bureau of Land Management, BLM/OR/WA/PL-96/006+1792, September 1995.

Mark, Stephen R. Historic American Buildings Survey documentation, HABS Nos. OR-145 (Oregon Caves Chateau), OR-146 (Oregon Caves Chalet), and OR-149 (Ranger Residence), 1990.

_____. Oregon Caves Historic District, nomination to the National Register of Historic Places, June 1991.

Newspapers

Ashland (Ore.) *Tidings*
Cave Junction (Ore.) *Illinois Valley News*
Coquille (Ore.) *Sentinel*
Corvallis (Ore.) *Gazette Times*
Crescent City (Calif.) *Del Norte Triplicate*
Grants Pass (Ore.) *Bulletin, Courier,* and *Oregon Observer*
Jacksonville (Ore.) *Times*
Medford (Ore.) *Mail Tribune,* and *News*
Portland (Ore.) *Daily News, Evening Telegram, Oregonian,* and *Oregon Journal*
San Francisco (Calif.) *Examiner*

Manuscript sources

Crater Lake National Park Museum and Archives Collections (Superintendent's Monthly Reports, 1928-1966)
Josephine County Historical Society, Grants Pass
National Archives and Records Administration, Pacific Northwest Region, Seattle, Record Group 30 (Bureau of Public Roads) and Record Group 79 (National Park Service)
National Archives and Records Administration, Pacific Sierra Region, San Bruno (Calif.), Record Group 79 (National Park Service, see especially Branch of Plans and Design)
Oregon Caves National Monument Museum and Archives Collections (chronological and topical files including correspondence, architectural drawings, master plans)

Oregon State Archives, Salem (Oregon Department of Transportation records, highway department general correspondence, 1921-33)
Oregon State University Archives, Corvallis (Arthur L. Peck Papers and Ralph Gifford Collection)

Interviews

Bruce W. Black, taped transcription, September 27, 1988, Corvallis
Florenz "Bud" Breitmayer, telephone, February 22, 1999, and interview notes, May 17, 2001, Forest Grove
Roger J. Contor, telephone, February 24, 1999
Glen Happel, telephone, December 2, 1997
Roland Johnsrud, telephone, August 25, 1999
Francis G. Lange, telephone, February 1, 1991

Appendix 1

Tour of the Oregon Caves Chateau

Projected length: 25-30 minutes

Materials: Two or possibly three photographs, mounted on foam core or similar

Prep work: Make arrangements with concession staff to show spaces such as food storage, the employee dining room (Little D), and a guest room

Suggested stops:

1. Outside main entrance (near the NHL plaque, but positioned to where visitors can compare photographs with cave entrance and Chalet breezeway)
2. Outside the food storage on path next to tree (at second basement level)
3. Inside Food storage (optional stop in the Little D)
4. Dining room (away from tables, but perhaps overlooking canyon)
5. Lobby
6. Guest room (second or third floor preferred, so that room has original furniture)

Theme statement: The Oregon Caves Chateau is an outstanding example of design with nature and therefore a National Historic Landmark.

Significance statement: Integration with one's surroundings (that is, unity with nature) has always been an important part of the park experience for visitors.

Suggested content:

This can be a difficult program to begin outside without some photographs. I start with introducing myself, then quickly summarizing with what historians aim to do (take selected parts of the past and interpret them in light of their importance to the present). This allows for a neat transition to the Chateau being a national historic landmark. I compare the number of properties on the National Register (75,000 nationally) with those being NHLs (some 3,000) and identify why the hotel is nationally significant (design with nature). That allows for a transition to discuss the building site being in a ravine between two streams (one active, the other inactive) due to the lack of places to build near the cave.

To reinforce how things have changed, it is then time to show older photos of the cave entrance and the "bench" on which the Chalet breezeway was constructed. These images allow visitors to get some inkling of change, but also see continuity in the site. This also provides the presenter an opportunity to summarize why, as L.S. Harrison states in the NHL theme study, the prime significance of the Chateau as a landmark is how the designer (Lium) creatively used the limited site and allowed it to dictate major architectural choices. On the practical side, one could mention that three concurrent events gave the Oregon Caves Company some incentive to build a hotel here: 1) construction of an exit tunnel; 2) government appropriations for a lighting system in the cave; and 3) widening of the Caves Highway.

Before leaving the first stop, I make sure the visitors notice the building appears to be only two stories. We then descend the steps, walking by the kitchen door and stop next to a tree. This allows the group to count six stories (hopefully), and I point out how the stream they saw gushing from the cave has disappeared. At this juncture I develop the significance statement a little by talking about why people would want to design with nature in

FIGURE 81. Perspective drawing of the future Oregon Caves Chateau; the existing guide dormitory is shown to the right. (Oregon Caves Company photo, OCNM Museum and Archives Collections.)

such a setting. The Port Orford cedar bark is a good device in this respect and is also very durable. One can also throw out an analogy about the variety inherent in nature, pointing to the varied architectural details (window sizes, etc.). The choices made in naturalistic landscaping might also be identified, through a comparison of the dry laid retaining walls (whose structural function is to permit the building of roads and trails in steep terrain) that allow the growth of moss and fern could be made with other types of material like concrete. We then enter the building.

While passing through the corridor with food storage lockers, it could be mentioned that the concession recycles, thereby linking Oregon Caves with other units in the National Park System. In order to reinforce significance again, there should be some allusion to how Lium succeeded in grouping functions (this being a service area) yet in a building that does not have any regular configurations. If Little D is added to the tour, point out the connection between the kitchen and this dining room through the dumbwaiter. There is a chance that staff at Little D will describe functions of this dining room and how it connects with the rest of the Chateau, perhaps by using the dumbwaiter.

Some warning about the low ceiling is advised when climbing the stairs to the dining room. Since there may be diners at tables, you will probably want to take the group across the stream. The stream is a good opportunity to talk about unusual architectural features and how the culvert allows water to run through it. Going to the window allows visitors to see where the stream reemerges in the canyon below them. This spot should also allow for a summary of the flood damage that occurred in 1964, and how Gust Lium supervised the crew that put the building back on its foundation. It makes for a fairly epic story of how Lium convinced the company stockholders that the damage could be repaired less than a year before he died. There may be time to discuss change due to flood damage before going up the center stairway.

Once in the lobby, it may be well to begin with why this space is so rich in architectural detail and with furnishings. Some features serve a structural function while others are merely decorative. Take your pick about what to point out; I usually focus on the "hand hewn" beams, the fireplace, and the photographs. The latter can be used to put the Chateau and Oregon Caves into regional context with promoting the Redwood Empire to the south and attractions like Crater Lake to the north. Photos of Lium and Sabin help some people better visualize the business enterprise that constructed the hotel.

The last stop is in a guestroom (the best ones above the lobby level), where the original Monterey furniture can be pointed out and some detail provided about it. By stating each room is different the building's significance can be reinforced, yet also highlight the use of simple materials such as fiberboard and wood moldings that serve the purpose of tying these accommodations with the park setting. Subsequent changes are evident (such as the sprinkler system and the fire escape) but these are not damaging enough to building integrity so as to disqualify the Chateau for landmark status. The idea of evoking a certain period of time through architecture and why this might be important could serve as a final thought. This allows the presenter to let visitors contemplate the differences between past and present (thereby linking the last stop with what the photos depicted at the first stop), and give added meaning to the word *landmark* as an orientation point to a part of our national heritage.

Appendix 2

**Widening Perception and the Viability of
Developing Show Caves**
John E. Roth

While most other cultures emphasized the religious importance of caves, the Western world underwent two significant changes in attitudes toward caves that ultimately expanded the reasons why people visit them. This made the development of Oregon Caves viable, irrespective of low population density in the surrounding area.

Caves retained their pre-classical importance to art and religion in ancient Greece and Rome. As with many other cultures of the time, the pre-Christian Romans believed that all humans originated from caves. This was expressed in their festival of Lupercalia on February 15 at the shallow cave called *Lupercal* on the Palatine Hill, where the legendary founders of Rome, the twins Romulus and Remus, were said to have been nursed by a wolf.

The Persian concept of absolute good and evil was introduced into Greece and among Judaic Essenes shortly prior to the Common Era (otherwise known as *Anno Domini*, or A.D.) A large part of its success and spread was because this dualism helped justify social stratification by the promise of a glorious afterlife. More egalitarian cultures believed in a democratic and balanced transactional reciprocity with the spirit, social, and natural worlds, one in which one's actions or non-actions could yield benefit or harm. By contrast, relationships under the concept of good and evil were more one-sided, with priests and kings dominating and controlling those lower down on the social hierarchy, lest they too turn to evil. One cannot be egalitarian or tolerant if one side is evil or prone to evil and the other side is good.

Since there could not be two opposite places for absolute evil or absolute good, this dualistic concept created a singular focus on divine order and paradise at high elevations and thus ultimately devalued the religious importance of the middle world of humans and the lower world of caves. That the heavens were chosen rather than caves or even mountains likely had something to do with access, in that they required help from priest-kings. The choice also had to do with their seemingly unchanging, orderly, and hence perfect state; the importance of astronomical events in the seasonal calendar of agriculture; but the heavens also being a place where priests, kings, and gods could make sure everybody was behaving themselves. Sanctuaries on peaks in Crete overshadowed the earlier cave shrines but subsequently declined in use as the locus of divinity and paradise was placed beyond Earth. The Roman philosopher Seneca, for example, told of some Greek miners who visited a cave where they saw huge rushing rivers and vast still lakes, spectacles that made them shake with horror. The land hung above their heads and the winds made a hollow whistle in the shadows, while in the depths, the rivers led nowhere but into the perpetual and alien night. Once they returned topside, the miners "lived in fear, for having tempted the fires of Hell."[1]

By late Roman times most caves were increasingly viewed in a negative light, in part due to being most distant from the sky gods, but also because caves were not perceived as materially useful. Heroes like Hercules and Aeneas did not go to caves for their enlightenment, but because caves accessed the land of the dead. Only the profit motive could induce anyone less than a hero to embark on such a journey.

The belief pervading the western world that caves represented sacred space continued to ebb by the third century. They were then seen as inhabited by demons, ghosts, witches, beasts, and savages believed to have false religions or none at all. In part because

---

[1] Donald Dale Jackson, *Underground Worlds* (Alexandria, Virginia: Time-Life Books, 1985), 27.

FIGURE 82. A view of Virgil's Grove at The Leasowes landscape garden (England), 1748.

the new religions of the western and Islamic worlds began in cities and large towns, the wild or rural landscapes in general were not as esteemed as they had once had been. People of the countryside became known as the *pagani* ("pagan") in Italy or "heathen," if they dwelled amid the heather in moors located north of Hadrian's Wall on the island of Great Britain. If heaven in the prevailing Judeo-Christian perception could be seen as an escape from the misery and evil associated with earthly existence, then nature could be beautiful or even sacred only if sanctified by recognized saints. If depicted at all, caves were usually seen as entry points to hell or part of hell itself.

During the Renaissance, attitudes of the classical world were reclaimed but also were selectively modified to suit new tastes during the Renaissance. Most religious associations with both natural and human places declined, thus aiding in the rise of capitalism and science as well as the rebirth of democracy. Political power went from church authorities to a rising mercantile class that pursued its search for wealth on heretofore uncharted seas and newly discovered lands.

Accompanying this shift was a change in the location of Eden, this time from the heavens to a middle world of the future. The slow rise of technology aided by science made the flatter natural areas more profitable, as these tracts could be measured and then transformed into fertile farmlands once again emblematic of Eden. Even some rugged places not suitable for mining or other extraction like timber could be perceived as interesting for the purposes of art, and in time, science and recreation. This re-conceptualizing of heaven produced focal points like water, outcrops, groves, and grottos in Renaissance gardens—at a time when the rich and powerful wanted to recall (however selectively) the classical past. Nevertheless, deep caves continued to be cast in a negative light.

The eighteenth century Enlightenment included both the enshrinement of rational thinking (hence the birth of geology and an acceleration in scientific achievements) over superstition, and a revolution in aesthetics called Romanticism. Not only did the Romantics expand the Renaissance vision of a manicured, but earthly, Eden to include even the wildest places, they also expressed an impulse to turn landscape into art. Romantics were able to accommodate a great range of sea- and landscapes within their aesthetic of the "sublime," where both dread and delight, as well as melancholy, attracted artistic interest. Edenic landscapes also possessed great size, age, and mystery. One eighteenth century writer expressed the widely-held view where

> "Even the rude rocks, the mossy caverns, the irregular unwrought grottos, and broken falls of waters, with all the horrid graces of wilderness itself, as representing Nature more, will be the more engaging, and appear with a magnificence beyond the formal mockery of princely gardens."[2]

Most Romantics were also democrats who felt that such natural "gardens" should be open to everyone, rather than just the elite. Caves and other representations of "wilderness" could now be seen in a positive light, as suitable subjects for painting and even literature.

The Romantic view of caves as part of the sublime helped to contrast those rigid and orderly gardens of the ruling classes, as well as their castles or other great monuments in the Old World, with the bigger and even older "gardens" and natural "monuments" of the New World. This contrast aided the efforts of those who advocated that public parks be established that fit the mold of how Romantics viewed their gardens and a cultural construction

---

[2] Anthony Ashley Cooper, Third Earl of Shaftesbury, *Characteristics of Men, Manners, Opinions, Times*, reprint of 1711 edition (Indianapolis: Liberty Fund, 2001), 220.

FIGURE 80. The "Gothic Chapel," a vignette from "Scenes in Mammoth Cave," part of *Picturesque America, II*, 1874.

called the sublime. Park areas in the United States were thus increasingly seen as symbolic of a new aesthetic, but also of a new democracy in a new nation.

Promoters of the Oregon Caves realized very early that the tour route had to conform to expectations attached to an Edenic landscape, one where getting around presented a challenge but visitors were compensated for their efforts by experiencing rooms of various sizes and seeing an ever-changing array of formations. Enlarged passages with curving trails resulted, ones similar in form to European carriage roads where visitors could walk upright or sit in relative comfort in carriages. Once the tunnels and electrical systems were in place, people on the tour did not have to carry their own light or backtrack and go against the flow of incoming tours.

What made possible and guided the development of Oregon Caves centered on a cave that could be profitable if there was even more of an Edenic garden both above and below. All this was possible because, by the early twentieth century, there had been a great increase in leisure time. The reasons people visited caves had also expanded beyond the religious, to rationale such as curiosity, recreation, exercise, nationalism, beauty, sublimity, sport, and science. The multiplicity of reasons and funding from government sources to increase the ease of access to Oregon Caves eventually brought a sufficient number of paying customers.

APPENDIX 2   229

FIGURE 81. "Adventurous guests outfitted in special pajamas to protect from precipitaiton and cold being welcomed by Geroge Sabin, General Manager," (Photo by Earl Dibble, 1930, OCNM Museum and Archives Collections.)

APPENDIX 3

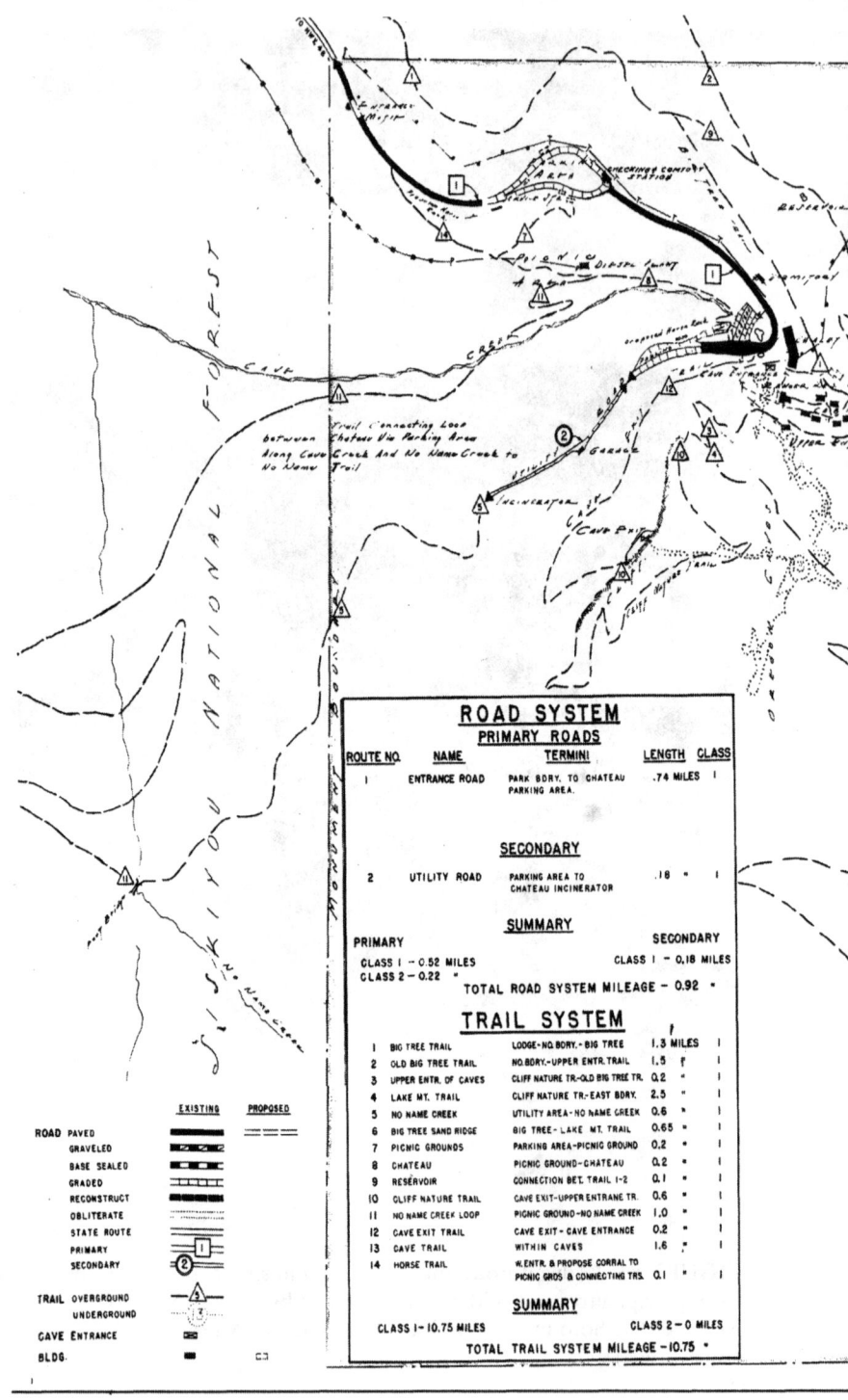

APPENDIX 3 231

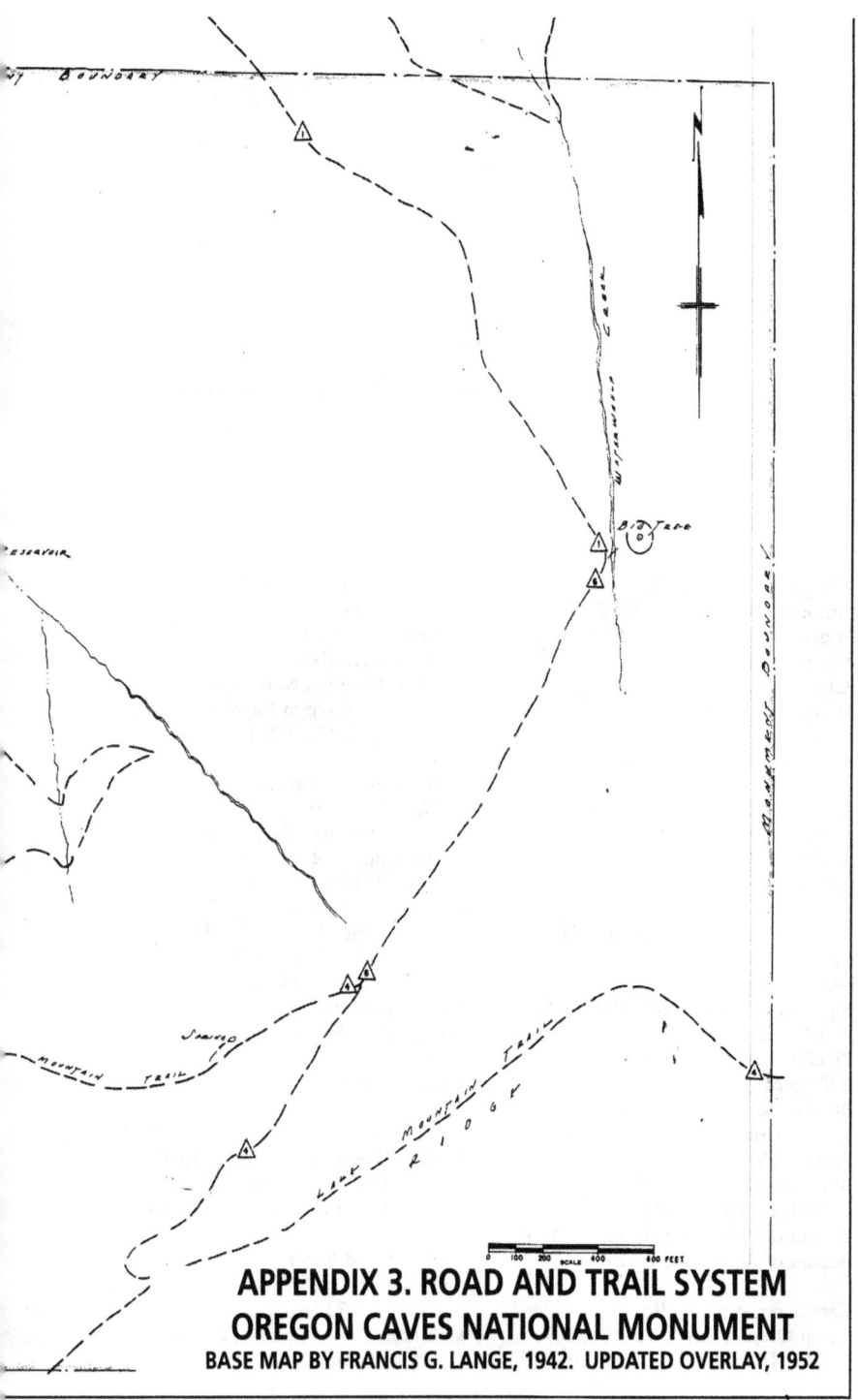

**APPENDIX 3. ROAD AND TRAIL SYSTEM
OREGON CAVES NATIONAL MONUMENT**
BASE MAP BY FRANCIS G. LANGE, 1942. UPDATED OVERLAY, 1952

Index

Albright, Horace, 86-87
Althouse (Oregon), 21-22, 24-25
Anderson, M.J., 48-50, 52-53, 55-56
Antiquities Act, 48, 51, 54
Ashland (Oregon) 48, 68
Athapaskan (Dakutebede, Shasta Costa) Indians, 18, 20, 21
auto camping, 68-70, 121, 189n23, 215n19
Applegate River (Oregon), 15, 17, 21, 26, 29
Applegate Trail, 16
Applegate Valley, 16, 20, 26, 28

Babyfoot Lake (Siskiyou NF), 142
Baker, Sam, 81
beaver, 15
Big Tree (Oregon Caves NM), 7-8, 102-03, 152
Bigelow Lakes (Siskiyou NF), 137, 156
Billingslea, J.H., 84-85
Bourne, Jonathon, 175n6
Buck, Clarence J., 74-75, 79, 81
Buford, Howard, 103, 213n7
Burch, Walter, 31, 36-37, 94, 151, 160, 175n8, 214n12
Bureau of Public Roads, 64, 66, 164
Bureau of Reclamation, 137

Cammerer, Arno B., 96
Camp Oregon Caves, 95-101, 109, 112, 156, 161, 163, 164, 200n35

Camp Wineglass (Crater Lake NP), 96
Canteen Company of Oregon (Estey Corporation), 138-39, 145-46
Canyon Creek (Siskiyou NF), 22
Carlsbad Caverns (New Mexico), 6
Cave Creek (Oregon Caves NM), 36, 79, 83-84, 86, 102, 104-05, 109, 114-15
Cave Creek Campground (Siskiyou NF), 137, 160
Cave Junction nee Caves City (Oregon), x, 4, 66, 95, 109, 111, 140-42, 153, 158, 164
cave tour, 3, 6, 9, 29, 54, 67, 79, 83, 86, 91-94, 113-14, 121, 123-24, 132, 134, 140-41, 143-47, 149, 152, 156, appendix 2
Caves Camp (Siskiyou NF), 76, 156
caves, perception of, 8, 30, 89-91, appendix 2
Cecil, George H., 76
Chamberlain, George, 52
Chinese (as miners), 23, 27, 171n23
Civilian Conservation Corps, 93-100, 102, 104-10, 112-15, 118, 127, 131, 147, 149, 152-55, 157, 161, 163, 165
Cliff, Edward P., 98
Cliff Nature Trail (Oregon Caves NM), 103-04, 152
Columbia River Highway, 59, 185n100
Condon, Thomas, 31, 147, 181-82n67

232

INDEX 233

Contor, Roger, xv, 134
Crater Lake National Park (Oregon), 8, 37, 48, 52, 72, 96, 99, 109, 113, 117-18, 121, 124, 133-34, 138, 144, 146, 163, appendix 1; Rim Drive in, 105, 108-09
Craters of the Moon National Monument (Idaho), 117
Crescent City (California), 14, 26, 28, 34, 42, 55, 66, 75-76
cultural landscape inventory, 154-55, 213n2

Davidson, Carter, 31, 160
Davidson, Elijah, xiv, 14, 28-31, 36, 106, 123, 158-59, 173-74n50
Davis, Chas, 144
Dean, Robert, 50, 180n52
Doerner, Armin, 96, 105-06
donation land claims, 26, 170n11, 172n35, 173n37
Doty, Cecil, 101
Douglas fir, x, 135
Dunham, Wayland, 123

Eight Dollar Mountain, 17, 142
Ellis, Frank, 53
Emergency Conservation Work, 6, 152
Exit Trail, 102-03, 134, 152

Fidler, William W., 29
forest reserves, 43-48, 54
Fort Hoskins (Oregon), 159
Fromme, R. L., 54-56
frontier, American concept of, 1, 3, 33, 43, 51, 54, 62-63
Fulton, Charles, 48, 179n43

Gifford, Ralph, 119
Gin Lin Trail (Rogue River NF), 159
Good Roads Movement, 58, 63-64
Glisan, Rodney L., 183n76
Grants Pass (Oregon), x, 5, 14, 16, 18, 31, 33-34, 36-40, 42-43, 45, 48, 53, 55-56, 59-60, 66-68, 76, 88, 111, 116, 121, 123-24, 139; Boatnik festival, 139; Caveman Bridge, 124; Commercial Club (Chamber of Commerce), 52, 56-57, 76-77, 124, 162; Riverside Park, 68
Grayback Camp (Siskiyou NF), xiv, 68, 70-71, 77, 80, 97-98, 100, 109, 137, 141
Grayback Creek, 60, 64, 70, 77, 79, 96, 98, 156, 161
Grayback Mountain, 29, 31, 135, 156
Grayback resort development, 71, 77, 80-81, 95, 98, 111
Graves, Harold, 121-22
Graves, Henry S., 57, 59-60, 62
Greeley, William B., 72
Gruber, William, 121-22

Happy Camp (California), 5, 18, 22
Harkness, Homer, 36-37, 94, 151, 175n7
Harrison, Laura S., 149, appendix 1
Hawley, W.C., 60
Hayes Hill (Oregon), 64
Henderson, "Uncle Jack," 37
Hermann, Binger, 46, 179n39
Historic American Buildings Survey, xiv, 161, 215n26
historic resources, definition of, xi, 3
historic resource study, goals for, ix, 1, 148
Horse Mountain (Siskiyou NF), 36
Holland (Oregon), 55, 64, 66, 77, 93
Hudson's Bay Company, 15-16
Humboldt Redwoods State Park (California), 117
hunting, in the vicinity of Oregon Caves, 4, 21, 58

Illinois River (Oregon), 4, 22, 24
Illinois River State Park, 142, 211n37
Illinois Valley, 4, 5, 14, 16-18, 20-22, 25-27, 29, 31, 34, 36-37, 45, 55, 59-60, 77, 83, 104, 136, 141-42, 151, 156, 161; farming in, 14, 21, 26-27, 142
Illinois Valley Visitor Center (Cave Junction), 141, 159
Indians (near Oregon Caves), 3-4, 14, 17-18, 21-22, 170n14
Indian reservations, 18-20
Indian removal, 18-20, 22, 158-59

Jackson County (Oregon), 15-16, 22, 25, 34
Jacksonville (Oregon), 15, 22
Josephine Creek (Siskiyou NF), 15, 22
Josephine County (Oregon), x, 4-5, 11, 13-17, 22-25, 28, 33-34, 43, 45-46, 55, 57, 59, 66, 88, 139-43

Kalmiopsis Wilderness (Siskiyou NF), 142
Karok Indians, 18

234 INDEX

Kerby (Oregon), 5, 22, 26, 34, 37
Kincaid, John, 182n69
Kiser, Fred, 81, 120-21
Klamath River (in California), 4-5, 17-18, 21-22
Klamath Mountains, 4, 16
Kneipp, Leon F., 196-97n84

Lake Creek (Siskiyou NF), 37, 100, 129, 131, 154, 157-58, 161
Lake Mountain, 102-03, 135, 151-52
Lake Selmac, 142
land frauds, 44-45, 49
landscape garden, 3, 89-90, 95, 126-27, appendix 2; Oregon Caves as an example of, 3, 11, 112, 116, 123-25, appendix 2
Lange, Francis G., xv, 8, 100, 104-11, 113-15, 153, 213n7, appendix 3
Lava Beds National Monument (California), 96, 99, 117, 163
Lium, Gust, 81, 85, 98, 112, 129, 138, 146, 163, 165, appendix 1

McClelland, Linda, xi, 150, 155
MacDaniels, E.H., 80
MacDuff, Nelson, 56
McLane, Larry, 36
McNary, Charles, 83
Mammoth Cave (Kentucky), 34, 41-42, 90, appendix 2
master plans, 8-10, 112-13, 128
Mazamas, 56-57
Medford (Oregon), 48, 58, 121, 123, 185n98
Meola, Edwin, 115, 213n7
Miller, Joaquin, 48, 50, 52
mining, 14, 21-25, 27-28, 43, 45, 58, 158, 159, 171n27, 172n33, 176n14, 214n16; technology of, 21-22
Mission 66, program called, 9, 127-29, 131-33, 156-58
Mitchell, G.E., 88
Munger, Thornton, 76
Myers, Jefferson, 180-81n55, 182n69

national forest maps, 71
national historic landmark, x, xi, 10, appendix 1
National Historic Preservation Act, x, xi, 128, 146, 148
National Parks Association, 133
National Park Service, x-xii, 6, 9-10, 71-72, 74, 86-88, 95, 97-98,
100-02, 104, 109-15, 118, 123, 127-29, 133-35, 137, 140-41, 143-44, 146-48, 151-53, 155-56, 158, 161-62, 164
National Register of Historic Places, x-xii, xiv, 10, 146-52, 154, 156, appendix 1
National Speleological Society, 133
Nickerson, Frank, 37, 182n69
No Name Creek (Oregon Caves NM), 81, 104-05, 151-52
Norris, William (Sr.), 29

O'Brien (Oregon), 5, 66
Ogden, Peter Skene, 15
Oium, G.O., 49-50
Operation Outdoors, program called, 137, 140
Oregon & California railroad grant, 46-47, 70, 175n2
Oregon Cavemen, x, 5, 123-24, 138-39, 162, 207n103
Oregon Caves Chalet, 78-81, 84-86, 102-03, 105-06, 111-12, 114, 132, 135, 138, 146, 149, 153, 161, 204n72
Oregon Caves Chateau, 11, 84-87, 96, 98, 101-02, 104-07, 109, 111-15, 121-22, 124, 131-32, 138-39, 146, 149, 152-53, 161, appendix 1; as a national historic landmark, x, 10, 144, 146, 149; Monterey furniture in, appendix 1
Oregon Caves Checking and Comfort Station, 101, 133, 141, 149, 154
Oregon Caves cottages, 80-81, 100, 107, 138, 146
Oregon Caves Game Refuge, 6, 74
Oregon Caves Guide Dormitory, 111-12, 138, 146, 149
Oregon Caves Highway (SR 46), x, 4, 6, 64-67, 77, 85, 109, 111, 120, 129, 131, 137, 141, 153-54, 160, 187n9, appendix 1
Oregon Caves Improvement Company, 38, 41
Oregon Caves National Monument (Oregon): cave restoration program, 12, 144, 146; circulars, 6, 71, 116; concession contract, 84, 86, 129, 132; development by the concessionaire, x, 3, 6, 11, 29, 56, 76-77, 79-81, 110, 113, 125, 131, appendix 2; discovery of, 28-30, 38; exit tunnel in, 82-84, 92, 134, 144,

INDEX 235

appendix 1; flood of 1964, 137-38, appendix 1; gates in, 134, 144; geology, 8-9, 91, 168n13; historic district, xi-xii, xiv, 10, 146-47, 149-50, 153-55; interpretation of, 133-34, 144, 183n77; ladders in, 34, 36, 42, 54, 81, 193n61; lights for cave tour, 53, 55-56, 81-83, 85, 92-93, 131, 134, 194n65, appendix 1; logging next to, 3, 135-37, 143, 163; main parking lot, 65, 101, 104, 107-08, 112, 131, 140, 153-54, 156, 161-62; mapping of, 50, 84, 113, 143; names for, 31, 38, 40; national park proposal, 56-57; part of local economy, x, xii, 10-11, 29, 35; photography of, 7, 37, 81, 86, 116, 119-21, appendix 1; proclamation of, 5-6, 48-53, 57; signs for, 109, 154; transfer to the National Park Service, 86-88; vandalism of, 31, 40, 50, 52-53, 92, 134, 180-81n55; water systems in, 75, 77, 86, 100, 131, 214n11
Oregon Caves Ranger Residence, 100, 130, 146, 149
Oregon Caves Resort, 71, 77, 84, 114, 121, 123
Oregon Conservation Commission, 52-53, 58
Oregon Mountain (California), 66
Oregon State Highway Commission, 64, 119, 131, 163; state parks as a responsibility for, 74-75, 118

Pacific Highway (SR 99), 59, 121
Page Creek (Siskiyou NF), 53, 199n19
Palmer, Joel, 20
Panther (Waterwhelp) Creek (Oregon Caves NM), 102
Patrick Creek (California), 66, 76-77
Patterson, Frank, 120-21, 136
Peck, Arthur L., 79, 85
Pepper Camp (Siskiyou NF), 156
Pinchot, Gifford, 51-52, 57
Portland (Oregon), 26, 28, 33, 37-38, 53, 55-56, 59, 71, 74, 114, 121
Port Orford cedar, x, 8, 79, 106, 215n21, appendix 1
Progressive Movement, 51
Provolt (Oregon), 29, 76

railroads, 25, 27, 31, 33-34, 42, 55, 63, 136
rancherias, 18

recreation centers, 6, 71, 73-74, 76
Redwood Empire Association, 66, 76, 116, 124, appendix 1
Red Buttes Wilderness (Oregon/California), 143
Redwood Highway (US 199), 66, 68, 76, 111, 121, 124, 141-42, 159
retaining walls, 105-06, 112, 114, 149, 153, appendix 1
Rogue Valley, 16, 22, 26, 34, 142
Rogue River timber withdrawal, 46
Rollins, Josephine, 22
Roosevelt, Franklin D., 87
Roosevelt, Theodore, 46, 48, 51
Rough and Ready Botanical Wayside (Oregon), 142, 211n37
Rowley, Richard W. "Dick," xiv, 92-93, 115, 123, 133-34, 147
rustic architecture, x-xi, 99, 127-28, 146-47, 150, 158, 161, appendix 1

Sabin, George, 78-80, 84-87, 114, 123, appendix 1
San Francisco (California), 26, 37-39, 43, 66, 75, 113-14, 128, 157
San Francisco *Examiner* expeditions, 37-41, 160
Save-the-Redwoods League, 75, 114
Sawyers Company, 121
Selma (Oregon), 4, 159
Shasta Indians, 18
Siletz Indian Reservation, 20-21, 159
Siskiyou Mountains, ix, 29, 43, 51
Siskiyou National Forest (Oregon), 4-5, 47-48, 52-53, 67, 88, 95-96, 98, 109, 134, 140, 151, 153, 160, 163-64, 199n32; Cedar Guard Station, 98, 156, 161; Redwood Ranger Station, 95, 100
Smith, Alonzo B. "Captain," 37-41
Smith, Vickers G., 54
Smith, Warren D., 123
Sowell, Richard, 183n32
Steel, William G., 37, 48, 58, 120, 185n97-98
Sucker Creek (Siskiyou NF), 22, 31, 36, 45, 59-60, 66, 70, 77, 93, 96-97, 135, 137, 156, 161, 185n100

Taft, William H., 52
Takilma Indians, 18, 20-21
Takilma (Oregon), 53
Teal, Joseph N., 52
Term Occupancy Act, 76
Timber and Stone Act, 36, 45

INDEX

Toll, Roger, 6-7, 86
trails, x, 3, 31, 36, 49-50, 54, 60, 64, 70, 73-74, 81, 94-95, 101-03, 113-14, 135, 150-52, 154-55, 161, 164, 201n41, 201n47, 201n50-51, 213n5

United States Exploring Expedition, 16
United States Forest Service, x, 5-6, 48-53, 55-57, 60, 62, 64, 70-81, 83-88, 94-100, 105, 110, 112, 116-17, 127, 129, 135-37, 141, 151, 158, 161, 163
University of Oregon, 31, 115

Veach, R.W., 48-50
View Master, xiv, 121-22
visitation, annual total at Oregon Caves, 3, 29, 53, 60, 65, 76-77, 83, 85, 111, 116, 131, 138, 140-41

wagon roads, 26, 31, 37, 40, 55, 60, 64, 66
Waldo (Oregon), 21-22, 24, 26, 66, 159
Watson, Chandler B., 48, 52, 181n67
Waugh, Frank, 79
Western Office of Design and Construction (NPS), 157
Wilderness Act of 1964, 143
wilderness areas, 72-74, 143, appendix 2
Wilderville (Oregon), 34
Willamette Valley, 16, 18, 26, 28, 71
Williams (Oregon), 5, 16, 27-29, 31, 34, 37, 39-40, 54-55, 64, 76, 102, 151-52, 156, 159-60, 186n104; proposed road connection to Oregon Caves, 55, 64, 188n19
Williams Creek, 14, 26, 28, 36

Young, Ewing, 16
Yreka (California), 18, 22
Yurok Indians, 18, 29

zoning, xi, 71, 147

www.ingramcontent.com/pod-product-compliance
Lightning Source LLC
Chambersburg PA
CBHW071707160426
43195CB00012B/1609